The Arsenal of Democracy

Edinburgh Studies in Anglo-American Relations

Series Editors: Steve Marsh and Alan P. Dobson

Published and forthcoming titles

The Anglo-American Relationship
Steve Marsh and Alan P. Dobson

The Arsenal of Democracy: Aircraft Supply and the Anglo-American Alliance, 1938–1942
Gavin J. Bailey

Post-War Planning on the Periphery: Anglo-American Economic Diplomacy in South America, 1939–1945
Thomas C. Mills

Best Friends, Former Enemies: The Anglo-American Special Relationship and German Reunification
Luca Ratti

Reagan and Thatcher's Special Relationship: Latin American and Anglo-American Relations
Sally-Ann Treharne

www.euppublishing.com/series/esar

The Arsenal of Democracy

Aircraft Supply and the Anglo-American Alliance, 1938–1942

Gavin J. Bailey

EDINBURGH
University Press

Edinburgh University Press Ltd
13 Infirmary Street, Edinburgh, EH1 1LT
www.euppublishing.com

First published in hardback by Edinburgh University Press 2013

Typeset in 11/14 Sabon by
Servis Filmsetting Ltd, Stockport, Cheshire, and
printed and bound in Great Britain by
CPI Group (UK) Ltd, Croydon CR0 4YY

A CIP record for this book is available from the British Library

ISBN 978 0 7486 4747 7 (hardback)
ISBN 978 1 3995 7095 4 (paperback)
ISBN 978 0 7486 4973 0 (webready PDF)
ISBN 978 0 7486 4975 4 (epub)

Contents

Tables

Acknowledgements

Much of the material in this book was improved as a result of discussion with colleagues at the annual Transatlantic Studies Association conferences held over the previous ten years, and I would like to express my appreciation for the helpful insights they have given, although I am responsible for the conclusions presented here.

Particular thanks are due to Professor Alan Dobson who provided valuable advice and assistance before, during and after my time as a PhD student under his supervision.

This book could not have been researched or completed without the help of my family, and I would like to thank my parents, David and Deirdre, for their support, my brother Keiron for his encouragement, and most of all my wife Em for enduring the unendurable for so long.

Gavin J. Bailey

Abbreviations and Glossary

2 Group	Light-bomber subordinate command within Bomber Command
ACAS	Assistant Chief of the Air Staff
AMDP	Air Member for Development and Production
AMSO	Air Member for Supply and Organisation
AOC	Air Officer Commanding
ASW	Anti-Submarine Warfare
ATP	Arnold-Towers-Portal agreement
BAC	British Air Commission
Bomber Command	RAF command conducting bomber operations based in Britain
BPC	British Purchasing Commission
C.-in-C.	Commander-in-Chief
CAS	Chief of the Air Staff
CID	Committee of Imperial Defence
CIGS	Chief of the Imperial General Staff
Coastal Command	RAF command for maritime operations in Britain
CRD	Controller of Research and Development
DCAS	Deputy Chief of the Air Staff
DRC	Defence Requirements Committee
DTD	Directorate of Technical Development
DWO	Director of War Operations
EATS	Empire Air Training Scheme
ECM	Electronic Counter-Measures
ERP	Expansion and Re-equipment Policy committee

Fighter Command	RAF command for the air defence of Britain
FO	Foreign Office
FR	Fighter Reconnaissance
FTH	Full-Throttle Height, the height at which aircraft engine superchargers operated without restriction
GDP	Gross Domestic Product
GR	General Reconnaissance (maritime patrol)
Group	USAAF unit of 3 squadrons, of approximately 72 fighter or 48 bomber aircraft in total. Larger RAF subordinate command.
IFF	Identification Friend-or-Foe
Luftwaffe	German Air Force
MAP	Ministry of Aircraft Production
MoS	Ministry of Supply
MTB	Motor Torpedo Boat
NDAC	National Defence Advisory Commission
OLLA	Office of Lend-Lease Administration
PAA	Pan-American Airlines
PR	Photographic Reconnaissance
PUS	Parliamentary Undersecretary
PWA	Public Works Administration
RAF	Royal Air Force.
RAFDEL	RAF Delegation in Washington
RFC	Reconstruction Finance Corporation
RN	Royal Navy
SBAC	Society of British Aircraft Constructors
SOE	Special Operations Executive
Squadron	RAF unit of approximately 16 aircraft
SWPA	South-West Pacific and Australia command
VCAS	Vice-Chief of the Air Staff
VLR	Very Long Range
USAAC	United States Army Air Corps
USAAF	United States Army Air Force
USN	United States Navy
Wehrmacht	German armed forces (typically referring to the German Army)

Wing	RAF unit of 2 or more squadrons
WO	War Office
WPA	Works Progress Administration

1 The Anglo-American Relationship and the Need for Historical Reinterpretation

> This little island will be ridiculously proud some ages hence of its former brave days and swear its capital was once as big again as Paris, or – what is to be the name of the city that will then give laws to Europe? – perhaps New York or Philadelphia.
>
> *Horace Walpole, August 1776*[1]

> I have come to the conclusion that they haven't any dollars left and I am convinced, if Congress does not make it possible for them to buy more supplies, they will have to stop fighting.
>
> *Henry Morgenthau, US Secretary of the Treasury, testimony to Congress during hearings on House Resolution 1776 in January 1941*[2]

These two statements encapsulate our fundamental understanding of the historical relationship between Britain and the United States to the present. Morgenthau's statement was made in support of the Lend-Lease Act in early 1941, a measure designed to relieve the exhausted British dollar exchange resources needed to purchase American supplies in World War II. The importance of that economic support is indicated by the critical dependence Morgenthau identified for it – without it, the British would be unable to continue their resistance to the Axis powers. This was a watershed moment, both in the history of the war and in the history of the Anglo-American relationship. British imperial decline and the rise of American power had been predicted, and then demonstrated. All that Walpole got wrong was the name of the capital city where the legislature giving laws to Europe would meet, an understandable mistake in the period before Washington, DC had been built.

Walpole's statement indicates that the underlying historical dynamic was perceived more than 150 years before Lend-Lease which would apparently confirm it. Even in the eighteenth century America was seen as a rising world power already on a path to surpass Britain, apparently the supreme power in the Old World after a series of victories against her European rivals in the Seven Years War. This prospect, of America eclipsing British power on an economic basis, had been predicted by many eighteenth-century writers on both sides of the Atlantic, and notably by Benjamin Franklin.[3] The revolution which was confirmed by the American Declaration of Independence in July 1776 would establish the United States of America as an independent nation by 1783. Over the next century the new nation would proceed to expand in terms of population, territory and economic development until it overtook Britain, the leading power of the industrial age, at the end of the nineteenth century.

History would seem to have vindicated the ideas of those eighteenth-century writers on the future of the transatlantic balance of power. Perhaps the most superficially resonant of those ideas might be the vision of American tourists viewing the imperial remains of London two centuries after the revolution.[4] Those tourists in London in 1976 would have perceived some strong references to the events of 1776. They might have viewed several exhibitions celebrating the bicentennial anniversary of the revolution, as well as other traditional attractions such as red-coated guardsmen marching on public parade, from regiments which had fought against the rebellious colonists in the revolutionary war.

These references would have been paralleled by the continuing celebration in the present of the pageantry and ritual originating during the period of British imperial power. The enduring nature of those traditions, or perhaps what Walpole described as ridiculous pride in former brave days, might well be seen in the similar military ceremonies celebrating Queen Elizabeth II's Diamond Jubilee in 2012. Those parades would reproduce the ceremonial displays of the last diamond jubilee for a reigning British monarch, that of Queen Victoria in 1897 at the very apogee of British imperial power and prestige.

But clearly the cultural and historical contexts are very different. Walpole and his fellow commentators were speaking as eighteenth-century Grand Tourists, viewing the ancient remains of Rome or Pompeii, rather than modern tourists in the age of mass air travel. In 1899, Victoria reigned as an empress over an empire upon which, geographically and symbolically, the sun never set. By 2012, the process of post-imperial decline was apparently long completed. Once more, behind the public displays of military pageantry, British officials were planning another round of cutbacks to the British armed forces and their global commitments, driven by the harsh financial reality after the 2008 economic crisis.

This balancing process between global commitments and economic overstretch would have been wearily familiar to British officials over the past century. It occurred in 1919 at the end of World War I, in 1945 at the end of World War II, in 1958 with the end of conscription, in 1969 with the withdrawal of military commitments from 'East of Suez', in 1991 at the end of the Cold War, and at numerous other intervals between and afterwards. Far from being a global empire, Britain had long since shrunk to a point where, even fifty years before 2012, an American official could observe with some truth that Britain had 'lost an empire and had not yet found a role'.[5]

And yet the military pageantry of 2012 might well demonstrate some small but significant indications that Britain had indeed found a role: one where the exercise of imperial power had been replaced by the exercise of military power within a close and enduring alliance. The guardsmen on parade in 2012 might well have experienced operational service in Afghanistan in the Fourth Anglo-Afghan conflict. But, unlike the three previous conflicts in that series of colonial wars culminating in the short war of 1919, British troops in the twenty-first century would not have been fighting to secure an imperial balance of power as they did in the nineteenth-century 'Great Game' between Russia and British imperial rule in India. Instead, they would have fought as perhaps the most powerful, but nonetheless undeniably junior, ally in a grand coalition headed by the United States. This had, indeed, become the implicit framework for British strategy ever since the 1998 Strategic Defence Review.

This metamorphosis into a close but unequal ally is symptomatic of an enormous and enduring change in the relationship between the United States and Britain. The power balance in the relationship may have followed the predicted course but the nature of the relationship did not.[6] In 1975–6, an American tourist in London during the bicentennial celebrations of the revolution might wonder why, as the introduction to one museum display put it, the British might take so much trouble to celebrate 'a humiliating defeat'.[7] Another guidebook answered this question by explaining that Britain lost a colony, '. . . but in fact, was handing over to the United States its ultimate destiny to assume one day the leadership of the English-speaking world'.[8] These explanations are entirely representative of our modern understanding. America did not just eclipse British power; according to these subsequent British commentators, it had succeeded to the global imperial role the British had previously claimed for themselves.

In 1775–83 the United States fought a successful revolution against British colonial rule. From the American perspective, this was a victorious war fought by a patriotic colonial militia in defence of the Whig and Liberal traditions of political liberty against an autocratic and tyrannical British government. From a British perspective, this was a war, fought to secure British power and parliamentary supremacy over colonial assemblies, which culminated in defeat, a defeat inflicted in a global conflict where Britain was isolated against a coalition of contemporary rival powers, notably France, Spain and Holland.

In 1812–14 there was a second Anglo-American war, driven on one side by British infringements of American neutral shipping rights during the enforcement of their maritime blockade during the twenty-year-long war against revolutionary, and then Napoleonic, France, and by aggressive American ambitions upon Canada on the other. The most memorable aspects of the war are some relatively insignificant spectacles: one British military expedition burned the presidential mansion in the new capital of Washington (later dubbed the White House after subsequent repainting); and another was decisively defeated at New Orleans before the signing of the peace treaty the previous month was known. The war did little but effectively confirm the status quo.

Despite the antagonisms towards British imperialism and colonialism that these conflicts helped embed in American popular belief, it remains a remarkable fact that, over the course of the nineteenth century, no further conflict took place between the two countries despite the rising power of the United States and the expansion of the British empire. During the American Civil War Britain and the United States were able to maintain a position of de facto neutrality despite provocations on both sides. Regardless of the arousal of popular antagonisms at various times, notably over the demarcation of the US–Canada border and a dispute over the boundary of Venezuela in 1896, the next instance of conflict involving the British and Americans was World War I. Then the two nations found themselves in a military alliance.

This conflict demonstrated the new power of the United States of America and the common strategic interests she shared with Britain but also confirmed the political constraints upon collaboration to secure those common interests. While the British entered the war in 1914 ostensibly to protect Belgium but ultimately to secure the European balance of power against German dominance, the entry of the United States into the war in 1917 was driven by German submarine attacks on American shipping. Both this and the concurrent protests against British maritime blockade policy recalled some of the issues that had been fundamental to the outbreak of the 1812 war. Despite the operation of such irritants on Anglo-American relations in 1914–17, America had eventually been pulled into a major European conflict alongside European powers, something Americans had long believed to be alien to their political ideals and national policy.

This had been caused by new political and economic developments. In the political sense, American leaders had recognised the common interest between America and the democracies of Britain and France rather than with the autocratic powers of the Central Alliance. In the economic sense, the burgeoning trade with the Allies had made the protection of that trade an American interest. In the Napoleonic era, Thomas Jefferson's ideas of restricting American trade with belligerent foreign powers held sway, albeit with limited success. In World War I, the economic expansion of the United States was matched by economic involvement in the conflict. Channelled into Allied hands by their blockade of

Germany, and massively expanded by Allied wartime purchases of munitions and supplies, economic relations made the success of the Allied war effort in the American national interest.

At the same time, these economic relations appeared to confirm the new dominance of the United States over the European powers, especially Britain. An important part of British strategy during the war was, effectively for the first time, the expansion and equipment of an army on the scale necessary to make a meaningful direct contribution to the defeat of Germany, a major European land power. Previously, Britain had relied upon naval strength for the protection of her territory and dominance of global maritime trade, with coalition partners providing the majority of the military means necessary to defeat her enemies. The scale of this new commitment prompted an extensive munitions and supply purchase programme in the US. Essentially, the British traded their financial exchange resources to mobilise the enormous industrial resources of the United States against the Central Powers. These financial resources were finite, however, and in 1916 the economist John Maynard Keynes warned the British government that the approaching exhaustion of convertible exchange reserves would realise Walpole's 1776 prediction: 'If things go on as at present, I venture to say with certainty that by next June or earlier the President of the American Republic will be in a position, if he wishes, to dictate his own terms to us.'[9]

Keynes would confirm this in a note to the US Treasury Secretary after America entered the war when he tried to get the United States government to assume responsibility for covering British and Allied expenditure in the United States. According to Keynes, British exchange resources were exhausted and, without American support in a matter of days, the whole financial fabric of the alliance would collapse.[10]

This demonstration of apparently critical financial reliance upon the United States provides a key example of how concepts of economic dependency were to inform historical understandings of both British power and the American role in relation to it during the twentieth century. If Britain was in decline and the United States on the rise, this was nowhere more clear than in the economic dependence of the British on America. This dependence, first indicated during World War I, would be confirmed during World War II and most explicitly during the evolution of Lend-Lease. It would be reiterated again in 1945 when Lend-Lease was terminated and Keynes himself was instrumental in negotiating a multibillion-dollar loan from the United States government to relieve the British foreign exchange position.[11]

On the American side of the Atlantic, involvement in World War I represented an exceptional experience and one which could not readily be reconciled to American political beliefs. Built upon the popular propaganda of revolutionary colonial politics, these were exemplified by George Washington's farewell speech, given at the end of his second term as American president in 1796, warning of entanglement in foreign alliances. This tradition demanded isolation from the internecine dynastic conflicts of the European Old World. The enduring appeal of this concept, together with a jealous perception of the powers of the legislature defined in the United States Constitution, was implicit in the failure of the US Senate to ratify American membership of the League of Nations in 1919. This not only terminated the prospect of American participation in President Wilson's project of a supranational institution to prevent a further world war but set the seal on a period of mutual suspicion in the transatlantic relationship.

For the next twenty years the British and French would struggle with limited success to keep the United States engaged as an active power in world affairs or, from a more suspicious American perspective, to secure their European and colonial positions against rival powers by co-opting American diplomatic and economic support. This was finally achieved in the crucible of World War II where President Franklin D. Roosevelt was able slowly to erode political and legislative constraints to support the Allies even before the Japanese attack on the United States Navy at Pearl Harbor in December 1941 brought America directly into the war.

A crucial element in the outcome of World War II was the development of a close Anglo-American alliance. Personified by the relationship between Roosevelt and British prime minister, Winston Churchill, the course of the war created new brave days for celebrating British national pride, as was demonstrated by the flight of wartime aircraft by the Royal Air Force's Battle of Britain

Memorial Flight over London during the 2012 jubilee celebrations. It also marked a clear watershed in British imperial decline, as the exercise of American military and economic power was fundamental to the defeat of the Axis powers and the achievement of British war aims.

After this conflict, the wartime alliance, together with many of the collaborative habits and institutions it had conceived, would endure. On the American side there was a realisation that leadership had now passed from Britain to the United States regardless of old dogma and suspicions. As Henry Luce, the publisher of the influential *Life* magazine, put it in 1941: 'In any sort of partnership with the British empire, Great Britain is perfectly willing that the United States of America should assume the role of senior partner. This has been true for a long time.'[12]

The perpetuation of wartime collaboration, with the United States as the senior partner, would be a fundamental element in the formation of the North Atlantic Treaty Organization (NATO) which, in turn, formed the keystone of western European security during and after the Cold War. In addition, British forces would deploy and fight alongside the United States in Korea, the 1991 Gulf War, the Bosnian and Kosovan conflicts in the Balkans during the 1990s, the 2003 invasion and occupation of Iraq, and the Afghan conflict which followed the terrorist attacks against America on 11 September 2001 (9/11).

Aside from the refusal of the British government of Harold Wilson to field forces for the Allied contingent in the Vietnam conflict, and, despite the bickering of senior commanders, commentators and sometimes politicians on both sides of the Atlantic during all of these conflicts, Britain has remained the closest and most reliable military partner of the United States. This military alliance, based on common values, in terms of liberal democratic political culture and strategic security interests, but also reflecting the habits and expectations born of decades of close and systematic interaction, remains the fundamental component of the so-called 'special relationship' between Britain and America which has obsessed politicians, pundits and academics in both countries.

Endless and cyclical commentary about the enduring nature of this relationship, and the periodic fluctuations within it, is perhaps less interesting than the manner in which the evolution of the relationship captures the historical process involved in the decline of British power. At its most basic level, it remains an exceptional fact that Britain and the United States have fought no war against each other since the conclusion of peace at the end of the 1812–14 conflict; the prior global hegemon accommodated itself to, and then gave way before, a new rival without the overt conflict that might have been expect by realists in international relations theory or ordinary cynics. This says something significant about the nature of the Anglo-American relationship and sets a problem for historians to explore and explain. If British power had been eclipsed by that of the United States, this remains a truism long since foretold and understood, and which does little to explain either the history of British statecraft which evolved in that lengthy period of decline or the continuing influence of the close military relationship between them in the present.

'Declinists', or historians attempting to explain modern British history by fundamental reference to British decline, have several problems to overcome. The most obvious of these is the issue of teleology, or the interpretation of historical events exclusively in the light of progression towards a known conclusion. This amounts to something more than simple hindsight and has a long pedigree, with one of the most recent examples being Francis Fukyama's assertion that history ended with the apparent global triumph of liberal capitalist democracy at the end of the Cold War. This triumph rendered other competing ideologies obsolete and thus ended the grand narrative of history.[13] Subsequent events, such as the post-9/11 'War on Terror' and the 2008 global financial crisis, might be seen to qualify Fukyama's thesis. In terms of decline as the decisive historical force in Anglo-American relations, the very existence of predictions such as Walpole's should give us warning. We know British power declined and America's power rose to eclipse it, but does this adequately explain every historical event involved in the two nations' long historical relationship?

This kind of binary approach, evaluating events and decisions on the basis of whether they fit with a predetermined conclusion, simplifies more than it can explain. This was a fact understood by critics of previous versions of similar teleological historical approaches. The best example to demonstrate this in historiography remains 'The Whig Interpretation of History' as deconstructed by Herbert Butterfield in 1931. This was based on the assumption by many nineteenth-century English historians that history would inevitably lead towards the triumph of the peculiarly British form of parliamentary democracy, demonstrated by the rise of British imperial power throughout the century following victory in the Napoleonic wars.[14] This approach was satirised in *1066 and All That* by Sellar and Yeatman who brought their comic 'Whig-ish' narrative of British history to an end in 1918 when British power was demonstrably eclipsed by the United States as Britain's financial dependence on the US became evident by the end of World War I.[15]

The ease with which this approach can lend itself to satire, as well as the fact that it was being satirised as early as the interwar era, indicate the shortcomings such magisterial simplifications can involve when it comes to offering convincing historical explanation. An understanding of relative decline is necessary but it is not sufficient by itself to understand the history involved.

Where many declinists differ from Sellar and Yeatman is in the point in time in which they fix the British eclipse by the United States. For most, taking their cue from Henry Luce, World War II represents the decisive point. There is one key reason for this: namely, the enormous political and diplomatic effort made to incorporate the US, then a neutral, in the materiel support of the British when they faced the catastrophes in their fortunes represented by the German successes of 1940. In May 1940, the British chiefs of staff made an appreciation of the strategic position in anticipation of the defeat of France, the possible loss of the British Expeditionary Force, and also the prospect of hostile intervention by Italy and perhaps Japan: '[We assume that the] United States of America is willing to give us full economic and financial support, without which we do not think we could continue the war with any chance of success.'[16] This remains the most fundamental of many statements that provide evidence of British strategic dependency on the United States during World War II and one which has been repeated and developed by historians since. These frequently reveal a perception of criticality associated with

American economic participation alongside Britain in the war: the sense in which it was indispensable to victory or, if absent, inevitable defeat. This is often extended from the achievement of victory to the separate and distinct achievement of British survival. As Joseph Lash has stated: 'In the autumn of 1940, Britain had only one hope of survival and of victory, and that lay with the United States.'[17]

Securing American aid was a primary object of British statecraft which was expressed through the financial, economic and political initiatives employed to obtain access to sufficient American supplies to defeat Germany. American supplies operated both in the economic sense to augment British resources and production and in the political and diplomatic sense of visibly involving the United States as a de facto ally in the British war effort. By the latter part of the war these objectives had largely been achieved and Lend-Lease supply allowed the British to develop – as a matter of optional choice – a level of war production which would never have been achievable without enormous external aid. But realising this objective took considerable time and much diplomatic effort to achieve. Not only had American capacity to manufacture armaments to be massively expanded but Britain had to establish and defend its claim on much of the resulting output.

The process involved merits detailed scrutiny as it describes the actual historical development of British dependency upon the United States. This book is an attempt to move beyond the assertions of the declinists by performing that detailed scrutiny on one specific area, namely the Anglo-American aircraft supply diplomacy involved in the provision of operational combat aircraft to the Royal Air Force in the run-up to the outbreak of war and into the mid-war period.

Why aircraft supply in particular, it might be asked? The issue of aircraft supply is particularly relevant to the larger picture of Anglo-American collaboration. The expression of Allied air power is central to the narrative of Allied materiel superiority which, in turn remains fundamental to the orthodox historical explanation of the outcome of the war.[18] This has recently extended to appreciations of how the perception of American economic potential informed Nazi policy before the war.[19]

The mobilisation of the United States economy for war production was undoubtedly successful, appearing to contemporaries as a 'production miracle'.[20] Between 1939 and 1944, US Gross Domestic Product (GDP) rose by an estimated 55 per cent, by which point the United States was making 40 per cent of the entire global production of armaments.[21] American aircraft and munitions production outstripped the combined efforts of the Axis powers in 1942.[22] John Keegan has referred to aircraft production as 'the most spectacular of all America's wartime industrial achievements'.[23] The raw statistics involved are staggering, with American production rising from 2,141 aircraft in 1940 to 96,318 in 1944. In the process, it outstripped British aircraft production, the flagship of their wartime national production strategy, in 1942. Between September 1939 and June 1945, Britain produced 123,819 aircraft; between July 1940 and June 1945, the United States produced 284,295. In the periods approximating to the war mobilisations of the British and American national economies, the United States produced more than double the British output despite the shorter time period involved and the apparent lack of the prior stimulus provided by British pre-war domestic rearmament.[24] Of this American output, the British Empire received a total of 36,182 aircraft.

This American potential was recognised by British supply diplomacy. Aircraft supply was at the core of British procurement plans in the United States and escalated in importance to the Allied war effort during 1940 as the outcomes of the fall of France and the Battle of Britain were largely attributed to the role of air power. British procurement of American aircraft had led the way in both British supply policy in the United States and also in the Roosevelt administration's rearmament and 'aid to the Allies' policies.[25]

By the end of 1940, British purchase contracts had been swelled by the assumption of French orders after the fall of France and by the increased strategic requirements following the catastrophic Allied defeats that year. At the end of March 1940, the Allies had ordered 4,600 American aircraft to be delivered by 30 September 1941; by June this rose to 10,800 aircraft, more than five times the total US production in 1939.[26] In November 1940, immediately before Lend-Lease, British orders totalled $1,985 million of which aircraft and their component systems accounted for $1,262 million. Future orders, involving the purchase of 26,000 aircraft which could only be funded by Lend-Lease, comprised $2.5 billion out of a total procurement of $3.2 billion. At this vital period in the evolution of the Anglo-American supply relationship, aircraft supply in the United States represented between 59 and 64 per cent of British purchasing plans by dollar value and 75 per cent of initial Lend-Lease appropriations.[27] As the British official history of wartime production states; 'The main claim on American supplies was from the outset conceded to the RAF.'[28]

Aircraft supply was given top priority in British economic needs from the United States and in the evolution of Lend-Lease to meet them. It has also been portrayed as symbolic of British dependence upon America and has been used by influential historians as a characteristic example of the larger strategic relationship between Britain and the United States. Corelli Barnett, for example, has used the British aircraft industry as a representative example of British decline and reliance upon America.[29] This apparent case study in abject dependence has been influential and, though challenges have been made to it, it has confirmed historical understanding of both British decline and the eclipse by the United States that exemplifies that decline.[30] Historians such as John Ellis and Paul Kennedy have adopted this perspective which is based upon economic determinism, or the idea that the war was won for the Allies by a material superiority provided by American economic might despite strategic misjudgements and poor operational performance on the battlefield.[31] The most trenchant of these ideas remain those of Barnett who, more than a decade after the first publication of his view that American economic aid was a 'life support machine' for the British war effort, repeated his unchanging opinion.[32]

> . . . I do not think one can overstate the importance of the whole British war effort being understrapped by the Americans. Again, as I point out in *The Audit of War*, in terms of vital pieces of industrial equipment, or actual industrial end-products, we were crucially and repeatedly dependent on America.[33]

This certainly reflects the tone of British diplomacy at the time. In 1940 this began to emphasise the criticality of American supplies to continuing British resistance: an approach characterised here as the critical dependency thesis. By the end of the year, the British had appealed for financial assistance to continue purchasing supplies in the United States after the imminent exhaustion of their dollar reserves; in Churchill's memorable rhetoric, to give the British the tools to finish the job themselves.[34] This resulted in the passage of the Lend-Lease Act of March 1941, which was explicitly defined as providing the British with the means of survival.[35]

In a deliberate irony to emphasise the fundamental change this represented in Anglo-American history, the development of Lend-Lease was replete with references to the revolution. These ranged from comments about how it made the British equivalent to the Hessian mercenaries hired by George III, to the very numbering of the bill, as House Resolution 1776, before it was presented to Congress.[36] Lend-Lease has encapsulated and defined the Anglo-American wartime relationship and contemporary understandings of it; as the British official history of wartime overseas supply observed: 'Lend-Lease, however, was far more than a matter of simple procurement. It was intimately connected with foreign policy and with military strategy; it profoundly affected the economic life of the country, and it was a very delicate issue in domestic politics.'[37]

The importance of Lend-Lease is attested to by the British reaction when the arrangement was terminated at the end of the war. In August 1945, the British found themselves, in Keynes's alarmist words, facing 'a financial Dunkirk' if there were no renewal of American economic aid.[38] This contemporary characterisation of the criticality of American aid has remained influential and has been emphasised, rather than refuted, by historical revisionists who have challenged other received wisdoms, such as the Churchillian influence on the history and historiography of the war.[39] The enduring perception remains that the British were bankrupt supplicants for American aid, aid that was to expand in scope and scale to a point where it became fundamental to the economic basis of the entire British war effort and to post-war survival.[40]

This Anglo-American dimension to declinism, and the sense of economic and military dependency which underpins it, forms a powerful influence over wartime history. Central to this interpretation is the operation of Lend-Lease and the Anglo-American supply relationship as a demonstration of the complete British political, diplomatic, economic and military dependence upon the United States.[41] Qualifications have been made to this: for example, A. J. P. Taylor and David Reynolds have observed that the passage of Lend-Lease was of little immediate benefit to British supply strategy in 1941 owing to the production limitations of the US armaments industry at the time.[42] These remain isolated footnotes, however, that have not challenged the dominant orthodoxy which remains based upon comparisons of raw statistical totals to the present. Richard Evans, in his recent history of the Third Reich, for example, has used the supply of American aircraft to the RAF in 1941 as a yardstick to measure the significance of American aid to Britain.[43] A detailed study of aircraft supply is therefore of fundamental importance in evaluating the larger wartime Anglo-American relationship.

The basis of this reinterpretation is the shortcoming of economic determinism as sufficient historical explanation. As Richard Overy has stated, 'The balance of economic product explains everything and nothing.'[44] Economic determinism has therefore already been recognised as insufficient to explain the outcome of the war, and the contemporary impact of the economic measures involved in American supply to Britain has been qualified by David Reynolds, A. J. P. Taylor, Alan Dobson and even the British official histories.[45] But this does not go far enough.

Economic comparisons between the combatants do not explain German successes in 1939–41 or Soviet defeats in 1941–2, any more than the production of large quantities of aircraft explains the eventual Allied air supremacy in 1944–5. The 'production miracle', by which Albert Speer and the German Fighter Staff tripled German single-engined fighter production in 1944 compared with the previous year, had no impact in wresting aerial superiority from the Allies.[46] Aircraft did not win the war by the simple fact that they were produced; to have any impact they had to consist of designs with a sufficiently competitive performance to have value in contemporary operational service. They also had to be equipped, manned and deployed effectively. The full complexity of this process has largely escaped attention in the accounts of economic determinism.

This lack of attention is reflected in Churchill's account of his reaction to the Japanese attack on the US fleet at Pearl Harbor where he dismissed the tortuous process involved in successfully deploying economic resources: 'All the rest was merely the proper application of overwhelming force'.[47] It might be observed that 'all the rest' amounts to the entire history of World War II from that point onwards. It might also be observed, perhaps in part as a consequence of this particular study, that the 'overwhelming force' involved did not necessarily originate where orthodox understanding often assumes that it did. Even Churchill's own account of the evolution of Anglo-American strategy admits that there were also substantive disputes about the 'proper application' of that force over issues such as the Anzio landing or the invasion of southern France.

This account is an attempt to rectify this problem by a critical examination of what the British wanted from American aircraft supply, how far they were able to meet those goals, and what affected the achievement of them. There are three key areas which this study will explore to expand and deepen our understanding of British aircraft supply diplomacy with the United States. Firstly, there is the issue of diplomacy itself; far too often it is forgotten that British supply policy in regard to the United States was conducted by diplomacy, determined by the tactics necessary to overcome political obstacles in order to achieve larger strategic ends. Secondly, there is the question of what contemporary British planners realistically expected in terms of aircraft supply and how they expected to employ it. Finally, there is the question of how successful American supply was in meeting those objectives, and what contemporary value it was seen to have as a result.

The issue of diplomacy reveals the complex and multifaceted issues involved. The political obstacles the British had to overcome were deeply embedded suspicions of Britain and British policy in the American body politic and in the minds of American service officers, administration officials, legislative representatives, journalists and, finally, in the minds of the American public. What the British needed aircraft for, and how much they needed them, informed their diplomacy but what determined it were the tactical manoeuvres necessary to attain their long-term goals. In this sense, the nature of British dependency on American aircraft supply will be seen to have been exaggerated for longer-term ends. Aircraft demanded as making the difference between successful resistance or defeat were, in fact, of much lower utility, and this was known to British officials at the time.

One explanation for this was the significance of the longer-term diplomatic objectives being sought. It will be demonstrated here that, ultimately, the British aircraft supply programme, which was fundamental to the evolution of Lend-Lease, was designed from the very beginning to incorporate the then neutral United States as a de facto co-belligerent providing economic support if not an open military alliance with Britain.

Diplomacy was not just conducted at the level of the nation states involved. It also involved industrial policy where, from an early stage, aircraft production planning involved the overstatement of objectives to impel the expansion of production under a sense of urgency. Aircraft production targets were understood to be exhortatory, being routinely used to stimulate future production more than they were relied upon to supply aircraft demanded by immediate plans. Sometimes these two aspects – international diplomacy and industrial diplomacy – could operate together but the immediately significant point here is that British planners knew at the time that production plans, and particularly those associated with American supply, were political instruments sometimes surprisingly disconnected from specific contemporary military requirements.

Even at this level, there are problems with the orthodox understanding. In short, the RAF was never able to rely upon promises of aircraft production and delivery from British industry. By 1942, RAF planners were cynically factoring in a 20 per cent reduction on British delivery promises from the Ministry of Aircraft Production (MAP) which was producing ‘realistic’ programmes as a consequence.[48] These problems were even worse when it came to American aircraft supply. Three key instances will be explored in this text: December 1940 when Lend-Lease was proposed; the summer and autumn of 1941 with regard to supply of aircraft from the Lend-Lease programme and also the increased need for heavy bombers; and finally, in 1942, when the successive abrogation of supply agreements culminated in the threat of the complete termination of American supplies of key types of aircraft. Ultimately, American aircraft supply would not meet the expectations of British planners at the time, and the consequent alternatives selected by British decision-makers, such as the decision to refocus on domestic supplies of heavy bombers in 1941–2, demand re-examination.

Another aspect of this diplomacy, which would become dominant by the mid-war period, was the relationship between the armed services involved, the RAF and the United States Army Air Force (USAAF).[49] To secure deliveries of promised American aircraft, the RAF had to justify their use to their main competitor for American aircraft production, an increasingly sceptical USAAF. Though it has long been understood that President Roosevelt appointed civilian officials, such as Henry Morgenthau and Harry Hopkins, to administer aid to Britain and overcome resistance from the US services, this resistance would prove remarkably resilient and finally, by 1942, become the dominant force in aircraft supply diplomacy. This USAAF influence threatened the termination of further supplies of American aircraft entirely now that the United States was a belligerent and had urgent supply needs of her own.

As a consequence, and in contradiction to the orthodox understanding of the supply relationship, in 1941–2 the British had to launch a little-known campaign to counter this resistance. Ultimately, this involved the supply of their own aircraft to the United States just to secure a greatly reduced level of supply from the Americans. As a result, the directionality of dependency can be seen to be two-way rather than simply operating to British benefit in isolation. This process also demonstrated how the British exploited what they considered to be their qualitative advantage over some important classes of American aircraft to supply the USAAF and drive an improvement in quality of American fighter aircraft, a process that would culminate in the deployment of the Mustang fighter with the Rolls-Royce Merlin engine, a development frequently identified as a decisive development in the employment of American air power.

The issue of quality is a key factor that has been largely ignored in the conventional wisdom. And yet the issue of comparative quality underlay the whole structure of aircraft supply diplomacy from the prewar purchase missions sent by the British to the United States to the aircraft exchange deals that lay behind the achievement of British supply objectives in 1942. Questioning British supply diplomacy from the 'top down' can give us a new perspective of how aircraft supply fitted into the critical dependency thesis propounded by high-level British statecraft. As will be seen in the first section of this analysis, a key component of that policy was the use of exhortatory targets in supply diplomacy. This revolves around a diplomatic strategy informed by *quantitative* analysis, and gives ground for scrutiny in terms of the numbers of aircraft involved and the numbers available as an outcome of that diplomacy. A new and further dimension is provided by a *qualitative* analysis of American aircraft supply, or the perceived value of American aircraft to meet the operational roles they were demanded for.

This represents a major and enduring problem for the conventional understanding built upon the comparison of raw statistical totals devoid of contextual evaluation. Mark Harrison has identified the interactive relationship between quality and quantity in wartime economic examination, yet the nature of the issue of 'quality' or 'value' is seldom explored.[50] Surprisingly, this issue has been well known at the macrocosmic and microcosmic levels in Anglo-American wartime supply, as the following examples, in terms of financial and military value, indicate.

At the broadest level, American supply has often been valued in terms of the financial exchange involved by citing the money appropriated, spent and then exported. The valuations associated with Lend-Lease are a notable example. Lend-Lease supply to the United Kingdom between 1941 and 1945 amounted to some \$27 billion against an approximate estimate of \$3.7 billion in British cash-purchased exports.[51] The nominal value of the figure of dollars spent in the US economy was brought into question immediately after the war when R. D. G. Allen compared US Lend-Lease supply to the United Kingdom with similar British reciprocal aid to the United States. While the dollar–sterling exchange rate was officially established at $4.035 to £1 during the war, Allen rejected this as having 'no relevance' to the appropriate relation for comparing dollar and sterling spending to establish the true value of the aid rendered.[52]

Allen established more representative grounds for comparison which accounted for the cost of procuring similar goods in the respective national economies of the United States and Britain. Owing to a variety of administrative and particular national differences, such as tighter cost control in British procurement contracts and the higher cost of labour in US shipyards, Allen suggested an average of $7 to £1 as the most accurate comparison of the respective purchasing power of the national currencies in procurement expenditure.[53] Allen's analysis engaged with the complexities of the differing national economic and internal industrial procurement contexts. It moved beyond the simplistic raw financial totals based on the official exchange rate to provide a more accurate perspective of the value of Anglo-American economic interaction. Allen's work on reciprocal aid and Lend-Lease remains seminal; yet his value-analytical approach has been ignored by the orthodox historiography of the Anglo-American relationship.[54]

The issue of value, or quality, was also evident from a 'bottom-up' investigation of American supply, as the example of tank supply to the British army in the Middle East during 1942 demonstrates. In early 1942, Sir Claude Auchinleck, the British commander-in-chief (C.-in-C.), indicated the sense of qualitative inferiority associated with British cruiser tanks by demanding a two-to-one superiority over their German equivalents.[55] In the light of those qualitative shortcomings, the raw statistics of tank shipments to the Middle East had little relevance to the operational capacity they provided. As the relevant British official history points out: '. . . comparisons of mere numbers seemed irrelevant and provocative'.[56]

By mid-1942, British strategy in Libya had begun to revolve around the issue of comparative tank numbers with a qualitative discount involved.[57] American tank supply would throw the problem into sharp relief. American-made Stuart tanks supplied in 1941 had already attracted favourable comment for their reliability but they offered no improvement over the firepower and protection of British tanks, and their operational range was worse. The arrival in Egypt in the spring of 1942 of the American Grant tank, which featured improvements in all these areas, introduced a clear qualitative differential over contemporary British tanks. The Grant was a substantial improvement on the Stuart and its British equivalent, the Crusader. Its greater operational capacity was reflected in Auchinleck's willingness to reduce the ratio of numerical superiority he demanded before beginning offensive operations from a two-to-one superiority over the German forces opposing him, and equality with the Italians, to three-to-two superiority over the Germans.[58]

Complaints about equipment quality could be a convenient rationalisation of less tangible problems with poor tactics, training and command which also contributed to inferior operational performance. Yet this represents a clear example of the importance of integrating a qualitative analysis, as it was understood to operate at the time, into any appreciation of the impact and significance of American supply to the British war effort. The qualitative inferiority of British tanks, and the contemporary qualitative superiority of American tanks, had a clear and demonstrable impact on operations, planning and strategy. The qualitative superiority of American tanks meant that their value cannot be understood by a quantitative account of their numbers alone.

This issue of qualitative value is equally relevant for aircraft supply. A history of planning within the MAP, written by the eminent economist Sir Alec Cairncross, succinctly indicates the problem with statistical reductivism absent a value-based analysis: 'Much of what was produced was, in our view, junk'.[59] And this was apparently in spite of the existence of a specific British industrial strategy of 'quality over quantity' in the aircraft industry, which has long been understood.[60]

Repeatedly throughout the history of British aircraft supply diplomacy, the RAF can be seen to operate a qualitative deployment policy where aircraft deployment was determined by their relative operational value. In this respect, quality was a chronic problem in terms of operational value to RAF planners but also in the negative impact it could have on Allied supply diplomacy. In the first instance, the RAF generally preferred their own aircraft made available by the massive investment in British domestic rearmament since 1936. Examples are legion and include the retention of the Spitfire fighter for domestic interception duties while American fighter types were relegated to overseas theatres against less formidable opposition. American heavy bombers were tried and found wanting at a critical period in supply diplomacy in 1941. American aircraft of all types, but particularly light bombers which were otherwise well regarded, lacked the level of modern equipment necessary for operational use without extensive and time-consuming modification. In some cases this British appreciation can be regarded as misplaced or overstated. But the key point is that British planners understood the relative qualitative value of aircraft to be a factor at the time. In all these instances given, the quantitative and qualitative constraints identified were known and subject to comment and debate at the time, and are not a matter for hindsight alone.

In Allen's case, he was a British official responsible for the compilation of Lend-Lease financial statistics. His evaluation of a \$7/£1 comparison was supported by the Treasury in 1943 when such statistics were a live issue in Anglo-American diplomacy during Congressional hearings on renewed Lend-Lease appropriations that spring.[61] In the case of American tank supplies, the inferiority of contemporary British tanks was both known at the time and has been an unexceptional understanding of mainstream military history ever since. In the case of aircraft supply, it is known that deliveries were lower than expected, and the quality of the aircraft sometimes questionable, but how this can be reconciled with the ambitious production plans of the time or the critical dependency asserted for American supply remains unexplained.

A closer investigation of the cumulative impact of these factors demands that we move beyond a binary, zero-sum appreciation of British dependency upon American resources. We need to grasp the nettle of explaining precisely what the British decision-makers of the time understood their dependency upon American supply to amount to. This is not in order to reverse the binary evaluation of the orthodox understanding for chauvinistic British benefit. Indeed, if anything, this study should emphasise the overriding ultimate strategic importance the British placed on American aid even after we have a more accurate understanding of the constraints which were known to limit the value of that aid at the time.

In July 1940 as the Battle of Britain began, Lord Lothian, the British ambassador to Washington and perhaps the most influential figure behind the British approach of asserting a critical dependency on American supply, told the American public that, 'In the long run we need airplanes'.[62] Five months later, President Roosevelt would respond with the policy of Lend-Lease, announced as a galvanising imperative to the American public: 'We must be the great arsenal of democracy'.[63] This study will attempt to evaluate these assertions by quantifying what the aircraft involved were needed for, how much they were needed, and how effectively they were able to meet this need. The answers which emerge provide some new and interesting perspectives, not only on wartime supply diplomacy but also the larger Anglo-American relationship which has been so enduringly shaped by the experience of intimately close wartime collaboration.

Notes

1. Horace Walpole, *Letters of Horace Walpole, Earl of Orford, to Sir Horace Mann; his Britannic Majesty's resident at the court of Florence, from 1760 to 1785*. Concluding series, Vol.2 (London: R. Bentley, 1843), p. 384.
2. Harold B. Hinton, 'No Dollars Left', in *The New York Times*, 29 January 1941.
3. Theodore Draper, *A Struggle for Power. The American Revolution* (London: Abacus, 1997), pp. 102–31.
4. Lawrence James, *The Rise and Fall of the British Empire* (London: Abacus, 1997), p. 96.
5. Robin Renwick, *Fighting With Allies* (Basingstoke: Macmillan, 1996), p. 184.
6. The literature on the development of the Anglo-American relationship

throughout the twentieth century is extensive. Some useful texts are Renwick, *Fighting With Allies*, Alan. P. Dobson, *Anglo-American Relations in the Twentieth Century* (London: Routledge, 1995) and David Reynolds, *Britannia Overruled* (Harlow: Pearson, 2000).

7. Foreword in British Library exhibition publication, *The American War of Independence 1775–1783* (London: British Museum Publications, 1975).
8. Foreword by C. D. Hamilton, in National Maritime Museum, *1776. The British Story of the American Revolution* (London: Times Books, 1976) p. 8.
9. 'Our Financial Position in America', memorandum by Keynes to Reginald McKenna, Chancellor of the Exchequer, 24 October 1916. Elizabeth Jordan (ed.), *The Collected Writings of John Maynard Keynes*, Vol. XVI (London: Macmillan, 1971), p. 201. Hereafter Keynes, *Collected Writings*, Vol. 16.
10. 'Note for Mr McAdoo', 20 July 1917. Keynes, *Collected Writings*, Vol. 16, p. 250.
11. Kathleen Burk, 'American Foreign Economic Policy and Lend-Lease', in Ann Lane and Howard Temperley (eds), *The Rise and Fall of the Grand Alliance 1941–45* (London: Macmillan, 1995), pp. 43–64; Robert Skidelsky, *John Maynard Keynes*, Vol. 3, *Fighting for Britain 1937–1946* (London: Macmillan, 2000), pp. 401–52. Hereafter Skidelsky, *Keynes Vol. 3.*
12. Henry R. Luce, 'The American Century', reprinted in *Diplomatic History*, Vol. 21, No. 2 (1999), p. 164.
13. Francis Fukuyama, *The End of History and the Last Man* (London: Penguin, 1992).
14. Herbert Butterfield, *The Whig Interpretation of History* (New York: W. W. Norton, [1931] 1965).
15. W. C. Sellar and R. J. Yeatman, *1066 and All That* (London: Methuen, 1930).
16. WP (40) 168/CoS (40) 390, 'British Strategy in a Certain Eventuality', 25 May 1940. The National Archives of the United Kingdom (TNA): Public Record Office, Kew CAB 66/7/48. Hereafter TNA references will be identified by departmental classification (ADM, AIR, AVIA, CAB, FO, PREM and WO).
17. Joseph P. Lash, *Roosevelt and Churchill 1939–1941* (New York: W. W. Norton, 1976), p. 256.
18. Williamson Murray, *The Luftwaffe 1933–45: Strategy for Defeat* (London: Brassey's, 1996), p. 139; Richard Overy, *Why the Allies*

Won (London, 1995), pp. 322–3; John Keegan, *The Second World War* (London: Pimlico, 1997), p. 178.
19. Adam Tooze, *The Wages of Destruction* (London: Penguin, 2007), pp. 658–59.
20. Hugh Rockoff, 'The United States: From Ploughshares to Swords', in Mark Harrison (ed.), *The Economics of World War II* (Cambridge: Cambridge University Press, 1998), pp. 81–2.
21. Alan S. Milward, *War, Economy and Society* (Harmondsworth: Penguin, 1987), p. 67.
22. Overy, *Why the Allies Won*, p. 192.
23. Keegan, pp. 177–8.
24. Figures from H. Duncan Hall, C. C. Wrigley and J. D. Scott, *Studies of Overseas Supply* (London: Her Majesty's Stationery Office, 1956), p. 5. Hereafter Her Majesty's Stationery Office abbreviated as HMSO.
25. Robert Dallek, *Franklin D. Roosevelt and American Foreign Policy, 1932–1945* (New York: Oxford University Press, 1995), pp. 172–5, 213; Hall, Wrigley and Scott, p. 28.
26. H. Duncan Hall, *North American Supply* (London: HMSO, 1955), pp. 121, 132.
27. November 1940 figures from Table 3, Hall, p. 212. April 1941 figures from Table 4, Hall, Wrigley and Scott, p. 108.
28. M. M. Postan, *British War Production* (London: HMSO, 1952), p. 230.
29. Corelli Barnett, *The Audit of War: The Illusion and Reality of Britain as a Great Nation* (London: Macmillan, 1987), pp. 125–58.
30. For example, the statistical basis of Barnett's thesis in the case of aircraft production statistics have been rejected by Jonathan Zeitlin, 'Flexibility and Mass Production at War: Aircraft Manufacture in Britain, the United States and Germany, 1939–1945' in *Technology and Culture*, Vol. 36 No. 1 (1995), p. 62.
31. John Ellis, *Brute Force. Allied Strategy and Tactics in the Second World War* (London: André Deutsch, 1990); Paul Kennedy, *The Rise and Fall of the Great Powers: Economic Change and Military Conflict from 1500 to 2000* (London: Fontana, 1989), pp. 113, 473.
32. Barnett, pp. 144–5.
33. Barnett interview in Richard English and Michael Kenny (eds), *Rethinking British Decline* (London: Macmillan, 2000), pp. 43–4.
34. Winston S. Churchill, *The Second World War*, Vol. III, *The Grand Alliance* (London: Cassell, 1950), p. 111.

35. Robert E. Sherwood, *The White House Papers of Harry L. Hopkins*, Vol. I, *September 1939–January 1942* (London: Eyre & Spottiswoode, 1949), p. 220; Warren F. Kimball, *The Most Unsordid Act: Lend-Lease, 1939–1941* (Baltimore: Johns Hopkins University Press, 1969), p. 189; Alan P. Dobson, *US Wartime Aid to Britain 1940–1946* (Beckenham: Croom Helm, 1986), p. 223.
36. Warren F. Kimball, '"1776": Lend Lease Gets a Number', in *The New England Quarterly*, Vol. 42, No. 2 (1969), pp. 265–7.
37. Hall, Wrigley and Scott, p. 117.
38. Skidelsky, *Keynes*, Vol. 3, p. 401.
39. David Reynolds, *In Command of History: Churchill Fighting and Writing the Second World War* (London: Penguin, 2005), pp. 174, 480; John Charmley, *Churchill's Grand Alliance: The Anglo-American Special Relationship 1940–1957* (London: Hodder & Stoughton, 1995), p. 18; and *Churchill: The End of Glory, A Political Biography* (London: Sceptre, 1993), pp. 421, 428.
40. Hall, Wrigley and Scott, p. 66.
41. For example, Charmley, *Churchill's Grand Alliance*, pp. 22–3, 45–6.
42. A. J. P. Taylor, *English History 1914–1945* (Oxford: Oxford University Press, 1992), pp. 513, 565; David Reynolds, *The Creation of the Anglo-American Alliance, 1937–1941: A Study in Competitive Co-operation* (Chapel Hill: University of North Carolina Press, 1982), p. 167.
43. Richard J. Evans, *The Third Reich at War* (London: Penguin, 2009), p. 243.
44. Overy, *Why the Allies Won*, p. 316.
45. Hall, Wrigley and Scott, p. 30.
46. Air Ministry, *The Decline and Fall of the German Air Force, 1933 to 1945* (London: HMSO, 1948), p. 309; Richard Overy, *The Air War 1939–1945* (Dulles: Potomac Books, 2005), p. 80; Murray, p. 254.
47. Churchill, *The Grand Alliance*, p. 539.
48. 'Review of Fighter Resources', October 1941; AIR 19/302; Sir Alec Cairncross, *Planning in Wartime: Aircraft Production in Britain, Germany and the USA* (London: Macmillan, 1991), pp. 20–4.
49. The US Army Air Corps (USAAC) until July 1941 when it became the USAAF. Both terms are used in the text according to the applicable date.
50. Mark Harrison, 'The Economics of World War II: an overview'; Mark Harrison (ed.), *The Economics of World War II: Six Great*

Powers in International Comparison (Cambridge: Cambridge University Press, 1998), p. 25.

51. Figures from Table 6, including Allen's estimate of $700 million for cash exports in munitions only for 1943 and 1943. R. D. G. Allen, 'Mutual Aid Between the U.S. and the British Empire, 1941–45' in *Journal of the Royal Statistical Society*, Vol. 109, No. 3 (1946), p. 253.
52. Ibid., p. 256.
53. Allen refers to a range of differential comparisons, ranging from $3 to £1 for motor vehicles and up to $10 to the £1 for certain ship-construction costs. Ibid., pp. 257–8.
54. For example, Alan Dobson utilises Allen's summary totals in his examination of Anglo-American wartime supply relationship. Dobson, *US Wartime Aid to Britain*, p. 1.
55. Auchinleck to prime minister, 30 January 1942. John Connell, *Auchinleck. A Biography of Field-Marshal Sir Claude Auchinleck* (London: Cassell, 1959), p. 446.
56. J. R. M. Butler, *Grand Strategy*: Vol. III, Part 2, *June 1941–August 1942* (London: HMSO, 1964), p. 441.
57. Auchinleck's plans were criticised on these grounds, Alanbrooke diary entry, 8 May 1942; Alex Danchev and Daniel Todman (eds), *War Diaries 1939–1945: Field Marshal Lord Alanbrooke* (London: Phoenix, 2002), p. 255.
58. Connell, p. 492; Butler, *Grand Strategy III Part 2*, p. 458.
59. Cairncross, p. 67.
60. Hall, pp. 322–3; Erik Lund, 'The History of Industrial Strategy: Reevaluating the Wartime Record of the British Aviation Industry in Comparative Perspective, 1919–1945' in *The Journal of Military History*, Vol. 62, No. 1 (1998), p. 79.
61. '. . . a rate which the Treasury consider to be correct'. CAB 21/1413.
62. Lord Lothian, NBC broadcast, 22 July 1940; H. U. Hudson (ed.), *Lord Lothian Speaks to America* (London: Oxford University Press, 1941), p.112.
63. James MacGregor Burns, *Roosevelt 1940–1945: The Soldier of Freedom* (San Diego: Harcourt, 1970), p. 28.

2 The Evolution of Transatlantic Aircraft Supply Diplomacy, 1938–40

> Is it possible to maintain a great Fleet and an immense Air Force requiring a vast labour force behind it, to sustain the dislocation of continued bombardment from the air, to provide munitions at a rate contemplated for Allies as well as ourselves, and at the same time to fight with an unlimited Army on the continent backed by an unlimited supply of materials?[1]

This was the question posed by Sir John Simon, the Chancellor of the Exchequer, as British rearmament policy took priority over normal trade in 1939. This development was long before the crisis of 1940 or the appearance of Lend-Lease in 1941, and indicates how concepts of the economic limitations on British military power stretch back into the pre-war period. The conundrum posed by Simon could be resolved only by national economic mobilisation on a scale beyond the Chamberlain government's initial preferences and eventually by plans for American aid on an enormous scale.

During the rearmament period between 1938 and 1940, British policy would have to grapple with this problem without American aid. Between 1932 and 1939 the strategic alignment of British defence policy changed dramatically. In 1932 Britain remained ostensibly wedded to the 'Ten-Year Rule', the assumption that no war with a major power could be expected in the next ten years, and military planning and expenditure were limited as a result. While the Royal Navy (RN) benefited from recognition of its continued global role and the Japanese naval threat in the Far East, the British Army and RAF had their horizons limited to imperial policing duties. The RAF had discovered an operational sphere to legitimise their continued independence in Air Control operations in Iraq and Somaliland. Within Europe, the relaxation of post-war Anglo-French tensions followed by the prospective outcomes of various international disarmament conferences had led to the completion of a plan derived from the 1923 Salisbury report for a force of fifty-two squadrons for home defence – defensive fighters and offensive bombers – being delayed until 1936. By 1934, the RAF had forty-two squadrons for domestic defence, four for naval and five for army co-operation respectively, and twenty-four squadrons overseas.[2] In 1936, the growth in international tension meant that the Salisbury report target was tripled to 124 home defence squadrons to be completed by March 1939.[3]

The years from 1935 to 1939, under the prime ministers Stanley Baldwin and then Neville Chamberlain, were marked by a primary focus upon air rearmament inspired by the growing German air threat. This was motivated by apocalyptic fears of the results of large-scale bombing attacks on civilians, and the perception among influential figures that an increased RAF bombing force could provide a deterrent to the outbreak of war and also offer an alternative to the enormous casualties associated with a large army commitment to the continent if it did. This marked a new evolution in British strategy which had previously been concerned with maintaining naval strength against potential competitors. In the words of Colonel Hastings Ismay, appointed Deputy Secretary of the Committee of Imperial Defence (CID) in 1936, '. . . the development of air power had revolutionised the position'.[4]

This development was an outcome of the defence planning conducted by the CID in the mid-1930s. The Defence Requirements Committee (DRC) of the CID had then been formed in 1932 to recommend remedial measures in British defence. An initial concern with Japanese aggression in Manchuria revived interest in naval rearmament, and the resumption of the construction of the Singapore naval base, but this had swiftly been overtaken by the focus on Germany. The DRC had been influenced by the opinions of two senior civil servants, Sir Warren Fisher of the Treasury and Sir Robert Vansittart of the Foreign Office (FO), who saw German rearmament under the new Nazi government of Adolf Hitler as the greatest threat to British interests.

Hitler's aggressive diplomacy, which progressively abrogated the remaining provisions of the 1919 Treaty of Versailles, bound the British into an escalating series of reciprocal rearmament initiatives. In March 1935 Herman Goring had publicly announced the formation of a new German air force, the Luftwaffe. This was quickly followed by Hitler's declaration later that month to Simon, then British Foreign Secretary, that the Luftwaffe had already reached numerical parity with the RAF.[5] Due to the absolute political imperative for domestic defence, combined with the perceived weakness of the RAF, the government was unable to reach any diplomatic settlement with Germany on air rearmament similar to the 1935 Anglo-German Naval Treaty. The result was a competitive escalation of industrial production.

The path of this escalation can be clearly measured in the diplomatic events that influenced the successive RAF expansion schemes in the rearmament period, as shown in Table 2.1. 'Scheme C' was prompted by Goring's claim of Luftwaffe parity; 'Scheme F' by Italian aggression against Ethiopia in 1935; and finally 'Scheme M' after Munich in 1938. The Air Staff's plan for 'Scheme J' was originally considered and rejected by the cabinet on the basis of the economic cost interfering with normal export trade; this was then modified into an accelerated 'Scheme L' which was an accelerated version of 'Scheme J' after the Austrian *Anschluss*.

The majority of these aircraft were to be based in Britain to confront the Luftwaffe; for example, 'Scheme C' involved a total of 1,512 aircraft in 123 squadrons, 83 per cent of which were to

Table 2.1 RAF pre-war expansion schemes[6]

Scheme	Date	Completion date	Striking force (Bomber Command)	Fighter Command
A	July 1934	March 1939	500	336
C	March 1935	March 1937	840	420
F	November 1935	March 1939	1,022	420
J	October 1937	June 1941	1,442	532
K	January 1938	March 1941	1,360	532
L	April 1938	March 1940	1,352	608
M	October 1938	March 1942	1,360	800

be split between the two main domestic combat forces of Fighter and Bomber Commands.[7] Just as the escalatory steps in the rearmament programmes were triggered by political pressure, their content was also influenced by political concerns. An early alliance between the RAF Air Staff and politicians on increases in bomber strength for doctrinal reasons and deterrence, respectively, was superseded by an increasing emphasis on fighter strength born of the political requirements for visible domestic defence.[8]

The RAF remained the primary beneficiary of rearmament spending when compared to the Army or RN. The Air Ministry's budget rose from £9.4 million, out of a total tri-service budget of £37.2 million in 1934 (or 25.3 per cent), to £109.9 million out of a tri-service budget of £260.4 million in 1939 (or 42.0 per cent).[9] This primacy was reflected in the figures actually spent which differed from the figures appropriated owing to various factors, such as the late delivery of aircraft or munitions against contract estimates. Air Ministry spending rose from £17.67 million in 1934 to £248.561 million in 1939, or from 15.5 per cent to 35.5 per cent of the combined defence budget over the same period.[10] Major Henry Pownall, Military Assistant Secretary to the CID, observed in 1934 how political concerns driven by the criticisms of a clique of back-bench politicians determined the relative neglect of the army: '. . . the balance is wrong. That the RAF have got too much. It is extraordinary the effect of (so-called) public opinion, the press, and the Lord Lloyd–Churchill group on the minds of ministers.'[11]

The factor limiting overall spending was the issue of available finance. The politicians and officials associated with the Treasury have been identified as an axis of decisive influence on rearmament policy.[12] These figures included Neville Chamberlain, first as chancellor and then prime minister, and Sir John Simon who succeeded Chamberlain at the Treasury in May 1937. The strategic preferences of these politicians were central to the balance of British rearmament policy.

Maintaining British financial stability was an article of faith for the national government formed in 1931 as a response to the Great Depression. This was exemplified by Chamberlain's success as chancellor in balancing the budget. That success was threatened by an adverse balance of payments being increased by the overseas' imports demanded by a substantive rearmament programme.[13] This would be compounded by the loss in capacity for earning foreign exchange caused by converting export trade capacity to rearmament production. Servicing an increasingly adverse balance of payments would eventually demand the liquidation of gold or convertible reserves to support Sterling, a process of disinvestment feared by politicians and economists alike for the resulting impact on the British economy. Finally, Chamberlain feared that increased domestic demand caused by rearmament would lead to inflation and a 'feverish and artificial boom followed by a disastrous slump' and repeat of the 1931 economic crash.[14]

While Hitler could exploit the capacities of a police state to benefit from draconian price and exchange controls alongside openly autarkic bilateral trading arrangements in order to manage enormous government spending on rearmament, the British government felt unable to abandon its liberal capitalist policies for political and ideological reasons.[15] This left British rearmament policy under substantial financial constraints. Significantly, and far from representing the conventional wisdom of a Treasury 'dead hand' limiting rearmament, these financial considerations acted in favour of air rearmament.

The tone was set by Neville Chamberlain, in his otherwise negative response to the 1934 DRC report, when he accepted the value of building up the RAF as a deterrent: '. . . we shall be more likely to deter Germany from mad-dogging if we have an air force which, in case of need, could bomb the Ruhr from Belgium'.[16] This was reflected in his arbitrary increase in RAF allocations in the resulting 1934 White Paper on Defence where he proposed an increase of £2.5 million in the RAF's allotment for the next five years at the same time as he cut back the amounts for the other services. Chamberlain's approach was not an isolated one at the DRC; with an irony lost on the later conventional wisdom of the Treasury role, Fisher even urged greater expansion of the RAF than the Air Ministry was asking for.[17]

One explanation for this might be Fisher's receipt of advice from Lord Trenchard, the first Chief of the Air Staff (CAS) and the originator of the 'Trenchard doctrine' of strategic bombing to break the morale of the enemy civilian population in war. Though the concept of strategic bombing of civilians pre-dated Trenchard's period as CAS (notably in the writings of the Italian, Douhet), Trenchard was instrumental in shaping the RAF's strategy around the concept and securing political support for it. Fisher and Chamberlain saw air power as the only force which could defend against and, more importantly, deter a possible German 'knock-out blow' or overwhelming pre-emptive attack on British civilian targets.[18]

The policy of deterrence was also informed by the issue of aircraft quality. The technical potential of the new types of heavy bombers demanded by Air Staff specifications in 1936 offered the promise of reaching German targets without the necessity of basing them in France or the Low Countries, with the diplomatic issues that would involve. A growing confidence in the ability of RAF bombers to deter future aggression was evident in Chamberlain's thinking that year:

> . . . I am pretty satisfied now that, if we can keep out of war for a few years, we shall have an air force of such striking power that no one will care to run risks with it . . . I believe our resources will be more profitably employed in the air, and on the sea, than in building up great armies.[19]

This political appreciation reflected thinking in the Air Ministry where figures such as Group Captain Harris, then Deputy Director of Plans, could advocate the complete abandonment of a 'continental commitment', or deployment of a military expeditionary force to France, in favour of the decisive potential of strategic bombing.[20] However during 1937 unquestioning Treasury encouragement of Air Ministry plans modified to become something more selective.

Initial rearmament plans had aimed at achieving parity with the Luftwaffe. But throughout 1936–7, this objective seemed to slip from the government's grasp as increasingly exaggerated estimates of Luftwaffe strength held sway. Part of the problem revolved around the issue of meaningfully quantifying air strength. Two fundamental aspects of this were the issues of reserves and aircraft quality. Reserves were needed to sustain losses in combat – by 1937 the RAF was aiming at a reserve of 225 per cent of its initial operational strength, and it was assumed that the Luftwaffe was following a similar policy. This more than doubled the number of aircraft required to be produced to reach a given front-line strength. Then there was the issue of quality: fabric-skinned biplanes could not be counted as equivalent to the new generation of higher-powered, stressed metal-skinned monoplanes with significantly better performance, payload, armament and range.

On the issue of aircraft quality, the RAF had rejected the option of increased production of existing types in favour of a more ambitious policy of ordering newer types featuring what they considered to be necessary technical improvements. This entailed a considerable delay in equipping and then developing the relevant production infrastructure in the British aircraft industry. While Germany was pushing ahead with similar designs, her production figures during the rearmament period were inflated by the inclusion of obsolete aircraft. As Richard Overy has observed,

> . . . many of the aircraft that the German air force counted as first-line during this period were of relatively poor performance and of doubtful military utility. Figures for gross strength or gross output are quite meaningless unless such qualifications are kept in mind.[21]

This was hard to quantify for estimates of the RAF strength required in response. This problem, along with the shortcomings of the RAF Air Intelligence branch at the time, made it difficult to assess just what force strength the RAF needed to counterbalance the threat from the Luftwaffe. Air Ministry figures for German air strength were felt to be consistently understated, leading to a loss of confidence on the part of officials such as Fisher and the adoption of alternative channels of private intelligence which informed both Vansittart within Whitehall and prominent external critics of Air Ministry policy such as Churchill. Both groups selectively leaked such secret information to the press to encourage increased air rearmament.[22]

In 1936 Baldwin had appointed Sir Thomas Inskip as Minister

for the Co-ordination of Defence, and Inskip had then responded to the political pressures for parity by recommending a new emphasis on air defence rather than deterrence by bombing.[23] In part this reflected a Treasury preference for fighter aircraft which were cheaper and quicker to produce than multi-engined bombers but it also reflected a shift in the balance of air-power policy towards defence rather than deterrence. This still left the government committed to an enormous programme of industrial investment to produce a strategic bomber force of unprecedented scale and striking power.

Despite the changes in strategic emphasis, Treasury limitations were constantly being modified under the pressure of escalation and still to the benefit of the Air Ministry. In 1937 a Treasury-imposed overall limit on defence spending of £1,500 million for 'financial rationing' was used primarily to enforce spending priorities within the services but the Air Ministry continued to benefit from a sense of priority within that limit. Financial orthodoxy was in retreat, most obviously in the form of the £400 million 1937 Defence Loan where Chamberlain reversed his previous policy of funding defence expenditure out of the normal taxation yield. Government borrowing for defence increased with a second Defence Loan in the following year when all Treasury limitation had effectively been suspended. By April 1938 the cabinet had accepted a policy of the Air Ministry ordering as many aircraft as the British aircraft industry could produce by April 1940.[24] This situation extended into the minutiae normally expected to provide a secure arena for Treasury supremacy when the Air Ministry successfully deflected Treasury attempts to revise the details of aircraft supply contracts to minimise industry profits.[25]

From this point onwards the scale of air rearmament was governed by the capacity of British industry to produce, based on the preceding capital investment of both the government and private enterprise in that industry. That this investment was ultimately relatively successful can be seen in the comparative total aircraft production figures in Table 2.2.

By 1939 British aircraft output had finally approached parity with that of Germany and, while this provided some confidence to the British government, it arrived too late to dissipate the lead

Table 2.2 Aircraft production by the major powers, 1932–9[26]

Year	Britain	France	USA	Germany	Italy	Japan
1932	445	n/a	593	36	n/a	691
1933	633	n/a	466	368	386	766
1934	740	n/a	437	1,986	328	688
1935	1,140	785	459	3,183	895	952
1936	1,877	890	1,141	5,112	1,768	1,181
1937	2,153	743	949	5,606	1,749	1,511
1938	2,827	1,382	1,800	5,235	1,610	3,201
1939	7,940	3,163	2,195	8,295	1,750	4,467

Germany had built up during 1934–38. In May 1938 political pressure over the slow pace of air rearmament lead to the dismissals of the Secretary of State for Air, Lord Swinton, and his deputy. Swinton had been well regarded at the Air Ministry but his policy of prioritising capital investment for the production of new aircraft types had not provided the immediate increase in output that was a political necessity.[27] By the time of the 1938 Air Estimates debate which caused Swinton's replacement, 'Scheme F' had been running for two out of the three years planned but only 4,500 aircraft out of the intended 8,000 had been delivered.[28]

In March 1938, one of Swinton's last initiatives was a response to an Air Ministry enquiry regarding the possibility of aircraft purchases in the United States. The slow pace of aircraft output from British industry was threatening the achievement of the planned RAF strength targets for March 1940 and, as a result, the dual issues of supplementary purchases of aircraft from America and the development of 'war potential' aircraft production in Canada came before the CID at the end of March 1938. While developing an infant aircraft industry in Canada was understood to be a longer-term issue, Swinton saw investigation of the off-the-shelf purchase of available American types 'of value to us' as a potential short-term addition to British supply that summer.[29]

Securing the funding for any resulting purchases was contingent upon overcoming the political reluctance to use the foreign exchange required. Swinton's proposal of a mission to the United States and Canada was approved by the CID, and came before the cabinet a month later. At this point the cabinet was considering moving from the existing 'Scheme F', calculated to complete by March 1939, and 'Scheme L', calculated to reach completion in March 1940. Overall, this demanded an increase of over 500 front-line aircraft in Britain and a further 474 aircraft overseas. Coupled with the requirement for reserves, this entailed a requirement for 12,000 aircraft to be produced over the next two years.[30] The provisions of 'Scheme L' were now expected to be 'substantially achieved' by March 1940 provided the required government capital investment was made. American purchases to supplement this programme were regarded as 'a contingent reserve'.[31] American aircraft supply was therefore viewed as a marginal supplement to a larger British programme but still important enough for the vociferous complaints of the Society of British Aircraft Constructors (SBAC) to be ignored.[32]

The cabinet discussions established a set of objectives and considerations that would remain a feature of British supply requirements throughout the war. Swinton's views of obtaining aircraft of sufficient quality and completing delivery in a short-term timescale to meet expansion targets would exist beside Chamberlain's view of American production as an 'insurance' against a possible loss of British output. These would remain lasting features of British aircraft supply policy in the United States. Two larger constraints were the financial and political limitations on American supply. While the financial limitations on overseas purchases on the British side would steadily be eroded, and then finally cast aside under the pressure of wartime disaster in 1940, the political limitations on the American side of the relationship could not be changed by British agency in isolation. This took the form of a hesitant progression from an unpromising start.

The Anglo-American relationship had deteriorated since the end of World War I and the rise of American isolationism following the rejection of the League of Nations by the US Senate. This left the British, as they perceived it, guarantors of the league and a Wilsonian peace settlement that the United States had retreated from. Bilateral tensions had also arisen with the Coolidge and Hoover administrations, notably over the Washington and London naval treaties which had even left Churchill with aggrieved suspicions. These had been deepened by diplomatic differences in the 1930s, notably over Japanese aggression in Manchuria and Roosevelt's adoption of economic nationalism at the 1933 London economic conference.

Domestically, isolationism had become a dominant factor in American politics. Traditional Anglophobia had now become allied with mid-western agrarian and protectionist interests and gained formidable influence in Congress and the Senate. The debt default of 1932, when the British and French were unable to make the annual instalments required by the 1923 settlement of their World War I loans, led to the Johnson Act of 1934 which prohibited further loans to defaulters. The extent of suspicions towards British statecraft had been revealed, and reinforced, by Senator Gerald Nye's investigation into the presumed manipulation of the United States into World War I by British-influenced business interests. Isolationists moved from an attack on the influence of the armaments industry on foreign policy towards limiting the powers of the executive of the federal government. Although the attempt to subject to a plebiscite Congressional power to declare war narrowly failed, this led to the 1935 Neutrality Act, renewed on a biannual basis until 1941, and which prohibited the export of munitions or implements of war to belligerents and the use of American shipping in war zones.[33]

Collectively, this legislation deliberately reflected the tenets of Jeffersonian economic statecraft in order to prevent American involvement in global, and specifically British, conflicts.[34] Removing these obstacles to the operation of the British global economy in wartime and drawing the United States into a closer relationship became primary objects of British statecraft during the appeasement era.

The policy of appeasement was contingent upon diplomatic satisfaction of some of the objectives of revisionist powers such as Germany, Italy and Japan at the same time as rearming to deter war. The British had been prepared to accept Hitler's abrogation of Versailles, his occupation of the Rhineland and the *Anschluss* with Austria. They were even prepared to offer economic aid and the return of overseas colonial territory to Germany. In the Mediterranean, the need to avoid driving Italy into the German orbit after Mussolini's aggression against Ethiopia had undermined the remaining credibility of enforcing collective security through the League of Nations. In 1938 Chamberlain attempted to detach Mussolini from Germany, leading to Anthony Eden's resignation as Foreign Secretary. In the Far East Japanese expansion in China and their threat to Singapore and Malaya led to the consideration of a diplomatic settlement though this was rejected because of the hostility it would provoke in the United States.

Within the narrow margins imposed by isolationism, Roosevelt supported appeasement through the offers of peace, stability and trade to Germany.[35] From a Whitehall perspective, just as Hitler's intransigent ambitions undermined any prospect of settlement with Germany, the need to conciliate the United States by avoiding a rapprochement with Japan prevented any accommodation with Tokyo. This produced little concrete progress, even when the British aligned themselves with American diplomatic opposition to continuing Japanese aggression in China, leading to increased British frustrations with US policy.[36] What the British particularly sought was the amendment of the Neutrality Act but, when this was renewed as a result of the Spanish Civil War in 1937, it perpetuated the embargo and shipping restrictions that the British wanted removed.[37]

Roosevelt was constrained by the genuine popularity of isolationism, his loss of authority resulting from the Supreme Court packing controversy and a renewed bout of economic depression. His famous 'quarantine speech' of October 1937, made in response to German and Italian intervention in the Spanish Civil War and expanding Japanese aggression in China, left Chamberlain dismissive: '. . . it is always best and safest to count on nothing from the Americans but words'.[38]

British access to the American economy was limited to a narrow window of cash purchases made before the outbreak of war. There was therefore little point in investing in any substantive programme of aircraft purchases even if this had been seen as desirable – the delay before deliveries could begin would leave the aircraft produced to be held hostage by the inevitable embargo. The consequent view of American supply as a short-term and marginal source of supply was reinforced by the promise of the eventual realisation of higher domestic output from domestic rearmament; the need for American aircraft was expected to diminish as British production increased.

The result of Swinton's initiative was the April–May 1938 mission to the United States led by Group Captain Weir, brother of Lord Weir, the industrial adviser to the Air Ministry, and which included Group Captain Harris and Sir Henry Self, the deputy undersecretary at the Air Ministry who would later lead the British Air Commission (BAC) in wartime New York. The mission's objectives were to investigate the Canadian aircraft industry with a view to building up war-potential production, and secondly to investigate the capacity of the American aircraft industry to alleviate current bottlenecks in British aircraft supply, notably in the area of flying boats, land-based maritime reconnaissance ('General Reconnaissance', or 'GR') and trainer aircraft.[39]

After touring aircraft plants, the mission reported that American military aviation was 'backward compared with British standards', in contrast with the much more developed state of civil aviation. After rejecting the Consolidated PBY (Patrol Bomber Y) amphibian (later called the 'Catalina') and the Boeing B-17 bomber after a limited inspection of the first squadron in US Army Air Corps (USAAC) service, the mission settled on two purchase recommendations. After Harris had been impressed by the speed with which Lockheed had produced an interior mock-up for his inspection, an order was placed for two hundred Lockheed Super Electra airliners adapted to operate in the general reconnaissance (GR) role (the B-14 'Hudson'), with an option for a further fifty for delivery by the end of 1939.[40] In addition the mission recommended the purchase of two hundred NA-16 Harvard I trainer aircraft based on the USAAC BC-1/AT-6 model from North American Aviation.

The 1938 purchases were limited, representing only four hundred to four hundred and fifty aircraft when compared to the 12,000 aircraft expected from domestic production over the same period, but they represented a significant financial escalation of British air rearmament policy. All purchases in the United States had to be funded by dollar payment, from exchange reserves or from the sale of gold, and therefore had a direct impact on the British trading position. Any American aircraft purchase programme was going to be expensive; the Hudson contract alone cost $25 million or about a quarter of the entire value of British exports to the United States in 1938.[41]

But finance was not a major consideration when the purchases were considered in cabinet. Swinton emphasised the necessity to meet RAF expansion targets but received support for diplomatic rather than for military reasons. Lord Halifax, who had replaced Eden as Foreign Secretary that February, observed that purchasing American aircraft would imply that 'America was behind us' and have 'a useful effect in Germany'; with the reverse being correct if the proposal was dropped. Oliver Stanley, the president of the Board of Trade, argued that a quick purchase would benefit the simultaneous negotiation of the Anglo-American Trade treaty.[42] This was concluded in November 1938 and fulfilled the ambitions of the US Secretary of State, Cordell Hull, to advance international co-operation and, by means of bilateral trade treaties, to avoid the conflicts generated by economic nationalism. Chamberlain's hesitancy over the political impact on the imperial preference trade system had been overcome by pressure from the FO to placate mid-west agrarian isolationists and to provide the 'appearance of solidarity' in Anglo-American relations.[43] Halifax argued that the political reasons for concluding the trade treaty outweighed the trade and economic considerations, and Chamberlain eventually agreed.[44]

> The reason why I have been prepared . . . to go a long way to get this treaty, is precisely because I reckoned it would help to educate American opinion to act more and more with us, and because I felt sure it would frighten the totalitarians.[45]

The purchase of American aircraft fitted into this larger political and diplomatic context. Just before his resignation, Eden had argued that the amendment of neutrality legislation in favour of countries fighting aggression would be an 'all important' gesture, making it clear that US economic resources were behind the Allies.[46] If this diplomatic dimension was a powerful influence on British supply, it was to be a determining influence on French supply policy which was to define Allied supply policy towards the United States.

If the British were concerned about their air strength compared to that of Germany, the French were almost desperate. After years of neglect, by 1936 the French air force was qualitatively and quantitatively inferior to the Luftwaffe.[47] This situation deteriorated further as the chaotic state of the French aircraft industry crippled French air rearmament. In January 1938, the new chief of the French Air Staff, General Vuillemin, reported to Guy La Chambre, the French air minister, that, in the event of war, he expected the French air force to be wiped out 'within days', leaving French cities at the mercy of Luftwaffe bombing.[48] Alongside Edouard Daladier, the French Minister of Defence, Chambre pushed through an ambitious air force expansion scheme known as 'Plan V', designed to achieve a front-line strength of 2,617 front-line aircraft by March 1939.

This seemed beyond the capacity of the French aircraft industry, and American industry was immediately considered as an alternative source of supply. Baron Amaury de la Grange was sent on a confidential mission to the United States in January 1938, three months before the Weir mission, to investigate the prospects of purchasing American aircraft to bolster the front-line strength of the French air force. De la Grange's objectives were far more ambitious than Weir's, with the hope that he could order 1,000 combat aircraft and also 'harness American industry to the French war machine'.[49] De la Grange was an acquaintance of the president and, during a visit to the president's estate at Hyde Park, Roosevelt encouraged a combined effort to improve French, British and American air power against Germany while warning that 'caution and discretion' would be required when dealing with Congress and the press.[50]

Following a formula which would become depressingly familiar over the next two years, de la Grange reported in February 1938 that the United States had little in the way of modern aircraft available. He recommended the purchase of a hundred Curtiss P-36 fighters, which were all that could be usefully supplied by April 1939, though this would require an investment of $1 million to provide the machine tools required.[51] This mission gave the first illustration of three factors that would shape Allied plans for American supply: firstly, the relative lack of available aircraft; secondly, there was the necessity for substantial capital investment to increase future production; and finally, there was the resistance of the USAAC. General Henry Arnold, the head of the USAAC, objected to the foreign sale of aircraft identical to those used by the USAAC. Arnold's opposition came into play when the French requested that a series of test flights of a P-36 be made by a French test pilot before the order could be placed in March 1938. After pressure from William Bullitt, the US ambassador to Paris, Roosevelt exercised his authority as commander-in-chief to order General Malin Craig, the US Army chief of staff and Arnold's superior, to direct Arnold to permit one short and secret test flight.[52]

Continuing French interest in the potential American aircraft supply became almost feverish as the Munich crisis developed in September 1938. The conclusion of the Munich agreement, accepting Hitler's annexation of the Sudetenland region of Czechoslovakia, has been represented as an example of the West being 'out-deterred' by Hitler.[53] Chamberlain's fear of German air attack paled into insignificance, however, when contrasted with the French position. French air force weakness had a direct impact on French diplomacy during the Munich crisis. Daladier, who became French premier in early 1938, was confronted with military views that were simply too bleak to be ignored. General Vuillemin had been 'distraught' about French weakness in the air, leaving General Gamelin, the French army chief of staff, to claim that Daladier had been driven to Munich by 'the air question'.[54]

Faced with such miserable appreciations, they looked for signs of US support beyond Roosevelt's speech on 16 August at Kingston, Ontario, which had been designed to raise doubts in Berlin over US intentions if war broke out.[55] La Chambre emphasised to Bullitt the near defencelessness of France against air attack, claiming that, if war began that October, the French would have a total of six hundred aircraft, with 240 British reinforcements, to face 6,500 German aircraft.[56] After Daladier confirmed to Bullitt that lack of air power had been the decisive influence on French policy at Munich, Bullitt returned to America to facilitate American aircraft supply as a means of bolstering French resistance.[57]

At the beginning of the Sudetenland crisis, Roosevelt had called in Harry Hopkins, the head of the Works Progress Administration (WPA) and later Secretary of Commerce, and asked him to conduct a survey of the aircraft industry on the US west coast. Hopkins was later to achieve great importance as Roosevelt's personal emissary and the administrator of Lend-Lease in 1941. He had a close relationship with Roosevelt which secured his access to power, a matter of prime importance in an administration riven by the jealousies and rivalries created by Roosevelt's deliberately chaotic leadership style. More significantly, he had substantial relevant experience in initiating large-scale New Deal programmes, including capital investment in industrial expansion and liaison with the armed services, which is often ignored in appraisals of his career.

The remit of these organisations extended to supplementing areas of the defence budget. The WPA and Public Works Administration (PWA), run by Hopkins's great rival, Harold Ickes, were often staffed by seconded and retired military officers. They funded everything from the construction of military roads and base facilities to the construction of new aircraft carriers. When General George C. Marshall was appointed deputy chief of staff in 1938, he was surprised to discover the PWA and WPA had already spent $250 million on War Department projects.[58] In 1938 Hopkins already operated at the developing intersection between the New Deal and rearmament policy.

Roosevelt wanted Hopkins to assess the capital investment required to increase the production capacity of firms that had missed out on the capital investment the French had provided to the Curtiss-Wright plant in Buffalo, New York, with their P-36 order earlier in the year.[59] The west coast states of Washington and especially southern California had become a new centre of the United States aviation industry. Firms based on the west coast included Boeing in Seattle, Consolidated in San Diego, and three in the Los Angeles area – Douglas at Long Beach, North American at Inglewood, and Lockheed at Burbank.

The result of Bullitt's diplomacy and Hopkins's mission became apparent during October when Roosevelt announced that he intended to ask Congress for $500 million in defence appropriations for the United States services. Roosevelt also discussed the possibility of evading the Neutrality Act by shipping aircraft parts for assembly in Canada and then reshipping them to France, though it became clear that this would be legally dubious and politically unacceptable. He also raised aircraft production targets to 15,000 aircraft per year, or more than eight times the actual US output in 1938.[60] Throughout November and December Roosevelt rejected military plans to build a balanced ground and air force with the broad range of equipment and logistical support the USAAC deemed necessary in favour of numerical deterrence. 'A well-rounded ground army of even 400,000 could not be considered a deterrent for any foreign power whereas a heavy striking force of aircraft would.'[61]

Roosevelt saw this striking force being built up by American industry but operated by French hands, and he began to take action to facilitate that objective. During his State of the Union address in January 1939, he identified the operation of the Neutrality Act and its potential benefit to aggressors as a problem to be addressed.[62] The previous December, Roosevelt had passed on a private assurance to Chamberlain that he was concerned with German air power and that Chamberlain would have '. . . the industrial resources of the American nation behind him in the event of war with the dictatorships'.[63]

Roosevelt's interest in substantive air rearmament intersected with the post-Munich French attempt to increase their air strength. Jean Monnet, a French businessman who had been deputy secretary to the League of Nations, visited the United States as a result of Bullitt's representations that October and was assured of Roosevelt's personal support. He returned in December to negotiate a second purchase contract to include orders for the most modern aircraft available in the near future. Monnet's objectives were to secure maximum output of American military aircraft production for France, adopt American mass production methods for the French aircraft industry, and arrange for the assembly of American aircraft in Canada to evade the provisions of the Neutrality Act.[64]

Daladier and La Chambre now had to confront the same financial issue which constrained British rearmament – the loss of convertible reserves needed to meet an adverse balance of payments. The new French finance minister, Paul Reynaud, while staunchly anti-Nazi, was reluctant to use the extensive French gold reserves to purchase aircraft. Reynaud believed that 'to defend the franc is to defend France', and opposed on financial grounds the post-Munich La Chambre–Daladier plan to purchase a thousand American aircraft.[65] Reynaud was overruled on the grounds of military deficiency: the French air force wanted three thousand aircraft by the end of 1939, and French industry was only expected to produce two thousand. As Daladier observed, 'Our aerial inferiority is tragic. One thousand American planes are necessary.'[66]

Monnet was then faced with the financial dimension from the side of the Roosevelt administration. In 1939 Hopkins was sidelined by illness after previous surgery for stomach cancer.[67] Roosevelt appointed Henry Morgenthau, the Treasury Secretary, and one of the figures in his closest circle, to facilitate foreign munitions orders through a liaison committee with representation from the US services. His appointment indicated Roosevelt's determination to ensure that his policy of aiding the Allies would be in the hands of a committed anti-Nazi and out of the hands of the unsympathetic State Department. It also indicated that a hard financial bargain would be driven. While Morgenthau was keen to help the French, he made it clear that substantive purchases were seen as earnest of French intent.[68]

Though Morgenthau rejected the idea of American loans to finance French-sponsored factories in Canada as a violation of the Johnson Act, he was to prove a valuable ally in the question of aircraft quality. Morgenthau accepted that the French required access to the latest types of aircraft ordered by the USAAC, and his efforts helped to overcome the USAAC's veto on the French testing the new and secret Douglas DB-7 attack bomber. The eventual French test flight of the DB-7 was to end in political controversy and generate the first direct confrontation between the divergent positions of the isolationists and the administration towards aiding the British and French.

On 23 January 1939, the prototype DB-7 crashed during a test flight at Los Angeles airport, killing two Douglas aircrew and injuring a French air force officer on board. The crash was exposed to the public, and the presence of a foreign military officer aboard instantly generated headlines throughout the press.[69] The DB-7 crash not only revealed the presence of a secret French purchasing mission but also exposed the willingness of the administration to supply advanced and even secret aircraft to the European powers. The Senate Military Affairs Committee had begun hearings on Roosevelt's air rearmament policy. Their main witness was Arnold who was able to defend the plan against isolationist senators on the basis that (contrary to Roosevelt's initial wishes) it built up a balanced USAAC force which included non-operational aircraft such as trainers. News of the crash broke during Arnold's testimony on 24 January and he was compelled to admit that approval of the DB-7 test flight had been granted against army wishes. Roosevelt's attempts to placate the committee with off-the-record talks at the White House backfired and increased isolationist anger when he allegedly asserted that the strategic frontiers of the United States lay on the Rhine.[70]

Roosevelt had more success defending the sale on economic grounds. The combined Allied orders represented a scale of investment and generation of industrial capacity that outstripped contemporary USAAC procurement. The $25 million Lockheed Hudson order made by the British had been the largest order placed with any American aircraft company to that point. In addition to the existing capital investment at Curtiss-Wright, the proposed French contracts included $2.25 million in capital investment for Glenn Martin to produce the GM-167 bomber. The French had now ordered 795 Pratt & Whitney Twin Wasp engines, guaranteeing production at a time when the company was considering closing the plant down owing to the lack of future orders.[71] When Roosevelt's dramatic call for 10,000 front-line aircraft in response to Munich had been cut by the USAAC to 3,000 aircraft, and his additional rearmament appropriation of $500 million for aircraft reduced to $180 million, the French expenditure of $60 million was a significant addition to American industrial potential.[72]

In total the Monnet mission resulted in the order of 555 aircraft for delivery between May and October 1939; one hundred more P-36 fighters, two hundred Harvard trainers, forty Chance-Vought dive-bombers, one hundred DB-7s and 115 GM 167 bombers. The reduction of the total ordered from the original plan of one thousand was imposed by the inability of American industry to produce any more aircraft of sufficiently modern types before the end of the year.[73]

One major bottleneck was the supply of modern engines. The French need for modern engines was so great that, not only was the use of five hundred Rolls-Royce Merlins (as used in the British Hurricane and Spitfire fighters) discussed, but the almost incredible idea of buying German Daimler-Benz DB 601 engines (as used in the Messerschmitt Bf 109) was also briefly considered.[74] To meet this demand, La Chambre expressed strong interest in securing delivery of five hundred Allison V-1710 engines which were in the process of development for the USAAC. He described the Allison in terms of criticality which was to become the stock-in-trade of Allied diplomacy: '. . . no single act could be of greater assistance to France and England than an immediate and great increase in the production of Allison motors'.[75]

In the broader sense, neutrality legislation was still the main obstacle to French hopes, with various schemes designed to exploit possible loopholes in the export of components made in French-financed factories being ruled out by the State Department in view of the impact on existing official expansion plans, and also the political furore the DB-7 crash had caused.[76] The French also considered various expedients to remove the Johnson Act, such as making a one-off down payment of $300 million in gold in an attempt to discharge their existing war debt, or selling French colonial possessions.[77] The legislative and political constraints on the administration did not alter Daladier's appreciation of the importance of American aid. As he put it to Bullitt immediately after the outbreak of war: 'If we are to win this war, we shall have to win it on supplies of every kind from the United States.'[78]

Much of this was to become familiar to the British in due course but they began from a different position which was also to shape their experience. The limited British purchase programme in 1938 reflected the British concentration on their own industry, and their ultimate confidence in it. In November 1938, an Air

Ministry planner, Group Captain John Slessor, completed a paper outlining the Air Ministry's perspective for the FO. He repeated the diplomatic importance of any demonstration of American sympathy for the democratic powers, with modification of isolationist legislation as a powerful deterrent to war and a demonstration of common interests in resisting the dictators. His view of the American aircraft industry and its future potential deserve repeating:

> The recent Air Mission has shown that it is easy to exaggerate the existing capacity of the US aircraft industry to provide immediate assistance to British air rearmament . . . [but] to decry the value of American support merely on the grounds that they cannot at present supply us with aircraft in sufficient quantities or of adequate quality, is obviously to take a ludicrously short view.[79]

Slessor's appraisal went on to outline the 'insurance' aspect of American supply to counter the impact of bombing attacks on British industry, and emphasised that modification of the Neutrality Act was not enough; ultimately some form of credit and repeal of the Johnson Act would be required. The Air Staff recommended the creation of the conditions needed for the modification or annulment of the neutrality legislation in the near future. This was significant. The Air Staff were separating the short-term and long-term significance of American aircraft supply and advocating a supply policy that utilised the former to realise the latter.

This involved the identification of American supply as a benefit for allies more than specifically British needs alone. This was evident in the advice given in February 1939 by Air Vice Marshal Wilfred Freeman, then Air Council Member for Development and Production (AMDP) responsible for RAF aircraft procurement, that American supply should be maximised while any available American aircraft should be made available to allies such as France or Poland, even if this prejudiced future markets for the British aviation industry.[80] This attitude endured even after the deterioration of the international situation provoked by the German occupation of the rump Czech state in March 1939 which resulted in the extension of British security guarantees to European countries, including Poland, and the final acceptance of a 'continental commitment' or the expensive cost of equipping an army expeditionary force for an implicit deployment to France.

What lay behind this view was a gradual but appreciable increase in confidence in British air rearmament after Munich.[81] The enormous preceding investment finally began to be reflected in production figures in 1939 as output almost tripled (7,940 compared to 2,827 aircraft in 1938) and reached near parity with Germany for the first time that year (7,940 compared to 8,295 aircraft). By the outbreak of war, the RAF was underway to achieve the Scheme M of November 1938: against a target of 2,549 aircraft in the metropolitan air force to be achieved by 1942, the RAF had 1,460 first-line aircraft available with two thousand reserves on hand. Deliveries were now matching, or sometimes exceeding, requirements, with 3,753 aircraft delivered in the first six months of 1939 as against 3,146 planned.[82] The slow development of new types meant that some of these were not the most modern aircraft. The bomber force was being built up with Whitley and Hampden medium bombers rather than with any of the new four-engined types of heavy bomber; or, worse still, with admittedly obsolete aircraft like the single-engined Fairey Battle bomber. Nevertheless the overall picture was encouraging and a vast improvement over the situation in 1936–38.

Airframe production was expected to rise from 750 aircraft per month to one thousand and then two thousand within eighteen months, provided the required imports of American machine tools continued. An ultimate target of 2,550 aircraft per month (including 250 from the Dominions) was accepted by the cabinet in September. The remaining bottleneck in wartime expansion was aircrew training which was expected to be resolved by the huge overseas training programme involved in the Empire Air Training Scheme (EATS) over the next two years.[83]

British unwillingness to buy American aircraft had been conditioned by the relationship between the British financial and military positions. The RAF perceived American aircraft to be of limited operational value and the Treasury saw them as expensive in foreign exchange. By investing in expanding British production instead, they could achieve the happy medium of economising on price, reducing foreign exchange expenditure and getting more-effective aircraft. This was spelled out by the British reaction to renewed French initiatives to exploit American supply immediately after the outbreak of war, which stressed the small scale of American industry and the limited qualitative value of the aircraft then available for production. As the French had a smaller air force but more gold, Simon suggested that it would be more appropriate for them to buy American aircraft.[84] At that point, British intentions were to conserve their foreign exchange reserves to last for up to three years of war.

Though the DB-7 crash caused a temporary reduction in visible efforts by the Roosevelt administration to aid the Allies, continued German expansion brought the removal of the arms embargo section of the Neutrality Act under increasing pressure. Removal would permit exports to belligerents under a 'cash and carry' clause which mandated that purchases were made in dollars, the title of ownership to pass to the purchaser, and that the goods were exported at the purchaser's risk. Roosevelt raised the issue in May, publicly stating that he wanted Congress to approve revision before the arrival in June of King George VI and Queen Elizabeth for the first state visit of a British monarch to America.

The power of the isolationists in the Senate compelled the administration to back away before an obvious defeat, and attempted amendments, which would have permitted the export of civilian goods with alternative military uses (such as aircraft), were abandoned.[85] This defeat indicated the continuing strength of isolationism, but also the priority the administration continued to place on aircraft supply to the Allies, and had provided clear evidence of where the main focus of attack against isolationist legislation would remain. The Allies had already entered upon a process of aircraft purchases in the United States regardless of the qualitative and quantitative constraints involved to encourage this process. Allied procurement policy and administration policy were complementary. Even though their ultimate objectives were similar, however, British procurement policy was to continue to be outstripped by French initiatives that, in turn, were driven by more pressing short-term military needs.

As tensions rose again in August 1939, without the credible possibility of another Munich settlement to delay the onset of war, La Chambre was faced with the continuing problem of the struggling French aircraft industry. Production had risen from the dire position before Munich but the air force stated that 2,800 aircraft and no less than ten thousand engines would be required on top of the existing domestic programme in the next six months. French officials placed no confidence in either British production claims or their willingness to deploy sufficient aircraft to defend France.[86] Another emergency purchase programme in the United States appeared to be the only answer.[87] Despite being one of the strongest advocates of American supply, Monnet stated that this target was beyond existing American capacity to meet, and advocated a joint Anglo-French programme to order everything available and, more importantly, to double or treble American capacity.[88]

Monnet's objective remained out of reach while the existing British policy of relative financial restraint remained in force. The prospect of immediate reinforcement, however, and the likelihood that the legislative obstacles would be overcome by a sympathetic administration, led to another French purchase mission which placed contracts to secure available American output until the end of 1940 regardless of the impact of an arms embargo. With assistance from Morgenthau, the French were able to overcome USAAC resistance to order the latest types of aircraft. These included the Bell P-39 fighter, then under development for the USAAC, and also the Curtiss P-40, a P-36 developed with the more powerful liquid-cooled Allison V-1710-C engine in place of the Pratt & Whitney R-1830 radial engine. The mission managed to order 550 further P-36s together with a hundred Allison-engined P-40s, as well as another 130 GM 167s, 270 DB-7s and two hundred Harvards.[89]

The British were encouraged to follow suit, and Lord Riverdale visited the United States and Canada in July and August at Roosevelt's behest. Riverdale's objective was to establish the organisation required for managing a programme of wartime supply from North America. This included arranging liaison with the Canadian procurement authorities and establishing a purchasing commission in the United States. The latter objective would fulfil the administration's desire for government-to-government contact over Allied procurement in the United States. This avoided repeating a central element in the isolationist thesis of financial concerns conniving with perfidious Allies to engineer American involvement in another European war. The intent of the administration to revise the neutrality legislation was made clear to Riverdale by his State Department contacts, though they stressed this would involve Congressional action.[90] In the meantime, the British placed follow-on orders for their 1938 contracts, including a further two hundred Hudsons and six hundred Harvards, as well as new contracts for 120 Brewster Buffalo fighters, accepting 'moderate performance type for early delivery', and fifty Consolidated PBY Catalina amphibians.[91]

The expectations encouraged by the administration were met when Roosevelt's renewed attempt to revise the Neutrality Act was finally successful after his recall of Congress in November. This ended the embargo and introduced 'cash and carry', but also maintained stringent restrictions on the travel of US citizens and US shipping in war zones to cover remaining points of isolationist criticism. The economic benefits expected from cash and carry placed a strong card in the administration's hand which effectively bought off isolationist senators such as Robert Taft, and left Hiram Borah making token public opposition.[92] Coupled with public support for the British and French stand against evident Nazi aggression now that war had actually broken out, the administration had the tactical advantage they had lacked a few months earlier. Sympathisers like William Allen White and Clark Eichelberger were able openly to form organisations to mobilise public opinion behind the issue of repeal.[93] Even Charles Lindbergh's pro-isolationist, non-intervention broadcasts at the time approved the sale of defensive munitions.[94]

The 1939 purchase missions had effectively worked within existing constraints, both political and industrial, to secure output from existing American capacity until the end of 1940. The next French initiative aimed far beyond this and sought to act as a catalyst to expand and mobilise latent American potential. Monnet took the lead by advocating firstly a joint Allied Purchase Commission to avoid inter-Allied competition, and secondly by advocating joint action with much wider objectives in mind. To this end he presented a joint balance sheet which detailed future Allied production against Allied targets. This was designed to 'shock' the British into participating in a purchase programme that was, for the first time, explicitly designed to realise American industrial potential.[95] Monnet's ambition was avowedly political, designed to demonstrate that 'the vast resources of America' were firmly and surely at the back of the Allies.[96]

Monnet's plan resulted in the creation of a joint Allied Purchasing Commission in New York headed by the Canadian businessman Sir Arthur Purvis to match Monnet's equivalent position on the Anglo-French Supply Council in London. Daladier began the next phase of the plan in November 1939 by calling on Bullitt for the delivery of ten thousand aircraft to give the Allies 'absolute dominance in the air'.[97] In a meeting with Bullitt, La Chambre and Monnet on 23 November, Daladier explicitly linked the concept of American aircraft supply with both his position as premier and with Allied defeat in the absence of US supplies: a 'peace of exhaustion and compromise' negotiated by appeasers like Georges Bonnet or Pierre Flandin would be followed by German domination of Europe.[98] It was clear that a thesis of critical dependence – making the difference between success or defeat – was already being built up by French diplomacy on American aircraft supply.

At this point, the British were more concerned with machine tool supply. The completion of the British industrial rearmament programme, including the final stages of air rearmament, relied upon the supply of American machine tools which would be diverted to the American programme at the expense of existing British plans. Nonetheless, British reluctance was steadily overcome by continuing French pressure. Daladier emphasised the importance of winning air superiority at the earliest possible moment, observed that the French were restricting their foreign exchange for the purchase of aircraft, and reassured Chamberlain that the plan would exploit the untapped potential of the American car industry rather than competing for machine tools.[99]

British agreement to assess the potential of the plan survived the disappointing report by Monnet's assistant in January 1940 that

American industry would be unable to meet Daladier's demand for ten thousand planes by April 1941; even after doubling engine production capacity, the maximum that could be built would be 8,400, and only 2,800 of these could be delivered by the target date, with the rest to follow by October 1941.[100] The Air Ministry was more pessimistic, concluding on the basis of their experience of industrial expansion that only 4,800 aircraft, including an allotment for spares, could be supplied by the end of September 1941. The residual output would be available to strengthen the Allied position in the third year of the war.[101] Significantly, the report noted that the estimated cost of $950 million for the aircraft, exclusive of capital investment, would cover all deliveries up to September 1941, and further financial liabilities would arise only by the spring of 1941.[102] This closely anticipated the chronology and capital costs that transpired in the development of Lend-Lease.

Meanwhile, after substantial consultation in the United States and negotiation with the French over the allocations of particular types, the Air Ministry presented a revised programme for the joint purchase of 4,700 aircraft which became the basis of the Allied purchase programme when it was concluded in April. The proposed orders are broken down in Table 2.3.

Significantly, the strings apparently attached to this capital investment looked further ahead than the purchase programme itself, with the Air Ministry observing that the creation of this

Table 2.3 The March 1940 purchase programme, including spares allocation[103]

Type (including subsequent British name)	British	French
Curtiss P-40 (Tomahawk)	280	200
Curtiss P-46 (later converted to P-40D Kittyhawk)	760	200
Bell P-39 (Airacobra)	0	200
Lockheed P-38 (Lightning)	300	500
Martin GM 187 (Baltimore)	500	250
Douglas DB-7 (Havoc; Boston I and II)	0	550
A-20 (Boston III)	200	0
Lockheed 37 (Ventura)	400	0
Consolidated B-24 (Liberator)	0	60
Vultee dive bomber (Vengeance)	0	200

involved the creation of new capacity on the condition that it would be available for Allied use during the war.[104] Although not spelled out in detail, this represented the first indication that some kind of undertaking existed that might go beyond the existing financial provisions of the Neutrality Act. This relative lack of immediate importance the British otherwise afforded to the plan was reflected in the recommendation that adopting the scheme would provide an insurance against the loss of Allied production capacity.[105]

A year before Lend-Lease was implemented, and three months before the fall of France and the British strategic isolation that followed, British appreciation of American supply had changed to embrace the concept of developing an American war potential that would only be realised more than a year later. Economic considerations in American supply policy were now already secondary to strategic concerns with expanding future aircraft supply. The pre-April 1940 American purchase programme still remained a marginal supplement to British planning, however.

In April 1940, the same month that the Anglo-French purchasing commission placed the orders for the joint programme, the Secretary of State for Air reported to the cabinet that, since the outbreak of the war 21,650 aircraft had been ordered in Britain, with 310 ordered in Canada and 1,320 in the United States, at a total cost of approximately £489 million ($1,970 million). The British share of the new purchase programme in America would add 2,440 aircraft at a further cost of £77 million; disregarding further upcoming orders from British industry, American orders amounted to 14.6 per cent of the total.[106] To indicate the disproportionate nature of the respective spending and the industrial capacities created, by July 1939 the Air Ministry had approved £31.2 million ($125.8 million) in government-funded capital expansion of the British aircraft industry, or seven times the $17.5 million proposed for capital investment in the joint Allied programme, with further capital investment in British industry to follow.[107] In the period when the joint Allied programme was under discussion between February and April 1940, the Air Ministry approved a further £2,348,000 (or $9.5 million) in capital investment in the British aircraft industry.[108]

The new joint purchase programme brought the administration back into conflict with the USAAC. Arnold himself was struggling to expand and rearm the USAAC with modern designs of aircraft according to Congressionally approved plans against a background of prior financial neglect and limited industrial capacity. Allied orders represented competition for scarce capacity with a direct and negative impact on USAAC plans. They also competed for the latest designs of USAAC aircraft, and the resolution of this competition provides further evidence of how pre-war supply diplomacy could inform later wartime developments.

The sharpest of these conflicts arose between the administration and the War Department over the supply of modern fighters for the joint Allied contracts. Roosevelt's appointment of a liaison committee, run by Morgenthau, to work with the Purvis commission removed Allied purchase requests from War Department administrative control.[109] Arnold's propensity for providing anti-administration critics with ammunition had been demonstrated in the DB-7 crash, following which Roosevelt had threatened him with a posting to Guam. His testimony to Congress in February–March 1940 seemed to be following the same pattern as he and his superiors in the War Department fought a rearguard action in an effort to secure USAAC primacy in aircraft procurement policy.[110] The Allies wanted access to test fly and then order newer types of fighter, such as the Lockheed P-38 and the Bell P-39, developed in response to USAAC specifications. These were believed to have the performance required for combat in 1941–2. P-36s from the original French order had seen combat against German Bf 109s by the end of 1939 and, while they were believed to have done relatively well, it was clear that they were technically outclassed.

In a repeat of the preceding clash over access to the DB-7, Morgenthau secured Roosevelt's approval for the Allies to get priority in P-40 deliveries and to order the P-38 and P-39.[111] He had clearly absorbed the Monnet–Daladier thesis of critical dependency, at least as far as the Allied joint purchasing programme was concerned, when he described it as possibly being 'the deciding factor' in Allied victory.[112] His price for overcoming USAAC resistance to the joint programme was to get the Allies to bear the research and development cost of new types.[113] This included the costs involved in upgrading American aircraft with the equipment such as self-sealing fuel tanks that had already been demonstrated as essential in combat. Getting the Allies to pay for the qualitative improvement of USAAC types was Arnold's price for agreeing to accept the release of new designs to the Allies. This came in time to allow the joint purchase scheme to be settled in April 1940 – just in time for the German conquest of Scandinavia and western Europe to change the path of the war and dramatically increase the importance of American supply.

Notes

1. David Dutton, *Simon: A Political Biography of Sir John Simon* (London: Aurum, 1992), p. 273.
2. Denis Richards, *Royal Air Force 1939–1945*, Vol. I, *The Fight at Odds* (London: HMSO, 1974), p. 8.
3. RAF squadron strength varied but can usually be assumed to be sixteen aircraft per squadron. Each squadron required up to 50 per cent reserves or even 100 per cent in overseas theatres, as well as wastage replacements for aircraft lost or destroyed during training or on operations. In addition, by 1940, Operational Training Units would be formed to train aircrew on operational types of aircraft, increasing the number of aircraft required to support a given number of squadrons.
4. Lord Ismay, *The Memoirs of General the Lord Ismay* (London: Cassell, 1960), p. 79.
5. Ian Kershaw, *Hitler 1889–1936: Hubris* (London: Penguin, 1999), pp. 549, 553; Dutton, *Simon*, pp. 197–9.
6. 'Summary of Pre-War Expansion Schemes – 1934 to 1939'; Sir John Slessor, *The Central Blue* (London: Cassell, 1956), p. 184.
7. Richards, *Fight at Odds*, p. 14.
8. Slessor, p. 166.
9. Figures exclusive of £12.7 million investment in Royal Ordnance Factories, largely for Army munitions production, in 1939. Sir Maurice Dean, *The Royal Air Force and Two World Wars* (London: Cassell, 1979), p. 72.
10. Appendix III, G. C. Peden, *British Rearmament and the Treasury: 1932–1939* (Edinburgh: Scottish Academic Press, 1979), p. 205.
11. Brian Bond (ed.), *Chief of Staff. The Diaries of Lieutenant-*

General Sir Henry Pownall, Vol. 1 (London: Leo Cooper, 1971), pp. 49–50.
12. Peden, pp. 17–23; David Edgerton, *Warfare State: Britain, 1920–1970* (Cambridge: Cambridge University Press, 2006), p. 18.
13. Peden, p. 63.
14. Keith Feiling, *The Life of Neville Chamberlain* (London: Macmillan, 1947), p. 292.
15. For Nazi economic policy in this period, Tooze, pp. 79–98, 208–59.
16. Feiling, p. 253.
17. Pedden, pp. 118–19.
18. David Dutton, *Neville Chamberlain* (London: Arnold, 2001), pp. 163, 171.
19. Feiling, pp. 313–14.
20. Malcolm Smith, 'The Royal Air Force, Air Power and British Foreign Policy' in *The Journal of Contemporary History*, Vol. 12, No. 1 (1977), p. 166; Henry Probert, *Bomber Harris* (London: Greenhill Books, 2003), pp. 70–1.
21. Richard Overy, 'German Air Strength 1933 to 1939: A Note', in *The Historical Journal*, Vol. 27, No. 2 (1984), p. 469.
22. Wesley K. Wark, 'British Intelligence on the German Air Force and Aircraft Industry, 1933–1939' in *The Historical Journal*, Vol. 25, No. 3 (1982), pp. 636–8; Overy, *German Air Strength*, p. 465.
23. Pedden, pp. 38–9.
24. Ibid., pp. 42–4, 50–2.
25. Sebastian Ritchie, 'The Price of Air Power: Technological Change, Industrial Policy, and Military Aircraft Contracts in the Era of British Rearmament, 1935–39', in *The Business History Review*, Vol. 71, No. 1 (1997), pp. 103–4.
26. Figures from Table 1, Overy, *The Air War*, p. 21.
27. Feiling, p. 350; Dean, pp. 56–7.
28. Postan, p. 16.
29. 'Supply of Munitions from Canada and the United States of America', 317th Meeting of the CID, 31 March 1938; CAB 21/766.
30. Postan, p. 18.
31. Cabinet 21 (38), 27 April 1938; CAB 23/93.
32. Dean, p. 97.
33. For the legislative impact of isolationism, Wayne S. Cole, *Roosevelt and the Isolationists 1932–45* (Lincoln: University of Nebraska Press, 1983), pp. 81–186, and *Senator Gerald P. Nye*

and American Foreign Relations (Minneapolis: University of Minnesota Press, 1962), pp. 60–152; Thomas N. Guinsburg, *The Pursuit of Isolationism in the United States from Versailles to Pearl Harbor* (New York: Garland Publishing, 1982), pp. 185–93.

34. Guinsburg, pp. 1–3.
35. C. A. MacDonald, *The United States, Britain and Appeasement, 1936–1939* (London: Macmillan, 1981), pp. 1–4.
36. MacDonald, p. 21.
37. Dallek, p. 139.
38. Feiling, p. 325.
39. Sir Henry Self, 'Report by DUS on the Results of the Mission to the USA and Canada in May 1938'; AVIA 10/119.
40. Sir Arthur Harris, *Bomber Offensive* (London: Greenhill Books, 1998), pp. 27–8; Probert, *Harris*, p. 79.
41. £20.5 million in British goods was exported to the United States in 1938, while the exchange rate fluctuated between $5 and $4.65 to £1, giving a notional equivalent of $95 million to $102 million.
42. Cabinet 26 (38), 25 May 1938; CAB 23/93.
43. MacDonald, pp. 24–5, 51, 85.
44. Ibid., p. 111.
45. Feiling, p. 308.
46. MacDonald, p. 18.
47. Robert J. Young, 'The Strategic Dream: French Air Doctrine in the Inter-War Period, 1919–39', in *The Journal of Contemporary History*, Vol. 9, No. 4 (1974), p. 68.
48. Robert J. Young, *In Command of France: French Foreign Policy and Military Planning, 1933–1940* (London, 1978): p. 210.
49. John MacVickar Haight, *American Aid to France, 1938–1940* (New York: Athanaeum, 1970), p. 3.
50. Ibid., p. 7.
51. Ibid., pp. 8–9.
52. Ibid., pp. 10–11.
53. Wark, p. 643.
54. Young, *In Command of France*, pp. 211–12.
55. Dallek, p. 163.
56. Orville H. Bullitt (ed.), *For the President Personal And Secret. Correspondence Between Franklin Roosevelt and William C. Bullitt* (London: André Deutsch, 1973), pp. 297–9.
57. John MacVickar Haight, 'France, the United States and the Munich Crisis' in *The Journal of Modern History,* Vol. 32, No. 4 (1960), pp. 350, 358; Haight, *American Aid*, p. 24.

58. Robert E. Sherwood, *Roosevelt and Hopkins* (New York: Harper, 1948), p. 76.
59. Sherwood, *Roosevelt and Hopkins*, pp. 67, 75, 100, and *White House Papers*, pp. 69, 97–9.
60. Dallek, p. 172.
61. Ibid., pp. 172–3.
62. Ibid., p. 179.
63. Cole, *Roosevelt and the Isolationists*, p. 301.
64. Haight, *American Aid*, p. 26.
65. Ibid., p. 45.
66. Ibid., p. 46.
67. Sherwood, *Hopkins*, pp. 92, 117.
68. Haight, *American Aid*, p. 82.
69. Cole, *Roosevelt and the Isolationists*, p. 297.
70. Haight, *American Aid*, pp. 93-96.
71. John B. Rae, 'Financial Problems of the American Aircraft Industry, 1906–1940', in *The Business History Review*, Vol. 39, No. 1, (1965), p. 113.
72. Dallek, p. 173; Haight, *American Aid*, p. 101.
73. Haight, *American Aid*, pp. 88, 101, 107.
74. Ibid., pp. 110.
75. Bullitt to Secretary of State, 12 April 1939; *Foreign Relations of the United States 1939*, Vol. III, *General, the British Commonwealth and Empire* (Washington, DC: US Government Printing Office, 1956), pp. 508–9 (hereafter *FRUS 1939* III).
76. Bullitt to Secretary of State, 29 April 1939; *FRUS 1939* III, p. 518; Hull to Bullitt, 7 March 1939; *FRUS 1939* III, p. 503; Hull to Bullitt, 7 March 1939; *FRUS 1939* III, p. 503; memorandum of conversation by Chief of the Division of Controls, State Department, 20 April 1939; *FRUS 1939* III, p. 516
77. Bullitt to Secretary of State, 13 February 1939; *FRUS 1939* III, p. 501; Haight, *American Aid to France*, p. 113.
78. Bullitt to Roosevelt, 8 September 1939; Bullitt, p. 368.
79. 'American Co-operation with Great Britain in the Event of War with Germany. The Neutrality Act and War Debt Settlement.', 12 November 1938. AVIA 10/120.
80. AMDP to CAS, 2 February 1939 and Freeman to 2nd DUS 'Purchase of munitions in USA in emergency', 8 May 1939; AVIA 10/120.
81. Douglas of Kirtleside and Robert Wright, *Years of Command* (London: Collins, 1966), pp. 37–9; Dean, p. 58.

82. Figures totalled from Table 3, Postan, p. 22.
83. J. R. M. Butler, *Grand Strategy*, Vol. II, *September 1939–June 1941* (London: HMSO, 1957), pp. 35–6, 39.
84. W.M. (39) 74th Conclusions, Minute 3; Confidential Annexe, 7 November 1939; CAB 65/4/6.
85. Dallek, pp. 184, 188–90; Cole, *Roosevelt and the Isolationists*, pp. 310–17.
86. Bullitt, pp. 373, 389.
87. Bullitt to Secretary of State, 28 August 1939; *FRUS 1939* III, p. 518.
88. Haight, *American Aid*, pp. 135, 143.
89. Ibid., pp. 139–40.
90. Riverdale to the Minister of Supply, 'Purchasing Commission in the United States and Canada', 17 August 1939; AVIA 38/39.
91. Draft telegram for Colonel Greenley from Sir Arthur Street, 15 January 1940; AVIA 10/122.
92. John Blum, *From the Morgenthau Diaries: Years of Urgency 1938–1941* (Boston: Houghton Mifflin, 1965), p. 118.
93. Dallek, pp. 202–5.
94. Cole, *Roosevelt and the Isolationists*, pp. 323–30.
95. Haight, *American Aid*, pp. 144–9, 188.
96. Ibid., p. 191.
97. Ibid., p. 157.
98. Bullitt to Secretary of State, 23 November 1939; *Foreign Relations of the United States, Diplomatic Papers 1939*, Vol. II (Washington, DC: US Government Printing Office, 1956), pp. 520–1. Hereafter *FRUS 1939* II.
99. W.P. 40 (40) reference W.P. (39) 47; 'Air Supplies from the United States of America' in 'Record of the Fourth Meeting of the Supreme War Council held on 19th December 1939'; CAB 66/5/20.
100. Haight, *American Aid*, pp. 175–81.
101. W.P. (G). 40 (38); memorandum by the Secretary of State for Air, 'Anglo-French Scheme for American Aircraft Production', 1 February 1940. AVIA 10/127.
102. Ibid.
103. Monnet to Purvis, 4 April 1940; 'Allied Purchases of Aircraft in the United States of America', 25 March 1940. AVIA 10/127.
104. 'Report by Anglo-French Mission on Aircraft Production in US', 25 March 1940; AVIA 10/127.
105. Ibid.
106. 3,760 out of 25,720 aircraft ordered in total; W.P. (R) (40) 150;

'Supply and Production. Ninth Report by the Air Ministry', 16 May 1940; CAB 68/6/30.

107. Appendix X and XI; memorandum by the Air Member for Development and Production, July 1939; W.P. (R) (39) 16, 'First Report by the Air Ministry', 23 September 1939; CAB 68/1/16.
108. Figures for February from W.P. (R) (40) 87, 'Supply and Production. Seventh Report by the Air Ministry', 8 March 1940. CAB 68/5/37. Figures for March 1940 from 'Eighth Report of the Air Ministry on Supply and Production, March 1940', W. P. (R) (40) 121, 15 April 1940. CAB 68/6/1. Figures for April from W.P. (R) (40) 150, 'Supply and Production. Ninth Report from the Air Ministry', 16 May 1940. CAB 68/6/30.
109. Haight, *American Aid*, p. 167.
110. DeWitt S. Copp, *Forged in Fire: Strategy and Decisions in the Air War over Europe 1940–1945* (New York: Doubleday, 1982), pp. 5–21.
111. Haight, *American Aid*, pp. 169–88.
112. Ibid., p. 196.
113. Ibid., p. 226.

3 The Diplomacy of Critical Dependency, 1940

> We are in an exposed position, and cannot be expected, alone and unassisted, to give our lives merely to save the rest of you. If you are unwilling to send us aid, you cannot compel us to fight your battle for you.
>
> *Herodotus' account of the Thessalian embassy to the Greeks before the invasion by Xerxes.*[1]

As France fell before the German onslaught in the summer of 1940, the British would adopt a similar position in their diplomacy towards the criticality of American aid to their continuing resistance. In his correspondence with Roosevelt, Churchill would repeatedly raise the prospect of British defeat without American aid.[2] At one stage, this approach was characterised by a Foreign Office official as '. . . rather like blackmail, and not very good blackmail at that'.[3] These assertions of critical dependency informed aircraft supply which remained at the forefront of the Anglo-American supply relationship through Roosevelt's 'all aid short of war' support for Britain throughout the crisis of 1940 and the evolution of Lend-Lease which followed. It can be assumed that this approach was a product of the exceptional circumstances of 1940 but, as Herodotus indicates, it had a long pedigree in diplomacy. The key point is to determine how far British supply diplomacy in 1940 reflected genuinely critical military needs, and how far it served broader diplomatic goals.

The starting point for assessing this must be the contemporary statements of the British chiefs of staff. In May 1940 they anticipated the imminent defeat of France and the entry of Italy into the war against them, and identified the need for American aid, including 'full economic and financial support', required to win the war.[4] One specific demand listed in the report was the supply of destroyers and motor torpedo boats (MTBs). Another was the supply of aircraft, and particularly fighters, including those in US Army and Navy stocks.

The story of the diplomacy which followed was to be the deliberate elision of three objectives of British diplomacy: the need for immediate reinforcement; the longer-term strategic need for American economic aid; and the desire to entangle the US directly in the British war effort. All these factors would become involved in the diplomacy to secure what might be termed the measures of 'immediate aid' identified in the chiefs of staff's appreciation. This elision was largely the responsibility of the approach adopted by Philip Kerr, Marquis of Lothian and the British ambassador in Washington from the outbreak of war up to his death in December 1940. With assistance from Monnet and Purvis in the Allied procurement bureaucracy, Lothian would adopt the Daladier thesis of 'critical dependency' upon America with great effect.[5] This operated in two directions. Firstly, it asserted the vital importance of Britain to American interests in a manner that transcended isolationist opposition. Secondly, it exaggerated the importance which the contribution of immediate American supply aid could make to continuing British resistance.

The thesis influenced Churchill's personal diplomacy with Roosevelt, the central channel for Anglo-American diplomacy, and culminated in the evolution of Lend-Lease. Appreciations of Lend-Lease have echoed this understanding of the British supply relationship with the United States down to the present day. The British diplomatic approach at the time has therefore done much to define current understanding of the Anglo-American supply relationship. But this often confuses the diplomacy of the time with the contemporary operational and strategic reality where the ability of the Roosevelt administration to meet the British requirements for long-term support and short-term aid in 1940 would prove problematic owing to political constraints, while the aircraft and munitions in question were known to be of insufficient quantity and quality to meet British requirements.

The resulting expectational gap between the rhetoric associated with American aid and the reality in 1940 would lead to contemporary criticism, not least by the Minister of Aircraft Production and even by Churchill himself. The existence of this gap left the British dependent almost entirely upon their own resources at the same time as they were claiming to be unable to conduct the war successfully without American aid. This represents a paradox at the heart of British supply diplomacy – aid being demanded and characterised as making a critical difference to British resistance when this was known not to be so – at the most critical period in the evolution of the Anglo-American alliance. This paradox requires exploration.

Allied supply policy had perceptibly changed with the adoption of the joint Anglo-French aircraft purchasing programme in April 1940. This change of intent was then accelerated by the catastrophic Allied defeats that immediately followed: the invasion of Scandinavia that month; the German offensive in western Europe in May; and the fall of France in June. This was followed by the Battle of Britain between July and October 1940, and then the Blitz, covering the period of German night bombing leading up to the redeployment of the Luftwaffe to confront the Soviet Union in June 1941. Throughout this period, the British stood alone against a German-dominated Europe, fighting off the Luftwaffe and the German U-boat blockade, while eventually apparently succeeding to secure the full economic aid specified in May 1940 with the evolution of Lend-Lease supply in March 1941.

There were four major items involved in supply diplomacy during this period: requests for aircraft, for destroyers, for arms, and for financial aid to overcome the limitations imposed by the Johnson Act. The supply diplomacy involved in securing these items can usefully be divided into three phases: the first crisis phase when French defeat seemed imminent and the outlines of the supply diplomacy which were to follow were established; a second intermediary phase roughly corresponding with the Battle of Britain where British supply diplomacy began to meet a response; and then a resolution phase in the winter of 1940–41, when Anglo-American supply diplomacy culminated in the Lend-Lease Act of March 1941.

Churchill's personal correspondence with Roosevelt during this period has been placed at the centre of British supply diplomacy, not least by himself.[6] Roosevelt had initiated correspondence with Churchill in September 1939 after Churchill had been appointed First Lord of the Admiralty. By means of this correspondence, Roosevelt sought to establish direct contact and exert some influence over British policy through the most hawkish member of a government still associated with appeasement.[7] The respective ambassadors in London and Washington were initially outside this channel of communication. While Joseph Kennedy was kept out of the loop because of his perceived defeatism, Lothian successfully gained selective access to it in January 1940 and then full access in July 1940.[8] Lothian then influenced the content and timing of these telegrams, and did so according to a pre-existing strategy of asserting 'criticality' through the US media and supplying 'proof' of British needs.

Though Churchill had attempted to conciliate Roosevelt by modifying British naval blockade policy as a result of the correspondence, its significance was initially limited while Churchill remained at the Admiralty.[9] This swiftly changed after Churchill replaced Chamberlain on 10 May as the result of reverses in Norway and the Labour Party's rejection of Chamberlain's leadership in a coalition government. Churchill's succession as prime minister coincided with the long-awaited German offensive in the west, as massive ground and air forces attacked Holland and Belgium, and encircled the Allied armies in northern France and Belgium. It quickly became clear that the Allies were on the brink of decisive defeat. In this crisis the Churchill–Roosevelt channel quickly became the primary means of communication in Anglo-American diplomacy, defined by Churchill's assertions of critical supply needs and the response of the Roosevelt administration to them.

Behind this correspondence, however, the British were well aware of the limited availability of modern combat aircraft in the United States. Output from the joint Allied procurement programme remained months away and, in the meantime, American production for earlier Allied orders largely comprised training or maritime patrol aircraft. The only other sources of supply were deliveries being made against USAAC orders and small numbers of other foreign orders for neutral nations such as Belgium and Sweden. These were known to have minimal combat value. On 8 May, two days before the German offensive in the west began, Arthur Purvis of the British Purchasing Commission (BPC) in New York had notified Whitehall that there was little point pressing for an acceleration in P-40 deliveries in the light of poor public opinion of Allied defeats in Norway. Though there was the prospect of diverting thirty-six P-36 fighters from Norwegian contracts due to be delivered between September and November 1940, which 'might be interesting for the French', of the remaining thirty-six single-engined A-17 attack bombers and twenty-four Northrop scouting aircraft, 'none . . . had any real combatant value'.[10] This should be borne in mind when British appeals for immediately available aircraft in May–June 1940 are considered: the British knew the limited number and value of the available aircraft.

The only alternative was the supply of aircraft which had already been delivered to the USAAC in exchange for deliveries from the Allied contracts when they began. This was raised by Halifax in the cabinet on 11 May after the scale of the German offensive in Holland and Belgium, which had begun the previous day, was beginning to become clear, and again on 13 May when the cabinet was discussing the material for use in Churchill's first message to Roosevelt.[11] Halifax reported Kennedy's frank advice to Lothian later that day: 'As he saw it, the winning of the war had little to do with changes of Government, or accusations of complacency or lack of drive, it was simply a question of whether one had enough aeroplanes.'[12] On the subject of diverting USAAC aircraft to the Allies, Kennedy's advice had been brutally frank: '. . . it was essential that the matter should be taken up immediately by the Prime Minister with the President direct. "You must pass the hat now", he said, "while the corpse is still warm."'

On 19 May Purvis explained to Whitehall the limited number of combat-capable USAAC aircraft available, consisting of 150 Curtiss P-36 fighters and 144 Northrop A-17 single-engined bombers.[13] Even if appeals at the prime ministerial–presidential level for USAAC aircraft were successful, these were the actual aircraft that would be involved; and by no stretch of the imagination could they be considered capable of repulsing the Luftwaffe by themselves. It is worth noting that the initiative for approaching the administration on the issue of diverting USAAC aircraft to the Allies was to come from the FO, and apparently in response to Lothian's assurances that American public opinion – if not Congress – was moving in favour of supplying the Allies.[14]

The manner in which the release of US aircraft entered the Churchill–Roosevelt correspondence indicates how the nature and timing of the appeals contained within them were directly informed by diplomatic objectives, defined by both the FO and Lothian's personal diplomacy in the United States. One of the key objectives involved was the search for visible signs of American support to bolster the French will to resist in May and June. When France was defeated, the surviving Anglo-American supply diplomacy retained the rhetorical assertions of criticality even when the particular British evaluation of the military value of the supplies in question was more limited.

Given the limited nature of procurement in the United States and the enormous investment in the domestic aircraft industry during the rearmament period, effective British air strength in the crisis of 1940 was entirely contingent upon the output of domestic industry. Fortunately for the British, this had been relatively successful. The position immediately before the German offensive of May can be established from a summary of the RAF position on 30 April.[15] British aircraft production in April exceeded one thousand aircraft per month for the first time. In total 1,130 aircraft were built that month, just exceeding planned output. American supply played a very limited part in this total; despite imports of American light alloy and steel being used to resolve some production bottlenecks, the only American aircraft imported were forty-four Hudsons. Even here, American supply represented a minor component of British output, as 175 British GR aircraft were produced that month. Overall, since the start of the war, the British had produced 3,740 aircraft, with two hundred Hudsons and seventy-three Harvard trainers being supplied from the United States in the same period.

One often-ignored aspect of the April supply figures was the delivery of five fighters from Canada by the end of that month.

Table 3.1 Production of the Hurricane and Spitfire, 1939–40[16] (average monthly production in brackets)

Period	Hurricane	Spitfire
1 September–31 December 1939	237 (59)	171 (42)
1 January–31 March 1940	314 (104)	128 (42)
1 April–30 June 1940	708 (236)	240 (80)
1 July 1940–30 September 1940	775 (258)	479 (159)
1 October 1940–31 December 1940	718 (239)	405 (135)

These represented the first five Hurricanes produced by the Canadian Car and Foundry Company in Montreal. The Canadian production line had been established as one of the longer-term results of the 1938 Weir mission to encourage the development of 'war potential' capacity for aircraft manufacture in Canada. In total the Canadian production line would deliver forty Hurricanes by the end of 1940. Though these Canadian Hurricanes initially required the shipment of British-built Merlin engines and British equipment for completion, in contrast to the American fighters supplied in 1940, they would actually see operational service during the Battle of Britain.

Production remained a political issue, however. Output figures in early 1940 had been affected by the slow production of new types, mostly of bombers but also by the delays involved in bringing the new shadow factories online which affected the output of all aircraft types. Table 3.1 indicates the increase in production of the two main single-engined day fighters, the Hurricane and the Spitfire, per quarter in 1940.

Hurricane production had expanded significantly, particularly after it replaced the Gladiator biplane on the Gloster production lines. But expansion of Spitfire production at the new Castle Bromwich shadow factory had proved more difficult, culminating in the takeover of the plant from Lord Nuffield, the Morris Motors magnate, by Vickers, the parent company of the original Spitfire plant at Woolston in Southampton.[17] Unease over the previous difficulties encountered in expanding production lingered after Churchill's assumption of power, and he quickly appointed his old colleague and press baron Lord Beaverbrook to head the new MAP. Following the example of the Ministry of Munitions in World War I under Lloyd George and Churchill, the MAP absorbed the Air Ministry's production, repair and development responsibilities.

Beaverbrook's appointment was apparently crowned with clear success as the production of aircraft, and specifically fighters, more than doubled in the course of the year. This reflected well on Churchill who credited Beaverbrook with 'clearing up the muddle and the scandal of the aircraft production branch'.[18] But, despite his reputation as having galvanised production during the Battle of Britain, Beaverbrook's new ministry relied heavily upon the skills and experience of the senior staff he inherited from the Air Ministry. As the increased production rates of the spring and summer 1940 indicate, the resolution of the remaining bottlenecks in the pre-war production plans were in hand before he took office.

Beaverbrook's dictatorial approach did increase production as the year progressed but this was a mixed blessing. Freeman observed that much of Beaverbrook's success involved exploiting the crisis atmosphere of the time to strip spares from depots and even operational units to boost production figures.[19] Criticism of Beaverbrook's tactics spread beyond the Air Ministry. Ernest Bevin was reported to have responded to a Churchillian observation on Beaverbrook's impact on production with the comment that 'magic is nine-tenths illusion'.[20] Aside from inflating actual production figures, the other legacy of Beaverbrook's focus on production statistics at the MAP was the use of exhortatory planning targets.

These used ambitious plans to inject urgency into production planning by aircraft firms.[21] This was evident from the very first comprehensive MAP production plan – the 'Hennessy Plan' – produced in September 1940:

> The Hennessey programme was a typical Beaverbrook enterprise. It did not attempt to estimate what the future production was likely to be. It laid down what production could be under perfect conditions . . . Beaverbrook did not claim that the programme could be fulfilled, and in fact it never was. It was, as he called it, a 'carrot' programme, something to strive for and never attainable.[22]

These became a feature of Anglo-American production planning, particularly after the catastrophic Allied defeats, which began in April 1940, demonstrated the importance of air superiority for modern military operations. The successful German invasion of Norway in April 1940 had revealed for the first time the difficulties of undertaking land and naval operations under German air superiority. The value of air strength and the supply of fighter aircraft were quickly recognised.[23] This was brought home decisively by the German attack on the west which began on 10 May.

This campaign, which saw Holland, Belgium and France defeated and the northern and western areas of France occupied by Germany, represented the first major contest between Allied and German air power. Although the French air force had over 4,800 aircraft on strength at the most recent count in February 1940, many of these were not deployed against the German attack in northern France and only 678 of the total were modern aircraft comparable with their German opposition.[24] Over 3,530 German operational aircraft, excluding transport aircraft and gliders, were used in the campaign, swiftly crushing the small Dutch and Belgian air forces in the first two days and then concentrating on the Anglo-French forces in northern France and Belgium.[25] By 20 May, German forces, which had broken through French lines in the Ardennes, had reached the Channel coast at the Somme estuary, prompting an Allied withdrawal to the northern Channel ports. This concluded with the evacuation from Dunkirk at the end of May, and the loss of northern France.

These shattering defeats caused a new intensity in appeals for American aid, with a notable emphasis on the criticality of American supply primarily originating from the need to keep France in the war. As Bullitt notified Washington after meeting Reynaud on 14 May: 'Reynaud then implored me to obtain additional aeroplanes from the United States. I told him I feared there were none to be had.'[26] Reynaud had then moved on to the need for the supply of old American destroyers for use against expected Italian submarine attacks on shipping after the anticipated Italian entry into the war. Reynaud was referring to the large number of World War I-era destroyers the USN (United States Navy) was reconditioning for use in patrolling the Neutrality Zone announced by Roosevelt after the Panama conference of Latin American nations in September 1939. To meet a perceived shortage of anti-submarine escort vessels, the RN had begun reconditioning similar vintage destroyers of their own while the destroyers and escorts from their expanded wartime orders were under construction. Though Churchill's early interest in the American destroyers at that time had been turned down because of the exchange costs involved, the FO had independently identified them as potentially available to the Allies under the apparent policy of benevolent neutrality intimated by the Roosevelt administration.[27]

These destroyers would become the central issue of British supply diplomacy until the conclusion of the Anglo-American Destroyers–Bases deal in September. They entered the picture as part of a triangular Anglo-French–American diplomacy, with Reynaud raising the issue with Bullitt on 14 May before Churchill's first appeal to Roosevelt for them on 15 May. The British were not just seeking to elicit American aid for themselves at this point. They were seeking to identify measures that could address the political crisis in France resulting from Allied defeats. As John Colville, one of Churchill's private secretaries, observed, '. . . it is vital to sustain French morale and give no excuse for a collapse'.[28] This was evident in Anglo-French diplomacy. On 16 May, the FO advised the British ambassador to France accordingly: 'Please suggest to the French government that they should make urgent and repeated appeals to the United States for assistance and support material and moral which may help them to turn the scale at this highly critical moment.'[29] On 13 June, Churchill met Reynaud for the last time at Tours and encouraged him to send a new demand to Roosevelt urging intervention: 'This appeal would be backed up from here by a statement of the position and a request for assistance to France.'[30]

Fighter aircraft were a particularly important element of this diplomacy, as can be seen in the constant appeals Reynaud made for RAF reinforcements and British fighters in particular. Early operations by the RAF in France had demonstrated both the high losses experienced by the bombers under German fighter attack and the relative effectiveness of the Hurricane as a fighter.[31] Though better than the main French fighter, the Morane Saulnier

MS. 406, the Hurricane was still considerably outclassed by the German Messerschmitt Bf 109E. This comparison tends to attract disproportionate attention from some aviation historians, however. The Hurricane could still fight effectively against the twin-engined Bf110C fighter and inflict substantial casualties on the more numerous bombers and dive bombers which represented the main offensive striking force of the Luftwaffe. The Hurricane therefore represented one of the few Allied fighters available in quantity that could fight on equal terms with most of the German aircraft involved.

During May the RAF had reinforced its contingent in France with twelve Hurricane squadrons, or approximately 192 aircraft. Additional detachments, amounting to another seven squadrons, were made available as the British sought to strike a balance between reinforcing France and jeopardising their domestic defence force, Fighter Command. [32] British fighter production had increased in the spring of 1940 to the point of allowing new squadrons, originally formed on obsolete types, to be largely re-equipped with Hurricanes and Spitfires. By May 1940, Fighter Command's available force had risen to forty-seven squadrons of which thirty-eight were equipped with Hurricanes or Spitfires.[33] At the loss rates experienced in the fighting in France, the commitment of just under half of Fighter Command's strength in modern fighters could be expected to be wiped out in ten days.

This level of savage attrition and imminent catastrophe provides the context of the initial messages in the Churchill–Roosevelt correspondence that May. Churchill was confronted by the political necessity for fighter reinforcement to counter the air superiority won by the Luftwaffe and also the strategic necessity, argued by Sir Hugh Dowding, C.-in-C. of Fighter Command, and Sir Cyril Newall, CAS, to conserve their own fighter defence force. In cabinet discussions on 8 June, Churchill identified the conservation of Fighter Command as vital to British survival, when he repeated the importance of British fighter strength to Reynaud: '. . . they afford the means by which we expect to prolong the war until the United States comes in, or even indefinitely, thus saving not only ourselves but France.'[34]

It seemed this dilemma might be resolved by accelerating the delivery of American aircraft by securing USAAC releases in exchange for deliveries from Allied orders in the United States expected in the autumn. Above all, the British wanted to secure visible signs of American aid to bolster French morale and keep them in the fight. This required a concerted diplomatic campaign both to facilitate whatever meaningful aid the United States could supply and encourage the administration to take bolder steps to assist.

This helps to explain the tone of Churchill's first message as prime minister to Roosevelt on 15 May. This listed Britain's 'immediate needs', consisting of 'forty or fifty of your older destroyers', 'several hundred of the latest types of aircraft', anti-aircraft weapons and increased allocations of steel for purchase.[35] Roosevelt's reply was unhelpful, referring to the need for Congressional approval for the supply of the destroyers which it was 'unwise' to ask for at that point. Accepting Roosevelt's response, Churchill then moved the supply of fighter aircraft to the top of the list of critical supplies: 'Our most vital need is therefore the delivery at the earliest possible date of the largest possible number of Curtiss P-40 fighters now in course of delivery to your army . . .'[36] Even here, Roosevelt's response was unpromising, with the USAAC understandably reluctant to relinquish their first deliveries of the only American fighter to be considered effective in modern air combat. At the same time as Churchill sent this message, Purvis responded to the enquiries previously prompted by Halifax with a repetition of the qualitative shortcomings of the aircraft already in service with the USAAC and already acknowledged by them to be obsolete.[37]

The prospects for the future might be brighter, as Roosevelt had used the developing crisis in Europe to secure Congressional support for a massive rearmament programme. On 16 May he appealed for the capacity to produce 50,000 aircraft per year, and emphasised that a large proportion of this capacity would be used to supply the Allies.[38] But this was rhetoric associated with production in 1941 and 1942; it was concerned with future potential, not current capacity which was limited and subject to political constraints. By 17 May the outcome appeared clear, and Alexander Cadogan, Vansittart's replacement as permanent undersecretary at the FO, pragmatically noted that there was little the United States could do to affect this battle. By 20 May, as the German armoured spearheads continued their advance, Churchill had decided that no further fighter reinforcement should be sent across the Channel; and now, after the defeat of France, attention was now focused on British strategic options.

Churchill's message to Roosevelt on 20 May reiterated the importance of the P-40s in view of the anticipated German assault on Britain but, as noted earlier, the response was disappointing. Aside from the fact that the USAAC P-40s would begin delivery only in June, Arnold was unwilling to relinquish the USAAC's P-36s which he regarded as essential for pilot training. One minor bright spot was Morgenthau's suggestion that the sale of surplus arms could be progressed separately from the demands for destroyers and aircraft. Reynaud had been continually pressing the administration for a visible commitment to the Allies and, on 22 May, Roosevelt had approved the sale of stocks of World War I-vintage rifles and French-designed 75 mm field guns held in storage, which would be finalised on 5 June.[39] But this would not take place in time to have any impact on events in France.

This initial phase of events concluded with the loss of the battle in northern France. Against all expectation, the British were able to evacuate their forces around Dunkirk between 26 May and 3 June. Though poor weather conditions hindered the Luftwaffe effort to attack the evacuation, part of the explanation for its success was the ability of Fighter Command squadrons to intervene directly in the battle area from their bases in southern England. A notable development was the entry into combat of the Spitfire squadrons which had been held in reserve for domestic defence until this point. These were the first Allied fighters to equal the Luftwaffe's Bf109E which had previously enjoyed a performance superiority over all the Allied aircraft it had faced. Experience later in the war, notably in Greece and Crete, would reveal how difficult naval evacuations of British forces could be when they were conducted under uncontested German air superiority.

The picture of larger crisis can sometimes obscure the limited commitment actually involved in the defeats in northern France.

An appreciation of the Allied fighter strength made by Monnet in early June revealed total Allied fighter strengths on 24 May to have been 1,668 British and 1,224 French. British losses between 10 and 24 May had been 194 against 138 replacements built, and French losses 354 against 154 replacements. The Allied loss of air superiority was due less to any lack of aircraft than to their inability to concentrate available resources at the decisive point. Nonetheless, despite the strategic defeat involved in the evacuation of the Allies from northern France, Dunkirk gave an indication that British sea and air power could operate successfully and largely independently of the fate of the French.

This becomes clearer when the only identifiable and credible event which could have represented a departure from Churchill's policy of resistance is considered. Between 26 and 28 May, the cabinet debated Reynaud's initiative to invite Italian mediation, with the implicit object of seeking terms. There was no revolt against Churchill's leadership.[40] This indicates that, despite Halifax's willingness to explore the diplomatic options available, Churchill was able to keep the cabinet aligned behind a policy of continuing resistance. This was undoubtedly popular with MPs in a manner that reflected their previous deposition of Chamberlain for his inability to win cross-party support as a war leader. It is significant that one of Churchill's most successful tactics in winning over potential opposition in cabinet at this time was to invoke the apparent capacity of the RAF to inflict substantial losses on the Luftwaffe.[41]

This was, however, the point at which the thesis of criticality, with regard to American aid, was to become firmly entrenched in British diplomacy. This was due to the influence of the British ambassador in Washington, Lord Lothian. His informal, journalistic style of personal diplomacy was designed to engender among his American audience a sense of direct involvement in British fortunes. As his biographer observed: 'He wrote articles rather than books, and their purpose was to present in clear language a summary of facts and considerations leading up to a conclusion.'[42]

Lothian had gained a reputation as an amateur diplomatist during his service as Lloyd George's private secretary and member of his 'Garden Suburb'. He then had moved on to inform opinion as a journalist, member of the Round Table (a precursor of the Royal Institute for International Affairs), and as a facilitator of contact between the establishment and the press. His reputation had initially prompted FO doubts about his suitability as ambassador.[43] Cadogan dismissed Lothian as 'a phrasemonger' on those grounds.[44] The operation of Lothian's leading analysis within a populist, journalistic approach in 1940 was probably best observed by Harold Nicolson who commented on the 'consummate ease' with which Lothian managed a press conference in October 1940 and the strategic message he got across in the process:

'[The] US came to understand that our interests and the strategic points of the Commonwealth were essential to themselves. It was a fine talk and it went well. Our press were delighted.'[45]

In March 1940 he acknowledged to Halifax that his speeches were 'somewhat indiscreet', but argued they were nonetheless successful because he knew the American mind well enough to deal frankly with controversial issues.[46] One way in which he did this was by the provision of the evidence necessary to convince American audiences. In January 1940, after a dispute with the US authorities over neutral shipping rights through the British naval blockade, he identified the material required: 'The United States will stand anything that we can prove to be really necessary for winning the war, but in future we shall have to prove it.'[47]

The supply of such 'proof', in the form of naval, military, scientific and even financial information to meet American requirements, became a feature of Lothian's advice to Whitehall for the rest of that year. Lothian's 'indiscreet' comments on controversial issues, calculated to exceed his brief from Whitehall in order to achieve a greater impact on the American public mind, would come to the fore in the evolution of Lend-Lease later in 1940. There can be little doubt, however, that his earlier statements indicate that his adoption of indiscretion as a diplomatic tactic was deliberate and was to be understood as such in the FO.

Another aspect of Lothian's method of personal diplomacy was the facilitation of personal contacts. This was not restricted to his dealings with the press. Lothian also advocated the exchange of secret technical information between Britain and the United States. In June 1940 he propelled the cabinet towards agreement to this exchange against Churchill's initial resistance. When arguing in favour of the proposal to the War Cabinet, Lothian's old colleague, Maurice Hankey, was astutely able to perceive Lothian's objective beyond the military and technical considerations ostensibly involved: 'What one wants to do is to get as many people as possible in the U.S.A. favourable to our cause, especially in the influential strata of society. Both the scientists and the military authorities fall into that category in present circumstances.'[48]

By the end of May, Lothian was consulting with pro-Allied pressure groups and pushing Whitehall for a specific statement by Churchill on what equipment the Allies most needed as a result.[49] By such means Lothian acted as a conduit for British supply diplomacy to be influenced by the requirements of American public opinion. The traction exerted by his approach was initially limited given the evident constraints on American assistance. This was demonstrated by Churchill's response to Lothian's suggestion that the rights for naval bases in British possessions be offered to the United States to encourage the administration to supply destroyers in May: 'The United States had given us practically no help in the war, and now that they saw how great was the danger, their attitude was that they wanted to keep everything which would help us for their own defence.'[50]

The combination of Churchill's attitude and Roosevelt's reluctance led to an impasse over the supply of the destroyers which lasted until August. During that time, Lothian's influence increased over the FO position as well as on Churchill's public statements and his diplomacy with Roosevelt. Lothian particularly advised Churchill to adopt a variant of Daladier's thesis of the criticality of American supply in his correspondence with Roosevelt. On 8 June, Lothian compressed the thesis to its essentials:

> The only effective argument is that we are fighting for civilisation with our backs to the wall, that if we go, future prospects of democracy will be very poor and that any assistance we can get immediately may make the difference between success and failure.[51]

This advice was upon tactics rather than a statement of final outcomes and, though it was firmly grounded in the circumstances during the fall of France, it indicated distinction between those tactics and the objectives sought. What made this more significant was the fact that Lothian's approach was not inspired by the catastrophe in Allied fortunes in May 1940 in isolation. He had prepared for his ambassadorship in 1938 by contacting Hankey, the recently retired chairman of the CID, and asked for a strategic appreciation of the effect on the United States of a collapse of the British Empire.[52] Lothian had been a close contemporary of Hankey's since his days as Lord George's private secretary when Hankey had run the Cabinet Office and War Cabinet secretariat.[53] Hankey had remained at the epicentre of Whitehall's strategic and defence bureaucracy until his retirement in July 1938, and would return to government in 1940 as a strategic adviser.[54]

The memorandum Hankey drew up was specifically designed to be used to influence American audiences, leaving Lothian, as he put it, 'adequately armed to talk to some of my American friends'.[55] The Hankey memorandum provided Lothian with the rationale of 'criticality' to demonstrate the strategic value of Britain to the United States. It did so in terms of critical outcomes which transcended the traditional ideological and Anglophobic suspicions that informed American isolationism by demonstrating that British survival and the continuing British war effort against the Axis was in American interest.

The supply of destroyers fitted directly into this thesis of criticality. In March 1940, Lothian had expounded to Halifax his theory of 'democratic control of the seas'.[56] This was a straightforward interpretation of Mahanist naval strategy which advocated Anglo-American naval collaboration to secure American defence. Speaking to Roosevelt on 17 May, Lothian threatened the keystone of Mahanist naval strategy by raising the spectre of the loss of the Royal Navy in the Atlantic.[57] This was characterised by the FO as justifiable 'blackmail' but linked the fate of the British fleet – and continuing British resistance – to the supply of the destroyers. Lothian went on to bring this scenario to the attention of the American public in speeches to Columbia University alumni on 4 June and in public at Yale University on 19 June.[58] This had understandable resonance at a time when the

British were preoccupied with the fate of the French fleet under the control of the Vichy government after the Franco-German armistice.

Throughout June, Lothian's argument, in favour of calculated generosity with regard to the offer of bases in British territory in exchange for the destroyers, steadily gained ground at the FO. By mid-July, his pressure was instrumental in a groundbreaking appreciation by the FO, arguing for 'foster[ing] a habit of cordial co-operation between the English-speaking countries' which was presented to the cabinet by Halifax on 18 July.[59] This also addressed the financial issue:

> . . . we are already heavily in debt to America as a result of the last war, and that we shall shortly be still further in her debt as a condition of winning the present war. We have no hope of ever repaying the enormous sums which will be involved, nor do well-informed Americans ever expect this of us.[60]

The memorandum also captured the basis of the diplomatic strategy which was already in de facto progress: '. . . not only do we require all the help we can get in the present, but the future of our widely scattered Empire is likely to depend on the evolution of an effective and enduring collaboration between ourselves and the United States'.[61] This provided the coherent statement of the basis for a policy which could override the objections of both the Admiralty and the colonial governments to the extent of the basing rights being demanded by the United States in exchange for the destroyers. The basis of a deal was agreed in August and it was formally agreed in September. Factors behind the progression of the deal were the growing realisation of its long-term political importance, as argued by Lothian and the FO on the British side, and a growing American perception of the capacity of the British to survive during the Battle of Britain, distilled in part by the reports of US military observers encouraged by Lothian. Finally, the interest of Frank Knox, Roosevelt's new navy secretary, in securing United States bases in the Caribbean provided the 'molasses' Roosevelt believed would be required to overcome potential opposition.[62]

Throughout this period, Lothian had been responsible for persuading administration officials, such as Knox, of the British need for destroyers by linking them with British survival and the fate of the British fleet.[63] This had progressively influenced administration officials in favour of the deal. By June, Morgenthau was certainly convinced by the Churchill/Lothian argument, believing that it was 'absolutely hopeless' to expect continuing British resistance without the destroyers.[64] The critical dependency thesis was clearly in evidence. So was the 'proof' fed to sympathetic media representatives. At Lothian's behest the United States media had been provided with increasingly detailed secret information on the British destroyer position and losses.

Though ostensibly addressing a major strategic need, the diplomacy involved deliberately ignored the capacity of the aid involved to meet the needs asserted. This is evident when considering the military value of the destroyers. The late conclusion of the deal directly undercut the chronological requirements, emphasised by Churchill to Roosevelt, which were to bridge the gap between the current crisis and deliveries from the British naval construction programme in 1941. Churchill had stepped back from the prospective deal in June, just as a German invasion of Britain appeared imminent following the loss of France. This implicitly undermined any causal link between the supply of the destroyers and continued British resistance. Even when the deal returned to the top of the agenda in August, the Colonial Office and the Admiralty – in theory the service department most concerned with obtaining the destroyers for vital operational needs – formed the mainstay of resistance to the American terms.[65] Churchill was prompted by Admiralty concerns privately to describe the destroyers as 'not vital' in complete contradiction to the rhetoric Lothian had encouraged.[66] Even a pragmatist like Cadogan, resistant to the periodic fits of Churchillian pique, agreed with Churchill when he claimed the destroyers were not worth the exchange demanded for them.[67] The military value of the destroyers would prove limited. In December 1940, Churchill downplayed a report on the problems and delays being encountered getting the destroyers into service when the future of British procurement in the United States was under consideration by the administration.[68]

Lothian's argument prevailed in the end, with the Admiralty accepting the offer of the bases being made 'as a gesture of good propaganda value' and the FO emphasising the 'wider political consideration' served by such practical evidence of the unity of interests involved.[69] In summary, this was supply diplomacy primarily concerned with political rather than military ends. Military requirements, and the capacity of US aid to meet them, were clearly and deliberately being overstated to service a diplomatic strategy designed to foster and facilitate American entanglement with Britain. The same dynamics were present in aircraft supply.

The most obvious example of this was an appeal for particular aircraft made in direct parallel with the appeals for destroyers. The supply of P-40 fighters was asserted as another measure that could make the difference between success and defeat in May 1940. Though that initial approach had been rebuffed, the P-40 returned to Churchill–Roosevelt correspondence in June as the first of them were produced at the Curtiss plant in Buffalo. On 1 June, at the same time as he extolled RAF successes over Dunkirk as providing hopes for the future, Churchill repeated his request for the P-40s, employing the exaggerated claims of combat results prevalent at that time in order to strengthen confidence in the operational performance of the RAF.[70] At this point, Churchill was extolling the RAF's achievement in the air battles over Dunkirk as 'the first real trial of strength between the British and German air forces': 'We had achieved our purpose and saved our Army, and there could be no doubt that this constituted a signal victory for the Royal Air Force, which gave cause for high hopes of our success in the future.'[71]

The British position was secured by Britain's own production. On 19 June, one month after his appointment, Beaverbrook was able to announce to the cabinet that aircraft reserves had risen to 755 aircraft, with production rising from 249 aircraft per week to 363 per week.[72] In contrast, the results of the appeals for American aid during this period remained limited. Roosevelt had approved the sale of surplus rifles and field guns to the French, followed by the sale of ninety-three obsolete, single-engined Northrop A-17 bombers, but there was no progress on priority items, such as the destroyers or P-40s.[73] Further appeals were made on the entry of the Italians into the war on 10 June, and again on the 15 June, with the supply of destroyers again being characterised as 'a matter of life and death'.[74] Meanwhile, the progress of the German offensive southwards led to the replacement of Reynaud by Marshal Pétain, the collapse of French resistance, and the Franco-German armistice of 21 June.

Despite the early start of a substantial purchase programme including the most modern combat aircraft available, American aircraft supply had done little to help the French stem the German assault. By 15 June, deliveries to France amounted to 223 Martin Maryland and 100 DB-7 bombers and forty Yale trainers.[75] But only 182 Marylands and fifty-five DB-7s had been assembled and delivered to the French air force to join the original 100 P-36s by that point. The American aircraft began to add to French air strength in the spring of 1940 at roughly the same time as production of French aircraft, such as the MS.406 fighter, picked up and the superior Dewoitine D.520 began delivery. The P-36s had done reasonably well, considering their performance inferiority compared to the German fighters, and the Marylands and DB-7s had demonstrated a better performance than their French equivalents in their brief combat careers. But American supply had proved to be too little too late to affect the course of events.

Roosevelt's apparent unwillingness to move beyond the surplus arms deal of June, and the discouraging responses to the Anglo-French appeals for aircraft and destroyers in the period May–June, left the British dependent upon their own resources. In one of his periodic rejections of Lothian's exhortations at the end of June, Churchill indicated the gulf between the rhetoric critical dependence involved in the initial stage of Anglo-American supply diplomacy and the reality which informed British decision-making: 'What really matters is whether Hitler is master of Britain in three months or not. I think not. But this is a matter which cannot be argued beforehand.'[76] The basis of Churchill's confidence remained the combination of British air and sea power which alone could defend Britain at that point. Any invasion attempt required the suppression of British air power and, between July and October, this is what the Luftwaffe tried – and failed – to do in the Battle of Britain.

The scale of this achievement bears repeating: the Luftwaffe concentrated approximately 2,600 aircraft in the struggle to gain air supremacy over southern England, and lost 1,733 aircraft between July and September 1940 without achieving success.[77] The RAF lost 915 aircraft in the same period. Despite intensive attacks, the strength of RAF Fighter Command grew throughout the battle; on 4 June, Dowding had 331 serviceable Hurricanes and Spitfires with thirty-six immediately available in reserve. By 11 August, he had 620 Hurricanes and Spitfires available, with 289 reserves.[78] Aircraft losses only occasionally outstripped output but. even then, did not consume available British reserves. Pilot losses were a genuinely greater worry for Dowding but even here it is possible to overstate the problem. Partly due to measures adopted to accelerate domestic pilot training in July, alongside the first products of the overseas Empire Air Training Scheme, at the peak point of shortage in fighter pilots experienced in mid-August, Fighter Command had over three hundred more pilots available than in mid-June.[79]

Fighter Command struggled to evolve an effective defence to the gradual shift of the German bombing effort to the night attack on urban areas which followed in October. This would be resolved only in the spring of 1941 with the increasing deployment of radar-equipped Bristol Beaufighter nightfighters along with an increase in radar-directed anti-aircraft guns. Nonetheless, by the end of September, and the onset of autumn weather conditions in the Channel, it was clear that the German attempt to follow up their continental victories had failed. Numerous factors were involved in the success of the British defence, including the force-multiplier effect of Dowding's integration of radar early warning, radio-controlled interception and anti-aircraft guns into a systematic organisation of centralised command and control. But the most fundamental reason of all was the basic success of the British aircraft industry to match the quality of German aircraft, to replace losses and to expand the strength of the British fighter defences.[80]

The loss of France caused an immediate change in the context of British appeals for American aid. The relative strength of British air power meant that the immediate objects of 'emergency aid' were of less military value to the British than they would have been to the French. The P-40s were a significant example. The British had taken over in toto the French purchase contracts in the United States just before the French collapse and, as a result, inherited the French orders for P-36s and P-40s which predated the joint programme of April 1940. Deliveries were expected to begin in September. At this point in August 1940, the suggestion was made, apparently as a result of the visit to London in July of Roosevelt's confidant, William 'Wild Bill' Donovan, that the British should receive the two hundred P-40s from USAAC contracts.

It is hard to accept that this offer was made with USAAC approval; if it was, their motives are difficult to discern, though it may have been another attempt to improve the quality of USAAC aircraft by swapping initial production variants, which lacked self-sealing fuel tanks, for aircraft later in the production run which came equipped with these as standard. It is more likely that Donovan raised the issue with Sir Arthur Salter, the chairman of the British North American Supply Council, after contact with Purvis on his return from London. In any case, the most important aspect of this offer was that, despite Churchill's repeated requests for these P-40s in May–June, the RAF turned the offer down.

The request had been relayed by the BPC to Sir Arthur Salter who, in turn, passed it on to the Air Ministry. Slessor, then Director of Plans, responded on 17 August: 'Our conclusion was that, as we are in a pretty strong position as far as the supply of fighters is concerned, we do not at present require these P.40s.'[81]

This took place the day before the heaviest day's losses to both the RAF and the Luftwaffe in the Battle of Britain.[82] Though Slessor referred to the 'insurance' aspect of American supply, by observing that the aircraft might be useful if held as a reserve against loss from German bombing of domestic production, it is clear that the apparent need for the aircraft had changed. Despite the enormous pressure the RAF was under at this point, American supply was not seen as the essential need that Allied diplomacy had claimed previously and British diplomacy was continuing to claim.

Roosevelt's selection as the Democratic candidate for an unprecedented third term as president on 19 July set the scene for an increase in the prospects for American aid. This would materialise in the form of increased aircraft supply by means of the '3,000-per month' scheme announced by Morgenthau and Purvis to the American press on 23 July 1940. The current capacity of the American aircraft industry was fully absorbed with USAAC orders and the existing Anglo-French purchase programme. The latter, which covered deliveries throughout 1941, would develop an expected capacity of approximately 750 aircraft per month. Any increase in production expansion for the British would conflict with the USAAC rearmament programme which had been launched by Roosevelt in May. An increased programme would also demand that the question of finance be addressed.

At the end of May, Roosevelt had appointed a National Defense Advisory Commission (NDAC), including the General Motors magnate William Knudsen who was charged with managing the industrial production required.[83] Achieving an increased programme required the integration of British plans with Knudsen's, and this could be achieved only by overcoming the resistance of the US services to what they saw as British competition for output. In June, Roosevelt had taken steps to position himself for re-election and reduce the opposition within the administration to aiding the Allies by introducing influential Republicans Frank Knox and Henry Stimson as the Navy Secretary and Secretary of War, respectively. Stimson, however, was impressed by Arnold's arguments of USAAC weakness, and clashed with Morgenthau over the priority given to British supplies. The War Department position remained that British procurement should be held at the level of 750 aircraft per month.

By this time 8,200 aircraft remained undelivered from the existing Allied contracts which were expected to end in October 1941. Another 4,200 aircraft were expected from continuation orders from those contracts up to July 1942, with an additional 1,500 in that period from the placement of new orders in May–July 1940.[84] At this point the MAP entered the lists to increase British supply expectations with an enlarged purchase programme, borne of Beaverbrook's own interest in realising the potential of American production. As A. J. P Taylor observed of Beaverbrook at this point: 'American resources, he believed, were limitless, and he was determined to mobilize them.'[85] The specific objective was to set out an expanded programme for American deliveries in 1942, following on from the conclusion of deliveries from the joint purchase programme. The MAP wanted to increase the figure involved from 750 to at least 1,250 aircraft per month.

Though this ambition was almost certainly derived from Purvis's influence, it initially involved Beaverbrook bypassing the BPC by sending his own representative, Morris Wilson, to place orders in the United States in June 1940. Wilson's initiative was soon absorbed within Purvis's structure as the British Air Commission (BAC), a branch of MAP, notably because Purvis had established a good working relationship with US officials such as Morgenthau. By mid-July Purvis was looking for Morgenthau's assistance to expand deliveries by 1,500 aircraft per month (the '1,250 per month scheme' plus 250 training aircraft excluded from the original calculations), giving a combined total of approximately two thousand aircraft per month. Morgenthau then encouraged Purvis to increase his target to three thousand aircraft per month, in part to overcome USAAC attempts to claim engines from the former French contracts the British had taken over.[86]

By committing themselves to paying for the capital investment required to achieve this, the British reduced USAAC fears of competing for allocations against a background of insufficient production. This secured Morgenthau's help, with Purvis helpfully employing the thesis of criticality, apparently under his own initiative.

> . . . deliveries against existing UK orders (including those taken over from the French under the assignment agreements) were absolutely vital to the successful conduct of the War and that if a report had to be made to London that these deliveries would be taken away the resulting discouragement would be so great as to profoundly affect the future conduct of the war.[87]

The whole concept revealed the process by which British objectives were subject to inflation by the British procurement officials in Washington and pro-British figures in the administration, notably Morgenthau. The initiative was suggested by Morgenthau to overcome War Department insistence on restricting British procurement to USAAC benefit, a situation that would become a major feature of British supply diplomacy in the years that followed. Although the RAF welcomed the prospects of increased American supply, Air Ministry involvement in this procurement diplomacy was minimal if not non-existent. If the production targets claimed did materialise alongside the British production target of 2,550 aircraft per month, the RAF faced the prospect of supply exceeding requirements.[88] The Air Ministry attitude was encapsulated by Slessor's post-war comment that the Air Staff did not accept the '3000 per month' scheme at face value.[89] This was another example of British supply plans being 'pulled' by interpretations of what was possible or desirable in Washington rather than 'pushed' by the specific needs of the British services.

What qualifies this further is the known practice of using exhortatory production targets which had already begun with the MAP's domestic production schedules. This understanding can be usefully extended to the similar US production plans under discussion at the same time. The '3,000 per month scheme' was drawn up as part of an effort by Purvis in particular to stimulate American production by the use of ambitious targets. It was accepted by Knudsen and the US administration because it promised to increase output beyond immediately foreseeable needs. Indeed, the objectives involved were almost entirely a product of the 'mobilisation' procurement diplomacy practised by Monnet and Purvis long before the fall of France. Sir Arthur Salter justified this approach at the end of July 1940:

> In general it is of urgent importance to 'talk big and at once' . . . The greater the over-estimate the greater will be the extension of America's productive capacity for armaments . . . If sufficient productive capacity is created now, it matters little how it is allotted. Its products will be available for our war effort, if by us – good; if by the Americans themselves – better still. The creation of this capacity, and the momentum of the output and the interests involved, may itself at the worst

> force a solution of our credit problem; at the best it will be a real factor in bringing the USA into the war.[90]

This was procurement diplomacy by acknowledged overestimation, entirely divorced from the short-term needs and assertions of immediate criticality which had ostensibly featured in supply diplomacy so far. The aim of this procurement plan was twofold. Firstly, it would generate the political momentum required to overcome the financial and legal obstacles in the way of the full employment of American economic power on Britain's behalf. Secondly, that momentum might suffice to involve the United States directly in the war. This was the rationale that justified the massive increase in expenditure involved, expenditure which it was clearly beyond British means to meet in the long term.

The British took over the French purchase programmes when France fell, at an additional cost of $600 million, at least $475 million of which was due on aircraft or aircraft-related contracts (engines, propellers, etc.). The British share of the Anglo-French scheme had now risen to $333 million (largely due to options and follow-on orders), with another $2 million for taking over a Belgian order for Brewster Buffalo fighters, and with a further $120 million for the British orders placed since the outbreak of the war. In addition to this, the British had committed themselves to taking over an Anglo-French scheme to build Merlin engines in the United States, costing a further $112 million. In total, the existing British aircraft procurement commitment had now reached over $1.1 billion and had become a major factor in the loss of British foreign exchange, due to the high advance and progress payments required before delivery of the aircraft later in 1941 and 1942.[91]

The programme was expanded again and the cost increased still further in August when Morgenthau pressured the British into placing approximately $500 million in continuation contracts. These covered the continued operation of the capacity employed on the joint Anglo-French programme beyond the original terminal date of September 1941 and up to March 1942, at an additional cost of approximately $500 million. In justifying their agreement, the BPC admitted the political dimension to this further commitment:

> The reason for this was that Morgenthau had represented to Purvis the importance of releasing the orders immediately in view of the US political situation . . . Reference to US political situation was a factor which BPC had to take into account even in the placing of orders.[92]

These continuation orders added a further 4,200 aircraft to British purchase contracts; by October a further tranche of 4,550 aircraft to be delivered between April and June 1942 at a cost of $673 million had been added to push the British total up to fourteen thousand aircraft inclusive of all existing cash-purchase orders. Estimates of the financial commitment were immense but clearly heavily weighted to the period when deliveries from the expanded programme would take effect. Of a total of $5.51 billion involved in the MAP purchase programme, $4.425 billion would be due after June 1941. The centrality of the aircraft programme to this scheme can be seen in the proportion of the total estimated purchase programmes of all the British supply departments, which amounted to $7.065 billion.[93] Aircraft supply represented 78 per cent of this supply programme. The new programme would now take the British beyond the limits of foreign exchange solvency, and precipitate an incipient financial crisis which would result in Lend-Lease.

The scene was set by a Treasury paper on the foreign exchange position presented to cabinet on 22 August 1940.[94] This noted how total foreign exchange in gold and marketable securities had declined from £775 million ($3.1 billion) on 1 January 1940, to £490 ($2 billion) in mid-August. While the loss of exchange between July 1940 and June 1941 had originally been estimated at £410 ($1.6 billion), this had been exacerbated by the French contracts both because of their extent and the more onerous payment conditions associated with them compared to British contracts. Now the Treasury estimated the loss of exchange to be £800 million ($3.2 billion) in the year July 1940–June 1941, or more than the existing reserve, some of which would need to be retained if Britain was 'to avoid complete financial dependence' on the United States. Although the Treasury had identified Allied gold holdings of £890 million ($3.6 billion), much of this might be impossible to access. This left the British facing the problem of holding out until US policy was clarified after the presidential election in November. Meanwhile, the British could expect to run out of gold for conversion into dollars to finance this programme by the end of December.[95]

Churchill announced himself willing to 'gamble' on the willingness of the United States to provide financial help on an extended scale. Beaverbrook agreed, articulating a policy of industrial brinksmanship:

> . . . we ought to do everything in our power to fill American factories with British orders. No American Government would dare to tell those factories to cease production, with all the consequences in the shape of unemployment and industrial derangement. Something had to be left to chance, and we ought to trust to the common-sense of the Americans, and their desire to see our cause prevail.[96]

After the removal of financial restrictions from consideration by the cabinet decision of 22 August, the detailed aircraft procurement scheme involved came before the cabinet on 6 September. Beaverbrook's proposal outlined the two options: one to increase American production to an eventual total of 1,250 aircraft per month; the second to increase it to three thousand per month. Both schemes would cost $450 million in capital and current expenditure by 31 January 1941, rising to $875 million and $950 million respectively by 30 June 1941. The eventual capital expenditure for the smaller scheme would be $475 million (essentially being completed by 30 June 1941) with a further cost of $1,500 million per year to cover the resulting output. In total, the 3,000-per-month scheme would cost $1,000 million in capital expenses, and $3,500 million per year to operate. Beaverbrook admitted that the objectives behind this scheme were clearly long term, with deliveries beginning in the second half of 1941 and additional deliveries from the larger scheme starting in 1942.[97] The Treasury made no bones about the implications of the plan:

> The cost of even the lower scheme is vast . . . There is no prospect of our ever having dollars to pay these sums, nor of our ever repaying those amounts, if lent to us by the USA. Production under either

> scheme depends upon the willingness of the American Administration to pay for it.[98]

Although the cabinet pencilled in qualifications to the plan, such as a review when the increased dollar expenditure became due or attempting to get financial assistance from the administration via Reconstruction Finance Corporation (RFC) loans for capital expenditure, Beaverbrook received permission to go ahead.[99] One consideration involved was that Morgenthau had already leaked details of the plan to the American press.[100] The press would be involved again as Lothian resorted to indiscreet personal diplomacy to help resolve the financial issue.

Lothian returned to Britain in October–November 1940, in part to lay the groundwork for a new British approach for American supply, to follow the conclusion of the presidential election in November. As he stated in his request to the FO to return home for a while:

> Public opinion here [in the USA] has not yet grasped that it will have to make far reaching decisions to finance and supply us and possibly still graver ones next spring or summer unless it is to take the responsibility of forcing us to make a compromised peace.[101]

To compel America to confront these decisions and resolve them in British favour, Lothian suggested a 'ruthless exposé of the strategic dangers' to disperse 'a fog of complacency' in a country 'saturated with illusions' about the British financial position.[102] The new departure from Lothian's preceding diplomacy was the extension of criticality to the larger and longer-term issue of finance. But the attribution of a critical responsibility for British resistance to US support remained. As Colville commented on Lothian's draft for Churchill's letter to Roosevelt appealing for financial aid, 'It is intended to make R. [Roosevelt] feel that if we go down, the responsibility will be America's'.[103]

Lothian's alleged comments, designed to prepare American public opinion at the landing stage on his return to New York on 22 November, are notorious. Sir John Wheeler-Bennett, one of his staff at the time, claimed that Lothian had baldly announced to the assembled press: 'Well boys, Britain's broke, it's your money we want'.[104] Lothian was compelled to defend his statements to Churchill but unrepentantly maintained that it was necessary to combat the illusions of American public opinion which remained 'the ultimate determinant'.[105]

The end result of the Lothian–Churchill initiative was Roosevelt's evolution of the policy of Lend-Lease, announced at a press conference on 17 December with the memorable analogy of lending a fire hose to a neighbour. This envisaged funding British supply in the United States through an administration-controlled and Congressionally approved procurement process. Roosevelt further outlined the ambitious aims of the programme on 30 December when he repeated Monnet's phrase about turning the United States into 'the great arsenal of Democracy'.[106]

Unlike the destroyers deal, which had been resolved by executive action to avoid legislative opposition, Lend-Lease openly confronted Congress with the administration policy to finance aid for the Allies on a major scale. That the administration could contemplate this step in early 1941 was, in part, due to Lothian's assertions of criticality not only taking hold in the administration but winning credibility with the American public. This permitted the growth of some level of bipartisan consensus behind the policy. An example of this was Wendell Wilkie's private confirmation of his support of the policy of aiding Britain before his unsuccessful challenge to Roosevelt in the Presidential election.[107]

French and then British diplomacy had adopted the thesis of critical dependency to secure a powerful ally, much as Herodotus claimed Thessaly had done thousands of years before. While the successful response to it was grounded in the reality of the German successes of 1940, it was also influenced by the diplomatic strategy adopted, notably at Lothian's behest: a strategy that operated distinctly from the military value of the supplies concerned. As the American press observed after Lothian's early death in December 1940, just before the announcement of the administration policy which would become Lend-Lease, 'We cannot recall that an ambassador from a great power has ever before addressed the American people directly, saying in effect, "If you help us we shall win; if not we shall lose".'[108]

Notes

1. Herodotus, *The Histories*, Book VII, trans. A. de Selincourt, revised A. R. Burn (Harmondsworth: Penguin, 1983), p. 502.
2. Notably on 9 June 1940. Winston S. Churchill, *The Second World War*, Vol. II, *Their Finest Hour* (London: Cassell, 1949), p. 355.
3. Reynolds, *Creation*, p. 115
4. WP (40) 168/CoS (40) 390, 'British Strategy in a Certain Eventuality', 25 May 1940; CAB 66/7/48.
5. This approach is developed in Gavin Bailey, 'Creating a Sense of Criticality: "Lothian's Method" and the Evolution of U.S. Wartime Aid to Britain', in Priscilla Roberts (ed.), *Lord Lothian and Anglo-American Relations, 1900–1940* (Dordrecht: Republic of Letters, 2010).
6. Churchill, *Their Finest Hour*, pp. 21–2; Reynolds details Churchill's efforts to use them in his histories while restricting their access by other authors; Reynolds, *In Command of History*, pp. 156–8.
7. Lash, p. 23–4; Warren Kimball, *Forged in War: Churchill, Roosevelt and the Second World War* (London: HarperCollins, 1998), pp. 35–9.
8. David Reynolds, *Creation,* p. 87; note from John Peck, Churchill's Private Secretary, 3 July 1940, in response to Lothian's requests in telegrams 994, 14 June 1940, and 1110, 24 June 1940, FO 371/24192.
9. David Reynolds, *Creation*, pp. 85–7.
10. Purco 106, 8 May 1940; CAB 85/14.
11. Meeting of ministers at the Admiralty, 11 May 1940; CAB 65/7/13.
12. Halifax to Lothian, No. 481, 13 May 1940; FO 371/24239.
13. Purco 131, 19 May 1940; CAB 85/14.
14. Lothian to FO No. 718, 13 May 1940; FO 371/24192.
15. 'Supply and Production: Ninth Report by the Air Ministry'; CAB 68/6/30.
16. Figures distilled from AIR 20/2039.
17. Leo McKinstry, *Spitfire: Portrait of a Legend* (London: John Murray, 2008), pp. 70–93, 141–8.
18. Churchill, *Finest Hour,* p. 561.
19. Anthony Furse, *Wilfred Freeman* (Staplehurst: Spellmount, 2000), p. 141.
20. Denis Richards, *Portal of Hungerford* (London: Heinemann, 1977), p. 195.
21. Cairncross, p. 20.

22. A. J. P. Taylor, *Beaverbrook* (London: Hamish Hamilton, 1972), p. 454. The programme marginally raised British production targets to 2,565 aircraft per month by June 1941 and 2,782 per month by December 1941. This included, however, a large increase in more complex heavy bomber production. Postan, p. 124.
23. War Cabinet 140 (40), 26 April 1940; CAB 65/6/49.
24. John Terraine, *The Right of the Line* (Ware: Wordsworth, 1997), pp. 119–20.
25. Air Ministry, *Rise and Fall*, p. 66.
26. Bullitt to Secretary of State, No. 659, 14 May 1940; Bullitt, p. 416.
27. Martin Gilbert, *Finest Hour: Winston S. Churchill 1939–1941* (London: Mercury, 1989), pp. 18, 31–3; memorandum by D. J. Scott, 28 February 1940; FO 371/24239.
28. Diary entry, 2 June 1940; John Colville, *The Fringes of Power: Downing Street Diaries, 1939–1955*, Vol. I, *September 1939–September 1941* (Sevenoaks: Sceptre, 1986), p. 171.
29. FO to Sir Ronald Campbell, No. 154, 16 May 1940; TNA: PRO FO 371/24192.
30. WM (40) 165; 'Meeting with M. Reynaud at Tours, 13 June 1940'; CAB 65/13/42.
31. Richards, *Fight at Odds*, p. 109.
32. Ibid., pp. 122–3.
33. Ibid., p. 65.
34. Gilbert, p. 483.
35. Churchill to Roosevelt, 25 May 1940; Warren F. Kimball (ed.), *Churchill and Roosevelt: The Complete Correspondence*, Vol. I, *Alliance Emerging October 1933–November 1942* (Princeton: Princeton University Press, 1984), p. 37.
36. Churchill to Roosevelt, 20 May 1940; Kimball, *Complete Correspondence* I, p. 40.
37. Purco 118, 15 May 1940; CAB 85/14.
38. Dallek, p. 221.
39. Purco 140, 23 May 1940; CAB 85/14; Haight, *American Aid*, p. 237.
40. The cabinet '. . . agreed that an approach on the lines proposed by the French government at the present time was unlikely to serve any useful purpose'; War Cabinet 145 (40), 28 May 1940; CAB 65/7/40.
41. Andrew Roberts, *The 'Holy Fox': The Life of Lord Halifax* (London: Phoenix, 1991), pp. 216–22.

42. J. R. M. Butler, *Lord Lothian (Philip Kerr) 1882–1940* (London: Macmillan, 1960), p. 240.
43. Alan J. Sharp, 'The FO in Eclipse 1919–22,' *History*, 61, No. 202 (June 1976), p. 206; John Turner and Michael Dockrill, 'Philip Kerr at 10 Downing Street, 1916–1921', in John Turner (ed.) *The Larger Idea: Lord Lothian and the Problem of National Sovereignty*, (London: Historians' Press, 1988), pp. 55–6.
44. Cadogan, diary entry, 27 November 1939; David Dilks (ed.), *The Diaries of Sir Alexander Cadogan 1938–1945* (London: Cassell, 1971), p. 234.
45. Nicolson, diary entry, 22 October 1940; Nigel Nicolson (ed.), *Harold Nicolson: Diaries and Letters 1939–1945*, (London: Collins, 1967), p. 122.
46. Lothian to Halifax, 11 March 1940; Churchill Papers, CHAR 20/15. The criticism refers to Lothian's speech to the Chicago Council of Foreign Relations, 4 January 1940. Hudson, pp. 47–63.
47. Lothian to Colonel Charles Kerr, 29 January 1940; GD 40/17/402, Lothian Papers.
48. Hankey, memorandum, 23 July 1940; FO 371/24256.
49. Lothian to the War Cabinet, Telegram No. 793, 22 May 1940 and Telegram No. 817, 24 May 1940; FO 371/24239.
50. War Cabinet 141 (40), 27 May 1940. CAB 65/7/36.
51. Lothian to Churchill, Telegram No. 931, 8 June 1940; FO 371/24239.
52. Typescript copy of Hankey's memorandum, 'The Value of the British Empire to the United States', 16 December 1938, Lothian Papers, GD 40/17/444; *see also* Stephen Roskill, *Hankey: Man of Secrets*, Vol. III, *1931–1963* (London: Collins, 1974), p. 371.
53. Peter Rowland, *Lloyd George* (London: Barrie & Jenkins, 1975), p. 418.
54. Ismay, p. 89.
55. Lothian to Hankey, 12 December 1938; GD 40/17/372, Lothian Papers.
56. Lothian to Halifax, 11 March 1940, Churchill Papers, CHAR 20/15; Lash, pp. 34–5.
57. Lothian to Churchill, Telegram No. 759, 18 May 1940; FO 371/24192.
58. Hudson, pp. 100–1; Reynolds, *Creation*, p. 115.
59. CAB 66/10/7.
60. Ibid.
61. Ibid.

62. Reynolds, *Creation*, p. 124.
63. Lash, p. 207.
64. Kimball, *Complete Correspondence* I, p. 49; Blum, p. 162.
65. Roberts, pp. 256–7.
66. Reynolds, *Creation*, p. 127.
67. Cadogan diary entry, 23 August 1940; Dilks, p. 323.
68. Churchill to Roosevelt, Telegram No. 3795, 31 December 1940, PREM 3/422/1. The report was sent via the U.S. naval attaché in London instead.
69. Director of Plans, Admiralty, 30 June 1940, and Halifax to Lord Lloyd, 19 July 1940; ADM 116/4409.
70. Churchill to Roosevelt, 1 June 1940; Kimball, *Complete Correspondence* I, p. 41.
71. War Cabinet 151 (40), 1 June 1940; CAB 65/7/46.
72. WP (40) 211, 'Aircraft Production: Memorandum by the Minister for Aircraft Production', 19 June 1940; CAB 65/8/41.
73. Dallek, p. 227.
74. Churchill to Roosevelt, 11 June and 15 June 1940; Kimball, *Complete Correspondence* I, pp. 43, 49–50.
75. Haight, *American Aid*, p. 244.
76. Churchill to Lothian, telegram No. 1304, 13 June 1940; PREM 3/476/10.
77. Air Ministry, p. 76; losses, from Richards, *Fight at Odds*, p. 190.
78. Richards, *Fight at Odds*, p. 156.
79. Though Fighter Command was 209 pilots below establishment pilot strength of 1,588 on 17 August, there were still 1,379 pilots on hand compared to 1,094 on 15 June; Appendix 10, Derek Wood and Derek Dempster, *The Narrow Margin: The Battle of Britain and the Rise of Air Power 1930–1940* (Tiptree: Arrow, 1967), p. 484; 'Royal Air Force Training', memorandums from the Secretary of State for Air, WP (40) 238, 1 July 1940; CAB 66/9/18, WP (40) 305, 7 August 1940; CAB 66/10/36, and WP (40) 447, 15 November 1940; CAB 66/13/27.
80. Overy asserts that production and intelligence were the critical factors; Richard Overy, *The Battle* of Britain (London: Penguin, 2000), p. 123.
81. Slessor to Sir Archibald Sinclair, 17 August 1940; AIR 19/173.
82. Alfred Price, *The Hardest Day* (London: Cassell, 1988), p. 9.
83. Dallek, p. 224.
84. Hall, Wrigley and Scott, p. 109.
85. Taylor, *Beaverbrook*, p. 428.

86. 'Memorandum of Discussion at Washington on July 24th.' Arthur Purvis, 12 August 1940. AVIA 38/14
87. 'Notes of Discussion in Washington on July 23rd'; AVIA 38/14.
88. ERP 21, 31 July 1940; AIR 20/5777; Slessor, p. 319.
89. Slessor, p. 309.
90. 'Armaments Programme' by Sir Arthur Salter, Chairman of the North American Supply Committee, 31 July 1940; CAB 115/78.
91. 'USA Aircraft Orders', undated but located within files associated with the assumption of French orders, June 1940; AVIA 10/126.
92. Self to MAP, Briny 296, 14 August 1940; AVIA 38/14.
93. Figures from BPC memorandum, 'Summarised Forecast of Payments on Proposed Programmes, as at September 1, 1940'; AVIA 38/14.
94. WM (40) 232; 'The Exchange Position'; 22 August 1940; CAB 65/14/23.
95. Ibid.
96. Ibid.
97. WP (40) 354, 'Creation of New Aircraft Capacity in the USA'; memorandum by the Minister for Aircraft Production, 3 September 1940; CAB 66/11/34.
98. WP (40) 355, 'Creation of New Aircraft Capacity in the USA', memorandum by Chancellor of the Exchequer; CAB 66/11/35.
99. War Cabinet 244 (40), 6 September 1940, 'Creation of New Aircraft Capacity in USA'; CAB 65/9/6.
100. *American Aviation Daily*, 25 July 1940; James H. Rowe Papers, box 6, folder Civil Aeronautics Authority; FDR Library. Research courtesy Professor A. P. Dobson.
101. Lothian to Churchill, Telegram No. 2063, 20 September 1940; FO 371/24246.
102. Reynolds, 'Lothian, Roosevelt, Churchill and the Origins of Lend-Lease', in Turner, p. 97; Butler, *Lothian*, p. 264.
103. Diary entry, 12 November 1940; Colville, p. 344.
104. John W. Wheeler-Bennett, *King George VI: His Life and Reign* (London: Macmillan, 1958), p. 521.
105. Lothian to Churchill, Telegram No. 2793, 23 November 1940; FO 371/24249; Reynolds, 'Origins of Lend-Lease', p. 100.
106. Dallek, p. 257.
107. Cole, *Roosevelt and the Isolationists*, p. 372.
108. Butler, *Lothian*, p. 315.

4 Lend-Lease and the Politics of Supply, 1941

There is a tendency among our people to rely more and more on American output of aircraft. That would be a mistake.

Lord Beaverbrook

The end of 1940 and first half of 1941 saw the devolution of supply diplomacy to a series of transatlantic personal missions concerning the implementation of American aid to Britain. These began as Lend-Lease, evolved at the end of 1940, and then became law in March 1941 after a series of Congressional hearings and extensive public debate. This personal diplomacy began with the Slessor mission of November 1940–March 1941 which would evolve into the Anglo-American 'ABC' staff discussions on joint Anglo-American strategy. These discussions would also settle prospective aircraft supply allocations between the RAF and the USAAC for the rest of 1941 in the 'Slessor agreement'. On the American side they would involve Harry Hopkins's first visit to Britain in January–February 1941, and then the despatch of Averell Harriman as Roosevelt's personal Lend-Lease expediter in March, and conclude with the first visit of General Arnold to Britain in April 1941. This last visit demonstrated how political resistance to supplying Britain would be increasingly assumed by the USAAC, and how the personal diplomacy recommended by Lothian was expanded to include the USAAC in an attempt to reduce that resistance.

The period was marked by continuing British appeals for immediate aid in the short term and the conclusion of a long-term aircraft allocation agreement as an integral part of the first Anglo-American strategic discussions. It also featured the exposure of the 'expectational gap', resulting from the existence of a qualitative deployment policy by the RAF, which was determined by shortcomings in aircraft performance. This policy involved the relegation of American aircraft to secondary roles and theatres which contradicted the assertions of the diplomacy employed to secure them, and threatened to inflame USAAC resistance to supply policy. The background for all this was the actual experience of American aircraft deliveries in RAF hands from pre-Lend-Lease procurement contracts.

At the end of October 1940, Beaverbrook notified the cabinet of the current British aircraft position. RAF strength had risen from eighty-eight bomber and fighter squadrons, with 884 aircraft available on 15 May, to 107 squadrons, with 1,222 aircraft available, on 25 October. Furthermore, and despite Beaverbrook's opposition, the need to supply the EATS and begin the reinforcement of the Middle East had led to 1,164 aircraft being sent overseas in the previous five months.[1] British aircraft supply was not only sufficient to meet defensive needs but had also begun to supply overseas theatres as well.

If British aircraft production had exceeded expectations and defied attempts by the Luftwaffe to cripple it, American production had become a source of disappointment. Deliveries from the existing French contracts were late. A significant example was the P-40 where British expectations, when they had taken over the French contracts, were that fifty would be delivered by the end of September. In fact, by the end of September, the British had received one which itself appears to have been the subject of a specific individual exchange deal for a Spitfire supplied to the USAAC earlier in the year.[2] Assembly of the American types, mostly at Speke near Liverpool or Colerne in Gloucestershire, was a lengthy process, and subsequent testing revealed shortcomings in performance and equipment. As a result of this, Beaverbrook offered some conclusions that attempted to correct inflated expectations of American aircraft supply which he himself had been guilty of raising.

> Deliveries of aircraft from the United States are disappointing in scale and limited in their value for the purposes of combat . . . There is

> a tendency among our people to rely more and more on American output of aircraft. That would be a mistake. On the contrary, the American situation shows the need for increasing our productive effort here. This is the true lesson which it has for us.[3]

On 24 December 1940, Beaverbrook reviewed the deteriorating delivery expectations of the existing purchase programme, observing that 'It is a most alarming document'. Delivery delays affected all the types originating from the earlier 1939 and 1940 Anglo-French purchase contracts that were scheduled to be delivered in the last quarter of 1940. Out of 428 aircraft ordered, 153 were expected to be delivered to the BAC in the United States between October and December 1940, yet only twenty-one had been received in Britain by the RAF. Beaverbrook's conclusion was inescapable. 'We cannot depend on any very large measure of assistance from the United States in the immediate future.'[4] By 26 December 1940, Beaverbrook had even lost patience with Purvis's strategy of attempting to maximise American supply: 'We are told over and over again that we get wonderful results from the Purvis Mission, but in fact he has nothing to his credit except a kindly disposition on the part of Mr Morgenthau, and that is easily bought at such a price.'[5]

This dissatisfaction extended beyond Purvis's personal efforts, however, and enveloped the whole concept of making diplomatic concessions to achieve the goodwill regarded as necessary to secure supplies. On 20 February 1941, Beaverbrook recited a litany of concessions made to the United States since World War I which had failed to secure American goodwill, concluding, 'If we give everything away, we gain little or no advantage over our present situation. Stand up to the Democrats!'[6]

Beaverbrook's annoyance was reflected by Churchill. In response to the Lothianesque statements of the British Consul General in New York on the critical importance of the American aid measures of the previous year to British resistance, Churchill complained to Halifax: 'We have not had anything from the United States that we have not paid for, and what we have had has not played an essential part in our resistance'.[7]

Clearly, there remained a divergence between the rhetorical

assertions of British supply diplomacy and the reality. The reality can be seen in the RAF order of battle at the very end of 1940. On 31 December 1940, Fighter Command had an operational strength of 829 aircraft available, Coastal Command 110, Army Co-operation Command 103, and Bomber Command 455.[8] Out of this total of 1,497 aircraft available for operations in the combat commands of the RAF in Britain, the only American aircraft which could be included were twenty-seven Hudsons in Coastal Command. This amounted to 25 per cent of Coastal Command's operational strength on that date and less than 2 per cent of overall RAF operational strength.

American aircraft supply had been largely irrelevant to the progress of the war in 1940. But this conclusion has been challenged by aviation historians in the specific technological niche of the supply of 100-octane aviation fuel which superseded the previous standard of 87-octane fuel during the Battle of Britain. This fuel is commonly regarded as both providing a performance benefit of critical importance to British fighters during the battle, and being supplied from the United States just in time to make this critical contribution. Richard Hallion has best summarised this understanding:

> . . . American suppliers delivered sufficient quantities of performance-enhancing 100 octane fuel to England in time for use by Fighter Command during the Battle of Britain, a contribution of profound significance to the operational success of both the Spitfire and Hurricane fighters.[9]

This understanding has been refuted, both in terms of qualifying the critical performance benefit provided by 100-octane fuel, which is often conflated with the introduction of the constant-speed, variable-pitch propeller that gave a significant improvement in the climbing performance of RAF fighters from the spring of 1940, and in the attribution of the origin of 100-octane fuel supplies used in the battle to the United States.[10] While the development of 100-octane fuel in the mid-1930s was unquestionably an American invention, when considering the wartime use of the fuel, the British had gone to some lengths to avoid being critically dependent upon American supplies. Air Ministry planning for the use of the fuel in wartime had begun in 1937, and had taken into consideration the embargo provisions of the Neutrality Acts.[11] As a result of this pre-war planning, the RAF had initiated a massive programme of investment in 100-octane fuel production, the majority of which originated outside the United States. This pre-war programme of production and storage permitted the introduction of the fuel to operational use just before the Battle of Britain. Far from representing a particular example of a critical and identifiably American contribution to the battle, the supply of 100-octane fuel confirms the larger context of the dependence upon British and British-controlled resources by British air power at the time.

This returns the focus of critical contribution to the issue of aircraft supply. The value of that supply was known to be divergent from the diplomatic rhetoric employed to secure it at the time, and this was not just a temporary problem for the British at the end of 1940 when dealing with the products of earlier orders. With the acceptance of the '3,000 per month' plan in July–September, the question of mobilising the American economy behind the British war effort had apparently already been achieved. This did not, however, represent a conclusion to either British aircraft supply diplomacy or the American resistance to it. The question of aircraft quality threatened to undermine the value of American supply just as the initiation of the massive procurement programme for 1941 and 1942 was secured by Lend-Lease.

This was manifested in the types of aircraft built and the standard of equipment they incorporated. The RAF had prioritised aircraft quality during the rearmament period, and this was reflected in the adoption of advanced monoplane aircraft and particularly the heavy bomber. In addition, aircraft designs were understood to require a process of constant updating and modification to reflect the changing needs of operational service. This process of modification required interrupting production lines to introduce these modifications, in other words reducing the quantity of aircraft produced to improve their quality. As Freeman had put it: 'The question – put in its simplest form – is, should we sacrifice quality to attain quantity?'[12]

The RAF had been generally successful when defending their qualitative agenda from pressure to adopt more easily produced types during pre-war rearmament. This dispute had arisen again when the MAP under Beaverbrook took control of aircraft production. As Freeman pointed out to Beaverbrook at the end of July 1940:

> I am convinced that it is no use equipping the Air Force with aircraft which are inferior to those of the enemy. There is in this country [Britain] a great belief in numbers, but numbers in themselves can achieve nothing if the equipment is inferior, since this inferiority will destroy the morale of our pilots.[13]

This was an issue of particular relevance to American production. The 1939–40 purchase orders had been placed to absorb the available production capacity of American aircraft firms and begin the process of expansion. This had involved the completion of deliveries within relatively tight timescales. To achieve this, the only option available to the Allies was to accept the production of types already in train or about to go into production as a result of the 1939–40 US rearmament programme. This meant that the RAF had accepted large numbers of aircraft which did not meet its qualitative standards in terms of performance and equipment. The types to be produced by the new capacity created for the '3,000 per month' programmes had not been specified. Initial plans had simply defined the kinds of aircraft to be produced: for example, 'single-engined fighter' or 'bomber'. As a result, for a short period, the British believed there was an opportunity to convince the United States to build British types.

This mattered to the Air Staff, as they preferred to see American bomber production take the form of British designs of heavy bomber rather than the American designs of twin-engined light and medium bombers that featured in the 1940 purchase programmes. The British also believed that their fighter designs, in the form of the Vickers-Supermarine Spitfire (which was a proven success and already in mass production) or the Hawker Typhoon (which was under development), were superior to American designs. If the Americans could be persuaded to build these types, the new production plans would turn out operationally effective aircraft when they peaked in 1942. Without making the attempt to do this, American production would consist of obsolete or ineffective types.

Changing this required overcoming the resistance of the US services. Air Commodore Baker, the RAF officer involved in negotiations with the Americans on standardising aircraft types for the new production programme, reported on USAAC resistance to British designs that September: 'It seems certain that for political and manufacturing reasons the US Government will require American rather than British aircraft to be built on a standardised programme.'[14]

It was hoped that the British position would be strengthened by the supply of scientific information to the US services. As part of his facilitation of personal contacts, Lothian had encouraged the dispatch of a scientific mission to the United States. The Tizard–Cockroft mission had revealed the full extent of British scientific research to the US services which, in general, was considerably more advanced than the contemporary American position. The development of the cavity magnetron, which permitted the development of centimetric radar and thereby provided the Allies with a major advantage over German radar developments for the rest of the war, was a case in point. This had gone some way to improving British credibility with the US services – as Baker observed, until then, they believed they had more to give than receive from the British.[15] But it had not proved decisive on the issue of aircraft procurement, and the USAAC held firm that production expansion should consist of American types.

Persuading the Americans to build British aircraft occupied considerable attention in the autumn of 1940, and the Air Staff were not above manipulating aircraft deployment policy to achieve this. Lothian had urged the acceptance of the small numbers of individual American idealists and adventurers who wanted to enlist in the British forces.[16] This included encouraging the RAF to accept American pilot volunteers after the fall of France. A private syndicate had recruited Americans for a new 'Lafayette Squadron' in the French air force to repeat a similar project from World War I. Lothian encouraged the RAF to enlist these volunteers who, with their successors, were eventually formed into three 'Eagle' squadrons in Fighter Command. Lothian's motive was primarily diplomatic, as his response to the War Office over their lack of interest in facilitating the enlistment of Americans in the British army indicated: 'I think the proposal should be encouraged for political reasons as every American who joins the British forces becomes a propagandist'.[17]

The first 'Eagle' squadron of American volunteers in the RAF, 71 Squadron, had been originally scheduled to be equipped from thirty obsolete American-made Brewster Buffalo fighters inherited from Belgian orders. The British had ordered 170 Buffaloes for themselves in 1939 to be delivered by the end of 1940, as Brewster was one of the few firms with spare production capacity at that point. The Air Staff were under no illusion about the comparative performance of the Buffalo, with the Assistant Chief of the Air Staff (ACAS) observing in January 1940 that the delivery criteria had meant accepting a type with 'quite a moderate performance'.[18] The Buffaloes had swiftly been relegated to equipping fighter squadrons scheduled to form to defend Malaya and Singapore but, in any event, deliveries from the British contract would not begin until 1941. This left the Eagle squadron saddled with the ex-Belgian Buffaloes which had been delivered to Britain in the summer of 1940.

The RAF's aircraft equipment and deployment policy was controlled by the Expansion and Re-equipment Policy (ERP) committee. At a meeting of the ERP committee in October 1940, the Deputy Chief of the Air Staff (DCAS) ordered 71 Squadron's Buffaloes to be replaced with British Hurricanes for diplomatic purposes instead. 'In my opinion, the best plan would be straight away to give the Eagle squadron Hurricane IIs or Spitfires, preferably the latter. This would be the best advertisement for British aircraft in the U.S.A.'[19]

There would eventually be three Eagle squadrons, all equipped with Hurricanes and then Spitfires during 1941, and their pilots would become some of the most vocal critics of US fighter quality when they were transferred into the USAAF in 1942. In 1940, however, the British failed to convince the US services to accept the construction of British types. This included the rejection of a proposal to build the Spitfire on the grounds that it would be obsolete in the eighteen to twenty-four months it would take to begin production.[20]

Resistance from the US services was not just evident over the issue of British types, it was also apparent over the issue of aircraft allocation. A major dispute over allocation policy arose in 1940 as a result of Lothian's campaign to encourage contact between the US and British military staffs. An American staff mission had been sent to London under Admiral Ghormley. The United States Army was represented on this mission by Brigadier General Kenneth Strong who reported, on his return to Washington in September, that the RAF, in the middle of the Battle of Britain during his visit, had more aircraft than pilots available. This did reflect the temporary situation for Fighter Command in August 1940 when pilot replacement had lagged behind losses. But it did not reflect the larger reality where RAF pilot output had been expanded to meet these losses. Nor did it reflect the expectations of 1941 where the supply of pilots would increase further as a result of the EATS coupled with expanded output in Britain.

Strong's statements represented an immediate problem for Morgenthau, however, as they contradicted the assertions of British diplomacy, regarding the critical need for American aircraft, and the administration's drive to aid the Allies, a policy he had been pushing through against strong political resistance.[21] Lothian (advised by Purvis) realised that a senior RAF officer with the knowledge, authority and prestige to rebut such USAAC criticisms would be able to assist the RAF in achieving their qualitative agenda and also to assist Morgenthau in securing allocations that might conflict with USAAC plans.[22] As it was then impossible to send either Sir Charles Portal, who had replaced Newall as CAS in October, or his deputy, Freeman, it was decided to send Slessor to Washington in November 1940.

Slessor's brief was to liaise with the administration and with US service departments over future procurement and planning issues but it was clearly understood that Morgenthau needed help to overcome resistance from the US services.[23] The attitude of the USAAC had been suspect for some time, as Newall had observed in March 1940: '. . . there is no doubt that the attitude of the

Services in America, when any concrete proposal is in question, is determined almost entirely by political considerations'.[24]

Dealing with this attitude meant bolstering Morgenthau's political influence which the British did by means of several individual initiatives designed to meet USAAC desires in 1940. A notable example was the request for a Rolls-Royce Merlin engine which the British originally wanted to swap for Allison engines (as used in the P-40) for testing. Writing to Rolls-Royce to confirm that he had been unable to secure the Allison, Freeman explained the priority given to the supply of the latest design of Merlin in political terms:

> . . . the matter has been taken up in the very highest circles, both in America, this country and in France, with the result that I have had to agree, in order to keep the Americans 'sweet', to the loan of two Merlin Xs for test purposes without any quid pro quo in the way of the loan of an Allison engine.[25]

Purvis made the positive political impact of the supply of the Merlin engines very clear when authority was granted to export them to the United States. Morgenthau and the president:

> . . . have spent continuous effort in setting the scene in such a manner as to obtain public and congressional support for the aircraft release necessary to meet our needs . . . The release authority telegraphed yesterday has served to strengthen my position with Mr Morgenthau and also Mr Morgenthau's position with the army.[26]

This was the principle behind Slessor's mission, and the political dimension involved was obvious to Slessor. 'This visit of mine is mainly a political business – a bright idea of Morgenthau's own conceiving.'[27] This did not mean that Slessor underestimated the potential of American production, as his 1938 memorandum quoted earlier indicates. Indeed, at the same time as he characterised his mission as political, he simultaneously recommended to Portal a full exchange of information with the Americans on production matters: '. . . we are largely in their hands over this matter, and if they don't play, we are sunk'.[28]

Although Slessor fully understood the ultimate importance of co-operation with the United States, he also understood the limitations restricting the results of that collaboration in the meantime. As a result of Purvis's adoption of Monnet's 'balance sheet' approach which listed requirements against production and defining 'deficiencies', ultimate US production targets at this point had now risen to four thousand aircraft per month to be achieved in the last half of 1942. With the twenty-six thousand aircraft in total expected from the British purchase programme to June 1942, and a further twenty-four thousand expected between July and December 1942, the 1942 production target now matched Roosevelt's public promise, made at the end of October during the presidential campaign, of achieving a production of fifty thousand aircraft per year to be made available to the Allies. With regard to these figures, Slessor sounded a note of caution. 'You will, I am sure, understand that this allocation is what we should like – in accordance with the target programme – and by no means necessarily what we shall get.'[29]

If this was the voice of weary RAF experience of optimistic production forecasts, the actual origin of the figures made them even more questionable as a valid yardstick for RAF planning. The figures were derived from Purvis's balance sheet of British deficiencies which established targets for additional American production, over and above British contracts and British production, of 4,300 operational aircraft in 1941 and 23,600 in 1942.[30] There was a clear divergence between these figures and RAF plans, however. Portal repeated Slessor's caution to Churchill at the time; '. . . the figures are intended to represent the target at which manufacturers should aim, and not an estimate of the requirements of our present programme'.[31]

This is significant, as the 'present programme' at this point in February 1941 was the ERP 21 plan drawn up by Slessor back in July 1940. This established RAF expansion plans at a target of 230 new squadrons to be formed by June 1941, of which a maximum of about a hundred were expected to be equipped with American aircraft. In figures, the RAF target was for 22,500 operational aircraft to meet wastage, training and the initial equipment of new units in 1941. To meet this target they expected to receive 5,600 operational aircraft from American contracts in 1941 (seven thousand less 20 per cent for delayed production and losses in transit) against a domestic production of about sixteen thousand (with a similar discount against production losses to bombing or other shortfalls).[32] This meant that the RAF was anticipating a deficiency of a thousand aircraft in 1941 rather than the 4,300 indicated by Purvis; and the RAF figure would actually be exceeded by four thousand aircraft if existing American deliveries and British production matched their targets.

While a need for increased aircraft supply from the United States in the future had been identified as part of the process in evolving Lend-Lease, American supply was primarily seen in the meantime as an 'insurance' against the loss of domestic production caused by enemy bombing. When the civilian agents of the MAP and BAC combined with Morgenthau to concoct the '3,000 per month' plan in July 1940, Slessor's response had been cool.[33] In other words, RAF plans in 1941 were expected to be met from the existing level of domestic production and Anglo-French purchase contracts and not by the results of the rhetoric of 'mobilisation' diplomacy. Even if these plans did mature on schedule in 1942, that would only be relevant more than a year into the future. As Slessor himself observed at the time, 'It must be remembered that the contribution of US industry to the air war will not make itself felt to a really important degree until the second half of 1941 and early 1942.'[34]

Slessor's production mission merged into the first Anglo-British-Canadian or 'ABC' staff conferences in Washington, held between January and March 1941, and which were almost exactly congruent with the passage of Lend-Lease through the legislature. These discussions established the broad pattern of Anglo-American strategy to be followed if the United States entered the war, notably on an agreed strategy of 'Germany first', or concentrating on defeating Germany before Japan, the other threat covered in the discussions. A key element in the ABC discussions was an agreement on air strategy and production allocation, incorporated in the ABC-2 paper issued two days after the agreed joint strategy paper in ABC-1. The production allocation aspect of ABC-2 was particularly important as it agreed an allocation policy for American- produced aircraft which the RAF itself recognised as generous.

As well as delivery of the twenty-six thousand aircraft associated with the British purchase orders, the ABC-2 allocations scheduled the continuing output from this capacity to the British as well as the entire output from any new production capacity created in the United States. This was subject to revision if the United States entered the war, on the preliminary basis that the output would then be shared equally between the British and America.[35] Though subject to later modification, the 'Slessor Agreement', as the ABC-2 allocations were subsequently known, formally accepted an RAF allocation consisting of the full delivery of the twenty-six thousand 'purchase contract' aircraft (including the twelve thousand involved in Lend-Lease), the continuing output from that capacity in 1942, and the output from subsequently created capacity.[36] This established a clear British primacy in aircraft allocation policy, earmarking for the RAF most of the fifty thousand aircraft expected to be produced in the United States by the end of 1942.

This appeared to be a major success for the attainment of British goals but it had required substantial modification of aircraft allocation policy for political reasons owing to the emergence of the expectational gap British supply diplomacy had created. The most obvious of these to arise during the Slessor mission revolved around the allocation and deployment of the Curtiss P-40 Tomahawk. The release of P-40s to the British was an issue of particular political significance for the administration, and one of the rationales advanced for justifying it to the USAAC and potential legislative opposition was the importance of gaining combat experience with the type. As part of this policy Morgenthau had insisted upon the transmission of combat experience in the original agreement to release the latest models of USAAF aircraft, made in April 1940, and this was repeated throughout the second half of 1940 as shipments of P-40s began that October.[37]

British responses to these inquiries were necessarily constrained by the fact that they had rejected the P-40 for service as an interceptor in Britain. The former French P-40s, christened the Tomahawk I by the RAF, were accumulating in MAP servicing units at the end of 1940. By January 1941 the RAF had decided to use the Tomahawk I to replace the Westland Lysander in Army Co-operation Command after essential modifications, such as the replacement of French instrumentation and the installation of armour and self-sealing fuel tanks. The Tomahawks would then perform fighter-reconnaissance missions for the British army units then in training in Britain. Tomahawk IIs, from the British section of the Anglo-French purchase contract (incorporating British equipment modifications such as self-sealing fuel tanks, armour and radio equipment), were to be shipped directly to the Middle East to be used as fighters to supplement, and eventually replace, the Hurricanes which would otherwise be sent there.

This employment did not reflect the rhetoric of the supply diplomacy which had been conducted to secure the aircraft in the first place. Exposure of the gap between that diplomacy and the RAF's actual use of the aircraft would represent useful ammunition for factions opposed to the administration's policy of aiding the British. Under pressure from Morgenthau, Slessor pressed Portal for a response that would minimise any potential political damage.

> In this connexion there have been several references in the press recently to the effect that the U.S. aircraft in England are not up to modern war conditions, and we are using them for training and subsidiary theatres. This of course is true but some carefully worded statement to explain the position to the U.S. press men in London might be desirable.[38]

Although Portal's response denied Slessor's assertions about American aircraft, emphasising the importance of the Middle East and the economy on shipping involved in exporting American aircraft there, it is clear that this was for public consumption and did not reflect the internal Air Ministry view represented by Slessor. The P-40 was not seen as an equivalent replacement for the Hurricane or Spitfire in Britain and was not employed as such. Morgenthau's repeated requests threatened to expose the reality that the British were not actively employing the supplies which he had expedited at some political cost.

In response to Slessor's appeals, the RAF could offer only Morgenthau misleading evaluations, such as the assertion that the P-40 had a performance 'equivalent to [the] Spitfire', which was contradicted by the RAF's deployment of the type.[39] Consequently, the use of the Tomahawk returned to the agenda of the ERP committee in January 1941 with the suggestion that a squadron in Fighter Command should be re-equipped with them. Four Tomahawks were then attached to 234 Squadron in January–February 1941 for the compilation of evaluation reports.[40] Though the squadron performed routine operational duties during this period, it did so with its existing complement of Spitfires, and the Tomahawks saw no combat.[41] The token deployment of the Tomahawk as a defensive interceptor in Britain was entirely driven by the need to address the expectational gap which arose when the deployment of American aircraft contradicted the diplomatic policy adopted to secure them.

This policy revealed the fact that the British were aware of the dichotomy between the imperative for further American aircraft supplies expressed by them at the highest political levels and the reality which was indicated by their reluctance to use even the most modern available American aircraft as substitutes for their main combat aircraft. As Slessor's commentary to Portal indicated, this required careful management. Slessor had been unimpressed with USAAC administration when he arrived in Washington, referring to it as 'hopeless'.[42] Other RAF officers held similar opinions of the apparent organisational chaos in Washington, with Air Commodore Baker concluding; 'The present situation is more than impossible – it is Gilbertian'.[43]

This meant that British supply objectives were being advanced in a confused situation involving institutional and personal conflicts which extended to sympathisers such as Stimson and Morgenthau. Regardless of British plans in Whitehall or the distinct objectives of the British procurement machinery in the form of Monnet and Purvis, objectives and means in Washington remained unclear and agreements could not be assumed with any confidence to be binding. In this situation of competitive chaos, underlying USAAC attitudes could play an influential role.

Though apparently brought under control by Roosevelt's earlier threats to ship uncooperative officers to Guam, and far from openly hostile to Slessor in person, Arnold's basic opposition to the full implementation of the administration's policy to aid the Allies was still apparent: '. . . Arnold remained the most visible reminder (most probably fed by Morgenthau's animus) of what had been perceived as War Department opposition to administration proposals for aircraft allocation.'[44]

This was apparent to his junior officers. Major Elwood Quesada, at the time one of Arnold's aides and subsequently a USAAF tactical air force commander in Europe, later admitted his role in obstructing British requests at Arnold's behest: 'Arnold was too shrewd to interfere openly with Roosevelt's wishes, but he knew that all sorts of small, mysterious obstacles could arise in the complicated procurement process'.[45]

At this point the first instance of competition for allocations of American aircraft arose. Under pressure from Chiang Kai-shek, the leader of the nationalist Chinese regime, for the supply of aircraft to use against the Japanese at the end of 1940, Roosevelt and Morgenthau had promised one hundred fighters. These were to be diverted from British contracts in exchange for two hundred aircraft from later production.[46] When Anthony Eden, who had replaced Halifax as Foreign Secretary when Halifax had in turn replaced Lothian as ambassador in Washington, described the deal to cabinet in January 1941, the political background and the financial discussions involving Morgenthau and the Bank of England's delegate in Washington were decisive.

> Mr Morgenthau had made it plain that the Administration were determined that they should go to China and the view of Mr Purvis was that in the present state of the financial negotiations between Sir F[rederick] Philips and Mr Morgenthau we simply could not afford a dispute with the latter.[47]

These aircraft were shipped to Burma later in 1941 and equipped the American Volunteer Group of the Chinese air force which entered combat against the Japanese during the Burma campaign in December 1941.[48] The Tomahawk's service in the RAF will be recounted subsequently but, at this point, it should be noted that, by the end of 1941, 542 Tomahawks had been shipped to the Middle East where they finally entered operational service against the Vichy French in the Syrian campaign in June 1941.[49] Portal waited until the Tomahawks had finally seen combat against the Luftwaffe in Libya later in that month before sending a belated expression of gratitude to Arnold.[50] In the event, the Tomahawk performed relatively well in combat, with a performance advantage over the Italian opposition it faced and also over the more numerous British Hurricane at lower altitudes. But when the German Messerschmitt Bf 109 appeared in Libya in the spring of 1941, it was outclassed for speed, rate of climb and performance at altitude, repeating the qualitative inferiority the Tomahawk had already experienced in Britain.[51]

The use and allocation of the P-40 were particular issues that arose during the Slessor mission but the larger issue of aircraft supply and allocation would arise separately as a consequence of the visit of Harry Hopkins to Britain in January–February 1941. Having resigned as Commerce Secretary after securing Roosevelt's nomination at the Democratic convention in July 1940, Hopkins had moved into the White House as one of Roosevelt's main speech-writers and personal confidant. At the beginning of January 1941, and despite his chronic ill health, Roosevelt dispatched Hopkins to London to act as his personal emissary and to establish a working relationship with Churchill. At that point, the position of US ambassador was vacant after Roosevelt's recall and dismissal of Kennedy before the presidential election. The Hopkins mission filled the void before John G. Winant took up his appointment as the new ambassador in February. Supply matters were at the core of Hopkins's mission. Roosevelt had charged him with establishing British needs, with particular reference to '. . . the urgent necessity of the exact material assistance Britain requires to win the war'.[52]

Hopkins was given privileged treatment in Britain, spending extensive time in company with Churchill, consulting with British ministers and being exposed to British decision-makers and British strategy. This took place against the background of the Blitz where Hopkins could see the results of Luftwaffe raids at first hand. His visit was regarded as successful on both sides of the Atlantic, and cleared the way for a personal meeting between Churchill and Roosevelt which eventually took place in August 1941. But the main context for his visit was the progress of the Lend-Lease bill through Congress which was taking place at the same time. Indeed, the thesis of criticality which Lothian had developed in the run-up to Lend-Lease was strongly evident during Hopkins's visit.

The British had two principal goals involved: to persuade Roosevelt (via Hopkins) to increase aid in the short term by means of immediate aid against a possible German invasion attempt against Britain later in 1941; and also to convince the administration that the change of longer-term British strategic focus to the Middle East, which was then taking place, was justified. Both these objectives featured in new iterations of the thesis of criticality which had been adopted in 1940. In his telegrams to Roosevelt, Hopkins continually stressed the importance of American aid in the short term. 'This island needs our help now, Mr President, with everything that we can give them.'[53]

While Churchill mentioned the importance of American aid in achieving air mastery, Hopkins was only given details of specific shortfalls in the existing supply programme. Examples included the Admiralty's need for accelerated deliveries of the Catalina flying boats ordered in 1939, and also propellers, armament and ammunition for the P-40 deliveries. This was a matter of deliberate policy; before Hopkins arrived, the cabinet office had organised information for his visit emphasising supply needs over the next few months.[54] Before the German attack on the Soviet Union in June, the prospect of invasion still remained, and this was a prospective threat that the British emphasised and that Hopkins passed on to Roosevelt.[55]

The context of imminent invasion lay behind the list of specific items of immediate aid that Hopkins brought back to Washington and which repeated many of the items mentioned in the crisis diplomacy of 1940. But it was notable that it did not touch on the issue of future allocations or the 1942 supply programmes which were attracting so much attention from British officials in Washington at the same time. Hopkins's list represented immediate aid issues associated with 'criticality' but, in terms of aircraft supply, they related to resolving specific problems associated with supplies from the previous year. Indeed, in some cases, they were the same issues that had not been met or resolved yet.

As Roosevelt's personal representative and the man who would shortly be placed in charge of Lend-Lease procurement and supply in Washington, this raised Hopkins to a position of decisive significance in the Anglo-American supply relationship at this point. Hopkins's return to Washington in February was followed by the dispatch of Averell Harriman, previously an adviser to Hopkins, to London as Roosevelt's Lend-Lease expediter in March. His terms of reference, as given by Roosevelt, were suffused with the same sense of short-term criticality that had informed the Hopkins mission. 'I want you to go over to London and recommend everything that we can do, short of war, to keep the British Isles afloat.'[56]

Harriman's mission maintained the connection between immediate American aid and British survival, with Harriman being critical of the scale and speed of existing plans to assist the British. Indeed, Harriman clashed with Churchill over the release of shipping losses to U-boat attack for this reason: Churchill wished to avoid public admission of heavy losses while Harriman saw them as an effective lever on American public opinion.[57] This remained a major determinant of British diplomacy as the Lend-Lease hearings took place, and the idea of critical dependency was regularly employed to justify the policy of funding aid to Britain. Morgenthau and Stimson testified in person on this issue, with Morgenthau summarising that, lacking American financial aid, there was 'nothing for Great Britain to do but stop fighting'.[58]

By this time, the progress of events and the reiteration of Lothian's thesis of criticality had successfully influenced public opinion to the point where legislative opposition from isolationism was marginalised. 'America First' delegates, who were called to testify during the debate, expressed sympathy for Britain and supported other forms of aid. Even the alternative bill put forward by isolationists Arthur Vandenberg and Robert Taft in the Senate extended dollar credits to the British. Isolationist opposition had been forced to concede the policy of aid to Britain.[59] Achieving this had also demanded the management of USAAC resistance, and Arnold's attitude in particular. This attitude would resurface as a result of the personal diplomacy of early 1941.

Hopkins's list of immediate requirements had partly originated in a late-night Churchillian session at Chequers. This did not go down well with the US services. As one US army officer commented to Harriman, 'We can't take seriously requests that come late in the evening over a bottle of port.'[60]

This scepticism was firmly in evidence when Arnold was presented with Hopkins's list of British requests. Marshall wanted Arnold to come up with a response that would avoid the administration imposing one on them. Arnold's opinion of the impact of the requests on USAAC plans was made clear on 6 March when he claimed that the list would 'eliminate' the objective of building up the USAAC to current targets.[61] Arnold's response was not welcome at the White House where his promotion was apparently being held up possibly as a result of his resistance to administration policy.[62] This represented an impasse which might have otherwise been broken only by his dismissal. That would clearly have enormous potential to damage administration tactics which were to obscure the conflict between rearmament justified for American defensive needs but used to supply the British ahead of the US services.

The timing of this particular outbreak of that conflict was particularly inopportune as it came immediately after the passage of Lend-Lease on 11 March and before Roosevelt had established any machinery to make it function. Hopkins suggested a way round this potential crisis by recommending that Arnold be sent to Britain to experience the same red-carpet treatment that he had received and that Harriman was now undergoing. As John Huston puts it: 'He [Arnold] would appreciate the extent and nature of British needs for American aircraft and gain sufficient credibility in the White House to avoid forced retirement.'[63]

The background was made clear to the British by Hopkins who informed them that Arnold had '. . . a tendency to resist efforts to give adequate aid to England'.[64] Arnold followed the route employed by Hopkins, Winant and Harriman, travelling by flying boat to Lisbon and then on to England. His visit, between

10 and 27 April 1941, also followed the pattern established by the previous missions. Arnold was granted access to the top level of British administration and military planning. He spent the obligatory weekend with Churchill, visited operational units as well as the headquarters of Fighter and Bomber Commands, experienced air raids on London and observed RAF fighter operations over France from a Fighter Command control centre. On the technical front, the British arranged a display of the American aircraft currently in RAF service, as well as the latest British aviation advance – a flight display by Gloster prototype jet aircraft powered by the Whittle engine.

Overall, Arnold's visit was a great success from a British perspective. On subjects such as the provision of pilots for ferrying aircraft to Canada and the conversion of civil flying schools in the United States to meet RAF training needs, Arnold proved co-operative with the requirements on Hopkins's list. He willingly accepted the RAF's preference for heavy bombers in preference to the light bombers involved in the contemporary American production and supply programmes. But there were areas of disagreement even if Arnold did not openly declare them at the time.

One clear issue was the matter of bombers: even though the RAF was being supplied with twenty American B-17s at this point, the British had not managed to make them operational. Arnold was also not impressed by his observations of Bomber Command at work. 'I think the British have much to learn about bombing.'[65] The quality of American aircraft designs was another issue. A meeting with Sir Henry Tizard, the Air Ministry's main scientific adviser, was not congenial. 'He [Tizard] thought that many of the [US] planes and some of the [US] engines might be thrown on the scrap pile.'[66]

Both these issues would quickly return to be major problems in Anglo-American aircraft supply. Another problem was the question of allocations. Arnold makes no reference to the ABC-2 paper or Slessor agreement in his memoir or diary at this point but his reference to British demands as 'exorbitant' indicates his attitude.[67] Arnold masked his scepticism but, in the meantime, noted down examples that seemed to provide evidence of the contradictions involved in British claims and their actual employment of American aircraft. Given the problems the British were having in getting operational the American aircraft they had received to date, this was not difficult. A specific example Arnold later gave was the sight of B-24 bombers lying idle before they were modified to begin service performing anti-submarine warfare (ASW) patrols for Coastal Command instead of bombing Germany as he expected. This would recur time and again in the future, and feed Arnold's suspicions that large allocations of American aircraft would be misused or left idle by the RAF.

A primary explanation for this was the lack of necessary equipment in the former French contract aircraft that were arriving at the end of 1940 and in the spring of 1941. The MAP summarised the problem with these aircraft in June 1941, which included the first deliveries of the B-24s that Arnold had noted in April. 'In general deliveries ready for delivery have no guns, ammunition, radio, armouring or self-sealing for tanks.'[68]

The P-40s had absorbed considerable diplomatic attention in early 1941, if only to counter American reactions to learning that they had not been used in combat. The Tomahawks were still plagued with maintenance and equipment problems at this point, with generator-drive failures repeatedly grounding them. Shortages of propellers and radios had interrupted Tomahawk deliveries while problems developing the Airacobra and Kittyhawk variants of the Allison engine led to the BAC referring to '. . . the failure of Allison engine production' by the summer.[69] The problems the RAF experienced with American aircraft in 1941, and the USAAF reaction to them, were to be summed up by Freeman to the MAP in September.

> A day or two ago General Royce, the US Air Attaché, complained bitterly, as had Mr Harriman some time ago, of the considerable time taken to make American aircraft which had been delivered to this country ready for operational units. This is, of course, an old story; that only makes the situation today worse. The Americans have on more than one occasion stated that they were starving their Air Corps of aircraft and if they eased up on deliveries this period of gestation would be their prime reason for doing so.[70]

All of this seemed to disprove British assertions of their urgent need for American aircraft and brought their position in allocation politics into question. Despite questioning the British position in his own mind at the time, Arnold was apparently convinced by his experience in Britain.

> One thing was apparent – either the British were actually in an awfully tight spot, and knew it, or they were deliberately trying to paint the picture as black as they could possibly to make it so that I would take that picture back to the President of the United States.[71]

In reality, however, Arnold had been forced to concede little ground. Assisting the RAF with ferry operations made little impact on USAAC requirements while directing RAF training demands to civilian flying schools in the US limited their potential claim on existing USAAC training facilities. Arnold needed little conversion to the importance of heavy bombers to strategic bombing; he was already wedded to the doctrine so far as War Department and US Army factionalism would permit it. More importantly, he was convinced of the capacity of US heavy bombers to perform it. Agreeing with British demands for increased heavy bomber production strengthened his hand in interservice conflict in Washington over the priority for heavy bombers. But it did not mean that he accepted an overriding British claim concerning the proceeds of that production, as events in the months after his visit to Britain would reveal.

All in all, Arnold's co-operation was predicated on his awareness of administration impatience with service resistance to its policy. He was also able to concede ground tactically in areas where he did not believe British requirements conflicted with USAAC interests. This certainly secured his position with the administration at a time when the overall strategy of supplying Britain could not be openly challenged – for the time being. Superficially, at least, the thesis of critical dependency had been vindicated again.

This success had drawbacks, however. In terms of Lend-Lease, it sponsored a perception that economic and military supply aid could be utilised only to meet deficiencies. The British had laid themselves open to this danger by their approach towards securing American supply in 1940. The statistical basis for British production planning in the United States deliberately stressed deficiencies between required targets in munitions production and the projected ability of British domestic production to meet them. This coloured the thinking of US service departments towards British requests for aid; Lend-Lease supply could be envisioned only once British supplies could be demonstrated to American satisfaction to be exhausted or inadequate, and not just when the British requested them.

This was paralleled by the equivalent perception in the area of finance. Convincing the legislative opposition of British financial exhaustion required proof that Britain was, in Roosevelt's phrase, 'scraping the marrow'.[72] This lay behind Morgenthau's pressure to sell off British holdings, such as the American Viscose firm, which was sold at a loss during the Lend-Lease hearings. This generated some resentment in Whitehall, because it appeared to illustrate a tendency to exploit the British position for American financial benefit at a time when the results of the administration's goodwill were questionable. At the time, Churchill informed Halifax that, '. . . it was impossible to continue to make concessions at short notice to meet the exigencies of United States politics'.[73] It was clear, however, that financial policy and aircraft supply and deployment policy remained subject to modification to secure the larger goal of Lend-Lease.

Throughout this period, and for some considerable time afterwards, aircraft supply was concerned with the deployment of aircraft from pre-war contracts. Lend-Lease itself could not increase aircraft deliveries until the contracts involving existing factories were completed and new production facilities constructed. Nor could it immediately resolve British financial problems associated with the massive pre-Lend-Lease purchase contracts.

The capital investment involved in the first stage of the Lend-Lease programme – the '1,250 per month' plan – involved a commitment of $475 million, $225 million of which would fall due before the end of 1940 and $250 million in the first half of 1941.[74] These requirements would form the heart of the interim finance crisis where the British struggled to cover the commitments made before Lend-Lease.[75] Although some of the British capital investment commitment was ultimately assumed by the US services as part of their rearmament programme, the vast majority of the capital costs incurred before the passage of Lend-Lease had to be borne by the British due to a promise made by administration officials during the Lend-Lease hearings.[76]

This problem was eventually resolved by two factors, financial and practical. The financial resources to cover the costs involved were finally met by the appropriation of Allied gold, including the delivery of South African gold which generated some Churchillian resentment, and the extension of a Reconstruction Finance Corporation (RFC) loan of $425 million in July 1941.[77] The practical help consisted of the continuing slow delivery of American aircraft. Despite the high advance and capital investment involved, as much as 50 per cent of the balance of British purchase contracts fell due when the aircraft were delivered. The slow and disappointing rate of delivery against these contracts which followed, reduced the monthly outgoings on the single largest procurement programme. In 1942, and even into 1943, the British would still be accepting, and paying for, the delivery of aircraft against orders made in 1940. This was a diminishing commitment but it was not a trivial one. In August 1942, for example, the British paid out $26.1 million against BAC contracts alone, more than three times the Ministry of Supply total for the same month to cover non-aviation supplies.[78]

The problem of continuing dollar payment for supplies after Lend-Lease led to substantial friction in the later war period, as the United States attempted arbitrarily to limit British dollar reserves and restrict British competitive exports to adhere to the accepted basis of Lend-Lease aid.[79] By establishing Lend-Lease as a measure necessitated by British financial exhaustion, Lothian grossly simplified the complex economic issues involved in the international British economy across the British Commonwealth and Sterling Area. The nub of the problem was identified by Churchill when he rebuked Lothian's November 1940 indiscretion with the press on finances: 'While it is generally understood that you were referring wholly to dollar credits, actual words attributed to you give only too much foundation to German propaganda to broadcast that we are coming to the end of our resources.'[80]

Warren Kimball has noted how this deliberate misunderstanding prospered, as the perception of 'bankruptcy' penetrated the thinking of administration officials favouring further aid to Britain. 'Many Americans, including Cordell Hull and Frank Knox, never really grasped the fact that Britain could run out of dollars without being bankrupt . . .'[81] This should be extended to consideration of the military procurement involved in Lend-Lease. Lothian's assertions of criticality within that diplomacy were obviously contradicted by the immediate value of American aid to the British war effort. As Kimball observed, 'As much as the leaders in Washington publicly talked about the Lend-Lease plan as a means of keeping England in the war, they knew full well that meaningful aid was a year or more away.'[82]

This reflected the provisions of the aircraft procurement programme which represented the lion's share of the initial cost of Lend-Lease. Even Lothian himself – no expert on munitions procurement – had admitted the problem:

> The Americans are sending over all they can in the way of airplanes and equipment. But, as you know, it normally seems to take about two years from the time you begin to lay down an airplane factory to the time when it comes into full production.[83]

After the interim finance crisis, aircraft procurement would be at the heart of Lend-Lease, with aircraft and their equipment accounting for $2 billion of the first Lend-Lease appropriation of $7 billion – the biggest single item within the programme.[84] Politically, diplomatically and financially, aircraft procurement had been central to the evolution of the Anglo-American strategic supply relationship in 1940–1. It remains to be seen what the British actually got for their money, and how it informed their air strategy.

Notes

1. WP (40) 427, 'Second Report on the Ministry of Aircraft Production', 27 October 1940; CAB 66/13/7.
2. Expectations on 23 June 1940 from 'USA Purchases. Estimated Deliveries of Aircraft up to December, 1940'; AVIA 10/126; delivery from Michael J. F. Bowyer, *Aircraft for the Few* (Somerset, 1991), p. 245. A single Spitfire I, serial L1097, was supplied to the United States in exchange for a P-39 or P-40 fighter in January 1940; FO 371/24250.
3. 'Second Report on the Ministry of Aircraft Production', 27 October 1940; CAB 66/13/7.
4. WP (40) 489, Appendix, 'Third Report on the Ministry of Aircraft Production', 24 December 1940; CAB 66/14/19.
5. Taylor, *Beaverbrook*, p. 439.
6. Ibid., p. 440.
7. Churchill to Foreign Secretary, 20 December 1940; CHAR 20/13.
8. Daily War Room returns, 31 December 1940; AIR 22/34.
9. Richard Hallion, *The American Perspective*, in Paul Addison & Jeremy Crang (eds.), *The Burning Blue* (London: Pimlico, 2000), p. 84.
10. Gavin Bailey, 'The Narrow Margin of Criticality: The Question of the Supply of 100-Octane Fuel in the Battle of Britain', in *The English Historical Review*, Vol. 123 No. 501 (2008).
11. 'War Reserves of Aviation Fuel – acquisition', AMSO memorandum for CAS, 29 January 1937; AIR 2/1686.
12. Undated memorandum by the Air Member for Development and Production (AMDP), 'Output of the Aircraft Industry: Quality versus Quantity'; AVIA 10/39.
13. Freeman, AMDP, to Minister of Aircraft Production, 29 August 1940; AVIA 10/125.
14. Air Commodore Baker to Freeman, 14 September 1940; AVIA 10/124.
15. Ibid.
16. Air Ministry memorandum, 3 July 1940; FO 371/24256.
17. Lothian to FO, Telegram No. 1092, 23 June 1940; FO 371/24256.
18. ACAS to parliamentary undersecretary, 15 January 1940; AIR 8/293.
19. Deputy Chief of the Air Staff (DCAS) note, 'Equipment of Eagle Squadron', ERP 49, October 1940; AIR 20/5777.
20. Postan, p. 121; precis of notes by Air Commodore Baker to Harold

Balfour, the Undersecretary of State for Air, for thirty-sixth meeting of the ERP committee, 4 September 1940; TNA PRO AIR 20/5777.
21. Slessor, p. 318.
22. Lothian to FO, No. 2247, 9 October 1940; AIR 19/473.
23. Sinclair to Beaverbrook, 17 October 1940; AIR 19/473.
24. CAS to Secretary of State for Air, 'Proposed appointment of two additional American Air Attaches in London.', S.3871, 11 March 1940; AVIA 10/122.
25. Freeman to Ernest Hives, Rolls-Royce, 24 March 1940; AVIA 10/122.
26. Purvis to Monnet, No.71 Purco, 26 March 1940; AVIA 10/122.
27. Slessor to CAS, 11 November 1940; AIR 8/446.
28. Slessor to CAS, 17 October 1940; AIR 8/446.
29. Slessor to Portal, 11 November 1940; AIR 8/446.
30. BPC memorandum 'British War Requirements 1941 and 1942', 4 January 1941; AVIA 38/14.
31. Portal to Churchill, 9 February 1941; AIR 19/473.
32. Portal to Slessor, X.418, 10 February 1941; AIR 19/473.
33. Slessor, p. 309.
34. 'US Air Production Programme', note by Air Commodore Slessor, 27 November 1940; AIR 8/446.
35. Slessor, p. 358.
36. In theory, the term 'Slessor Agreement' was applied to a revision of the ABC-2 programme in May 1941 but it is apparent that the term was applied to the ABC-2 allocations at the time and subsequently by RAF officers, including Slessor himself. Slessor, pp. 358, 404.
37. Purco 90, 22 April 1940; CAB 85/14; Pursa 177, 25 October 1940; CAB 115/78.
38. Slessor to CAS, 4 December 1940; AIR 8/446.
39. Comment by Group Captain Sorley; MAP 2821, 11 December 1940; AVIA 38/732.
40. Air Member for Supply and Organisation (AMSO), 'Equipment of a Fighter Squadron with Tomahawks', 90th ERP committee meeting, 19 January 1941; AIR 20/5777.
41. 234 Squadron ORB, January–February 1941; AIR 27/1439; trials reports in AVIA 15/921.
42. Vincent Orange, *Slessor: Bomber Champion* (London: Grub Street, 2006), p. 79; Slessor, p. 321.
43. 'Standardisation', Air Commodore Baker to C. R. Fairey, 7 October 1941, AVIA 38/483.
44. John W. Huston (ed.), *American Airpower Comes of Age: General*

Henry H. 'Hap' Arnold's World War II Diaries, Vol. I (Maxwell Air Force Base: Air University Press, 2002), p. 107.

45. Thomas Alexander Hughes, *Over Lord: General Pete Quesada and the Triumph of Tactical Air Power in World War II* (New York: The Free Press, 1995), p. 72.
46. Dallek, pp. 269–70.
47. 'Supply of Aircraft to China from the United States', Memorandum by Sir Anthony Eden, the Foreign Secretary, WP (41) 13, 27 January 1941; CAB 66/14/35.
48. Daniel Ford, *Flying Tigers: Claire Chennault and the American Volunteer Group* (Washington, DC: Smithsonian, 1991); Christopher Shores, Brian Cull and Yasuho Izawa, *Bloody Shambles*, Vol. 1 (London: Grub Street, 1998), pp. 235–73
49. 516 Tomahawks were exported direct from the United States to the Middle East, with another twenty-six re-exported there after initial delivery to Britain; figures from AIR 20/2039.
50. CAS to Harris, Air Ministry BRITMAN X970, 6 July 1941; AVIA 38/476.
51. Lord Tedder, *With Prejudice* (London: Cassell, 1966), p. 202.
52. Sherwood, *Hopkins*, p. 239.
53. Hopkins to Roosevelt, 14 January 1941; ibid., *Hopkins*, p. 245.
54. CAB 21/1406.
55. Sherwood, *Hopkins*, p. 257.
56. W. Averell Harriman and Elie Abel, *Special Envoy to Churchill and Stalin 1941–1946* (New York: Random House, 1976), p. 3.
57. Ibid., p. 25.
58. Kimball, *Unsordid Act*, p. 189.
59. Cole, *Roosevelt and the Isolationists*, p. 415.
60. Harriman and Abel, p. 15.
61. Huston, p. 130.
62. Ibid., p. 131.
63. Ibid., p. 132.
64. Ibid., p. 135.
65. Arnold diary entry, 17 April 1941; Huston, p. 147.
66. Arnold diary entry, 22 April, 1941; Huston, p. 157.
67. Arnold, p. 233.
68. Sir Henry Self to MAP, No. 150, 18 June 1940; AVIA 10/126.
69. BAC memorandum to C. W. Milner, 1 February 1941; AVIA 38/794; BAC memorandum to MAP, 19 June 1941; AVIA 38/452.
70. Freeman to Sir Charles Craven, 24 September 1941; AIR 20/1834.
71. Arnold, p. 235.

72. Warren F. Kimball, '"Beggar My Neighbour": America and the British Interim Finance Crisis, 1940–41', in *Journal of Economic History*, 29, 4 (December 1969), p. 770.
73. War Cabinet 29 (41), 17 March 1941; CAB 65/18/8.
74. 'Summarised Forecast of Payments on Proposed Programmes, as at September 1, 1940'; AVIA 38/14.
75. Hall, Wrigley and Scott, pp. 98–100.
76. Kimball, 'Beggar My Neighbour', p. 771.
77. Blum, p. 241.
78. CAB 115/317.
79. Dobson, pp. 126–84; Woods, pp. 87–93.
80. Churchill to Lothian, Telegram No. 3233, 27 November 1940; FO 371/24249.
81. Kimball, *Unsordid Act*, p. 237.
82. Ibid., p. 147.
83. Lothian to Aikman, 1 July 1940; GD 40/17/398/121, Lothian Papers.
84. Hall, Wrigley and Scott, p. 134.

5 The Limits of Dependency: American Aircraft in Action, 1940–2

By 1942 Britain had become dependent on American supplies.

Warren Kimball[1]

It was clear that we depended heavily on American aircraft, but the rate of delivery often proved to be disappointing.

Lord Tedder[2]

These statements, made by the authoritative historian of Lend-Lease and the RAF C.-in-C. in the Middle East, respectively, point to the dichotomy that remains at the core of American supply to Britain. Kimball's observation reflects the axiomatic understandings of conventional historiography, while Tedder's statement reflects the frustrations he felt as the primary beneficiary of American aircraft supply to the RAF in 1941–2. Both these statements are true but require reconciliation, or at least some form of quantification, to learn the extent of contemporary British dependency upon American supplies.

By the spring of 1941, the British had apparently achieved their main objectives with regard to American supply. The 1940 purchase programme had occupied most of the available capacity of the American aircraft industry. Future production seemed to have been secured as a result of Lend-Lease while the Slessor mission had established an agreed plan to allocate up to 50 per cent of that production to Britain. The total number of American aircraft ordered was certainly impressive – over twenty-two thousand by the end of 1940. Resistance from the USAAC to British procurement and allocation had apparently been addressed by the high priority afforded to the British by the administration and development of personal contacts between the United States and British services which culminated in the Arnold mission of April 1941. An increasing flow of American aircraft now seemed assured.

Richard Hallion has observed that the 1940 purchase orders represented a near duplication of the United States military inventory.[3] If, as Hallion indicates, this can be taken as a measurement of the extent of American assistance to Britain, then a detailed investigation of the utility of those aircraft to the British can establish the actual value of that assistance to British air strength. The supply of heavy bombers and fighters will be addressed in detail subsequently; the employment in Britain, the Middle East and Far East of twin-engined light and medium bombers will be addressed in this chapter.

Charting the development of RAF deployment policy involving the aircraft associated with the 1940 purchase programme indicates the extent to which American aircraft supply was subject to limitations: quantitative limitations based on the slow production and delivery of aircraft; qualitative limitations affecting their performance and equipment which dictated their utility during operations; and finally political limitations which were expressed through the competition the British were subjected to for aircraft allocations at the highest level. All these factors were to determine British deployment policy and inform supply diplomacy.

The pessimism Beaverbrook had expressed at the end of 1940 is largely confirmed by a detailed examination of RAF aircraft deployment policy. This was largely determined by the ERP committee which met at regular intervals at the Air Ministry. While aircraft deployment could be decided on an ad hoc basis by C.s-in-C., the ERP committee determined the outlines of RAF policy down to the detail of scheduling the establishment, re-equipment or disbanding of individual squadrons on the basis of current aircraft supply plans. A close study of the development of the ERP committee's policy towards American aircraft supply from the first comprehensive consideration of the issue in July 1940 confirms the gap between the assertions of British supply diplomacy and the reality of the deployment policy that lay behind this.

On 25 and 27 July 1940 the ERP committee decided to replace the obsolete Fairey Battle light bomber squadrons in 2 Group of Bomber Command based in Britain with the Douglas DB-7/A-20.[4] The DB-7 had been central to French supply contracts in the United States, and the British had inherited purchase orders for 237 early variants of the type. These were divided by the British into 138 Boston Is and IIs and ninety-nine Havocs. A further 781 Boston IIIs were due to follow from the joint purchase programme of 1940. The Boston IIIs included design and equipment improvements to British specification.[5] The Boston IIIs were essentially to be adopted as light bombers but the process would prove lengthy and problematic.

Although the Battle was considered so obsolete that, by March 1940, it was already being officially listed as a trainer instead of a light bomber, the perceived ability of initial Boston supplies to replace it was limited.[6] The deployment policy decided by the ERP in July 1940 was to maintain the Battle squadrons, many rebuilt and re-equipped more than once because of heavy losses in the French campaign, until the end of the potential invasion period in October. From this it can be seen that the supplies of DB-7s from the French contracts which were being delivered in 1940 were not considered as immediate substitutes for British aircraft – even the most obsolete ones at the beginning of the Battle of Britain. After that October, the eventual re-equipment from British Boston deliveries could begin.[7] The Boston IIIs anticipated to meet this requirement were scheduled to arrive in May 1941.[8] Subsequent tests with the early French DB-7s, used as trainers in Battle squadrons rebuilding in Northern Ireland in late 1940 and early 1941, revealed equipment shortcomings, such as the lack of self-sealing fuel tanks, defensive armour and armament, and the need for new bomb-release equipment to use British bombs.

The other main types of light bomber to be supplied were the Martin GM 167 Maryland and its anticipated successor, the GM 187 Baltimore. These were selected by the ERP to equip light bomber squadrons in the Middle and Far East according to decisions made in September and October 1940.[9] The limitations of the DB-7 for that role were recognised in its short range and single-person cockpit (which was regarded as imposing navigational difficulties). These features rendered it less useful as a bomber for the longer-range anti-shipping operations expected in defending Malaya against the Japanese. That need would be met by the shipment of Baltimores when they became available in the future. Though the DB-7 was therefore considered to have significant limitations as a bomber, its relatively high performance indicated it had potential as a nightfighter. This was a particularly important need during the Blitz, the Luftwaffe's campaign of night bombing of British cities between November 1940 and June 1941.

At a time when the RAF was struggling to field an effective twin-engined radar-equipped and directed nightfighter, failed dayfighters, such as the Boulton Paul Defiant, and even successful dayfighters, such as the Hurricane, were being pressed into service as nightfighters. The early DB-7s played no part in the development of the radar-equipped nightfighter which, in 1941, was slowly to solve the problem of night interception. Although relatively fast and well regarded for its handling qualities, the DB-7 could not compete with the performance provided by either the Bristol Beaufighter or the later de Havilland Mosquito which made them the most effective nightfighters. The Havocs were initially pressed into service carrying the long aerial mine (LAM), a bizarre and ineffective weapon to be towed along the route of the German bombers. By the middle of the year they were employed more profitably as intruders, patrolling at night over active enemy air bases in the hopes of attacking German bombers on take-off or landing.

Intruding at least represented something approaching the effective use of the aircraft for nightfighting operations. Equally ineffective, and only slightly less bizarre than the LAM operations, was the use of the Havoc (and then the Boston as Havoc supplies ran down) as a Turbinlite nightfighter in 1941–2. Turbinlite Havocs and Bostons had radar installed but, in place of any offensive armament, were equipped with a powerful fixed searchlight. Upon completing a radar-directed interception of an enemy aircraft, the Boston pilot would illuminate the target for one or two accompanying Hurricane fighter pilots to attack. These operations relied upon formation flying and co-ordination at night that were exceptionally difficult to obtain in practice, and were unsurprisingly both ineffective and unpopular with the aircrews as a result.[10]

Perhaps best understood as an attempt to give Fighter Command's large single-engined dayfighter force some nightfighting capability, Turbinlite operations were eventually recognised as a waste of resources and the squadrons involved disbanded at the beginning of 1943. This left a requirement, however, for a continuing supply of Bostons to meet the equipment and wastage replacement of the Turbinlite force throughout 1941 and 1942. From one flight (half a squadron) involved in LAM operations at the end of 1940, the Boston nightfighting force would eventually grow by the end of 1941 to three squadrons of intruders with twenty-two crewed and serviceable aircraft, and a further four Turbinlite squadrons with thirty-one aircraft crewed and serviceable. This represented seven out of 105 squadrons in Fighter Command on 31 December 1941, with fifty-three out of 1,236 crewed and serviceable aircraft.[11]

While the need to maintain the Boston nightfighter commitment was to be a feature of British supply diplomacy, notably in 1942, it must be borne in mind that they represented 4.3 per cent of the total Fighter Command strength at the end of 1941. Though they represented a larger proportion of the available nightfighter strength (fifty-three out of 429 or 12.4 per cent of crewed and serviceable aircraft), the Boston force was not comparable in size or effectiveness to the twelve squadrons of Beaufighters (132 aircraft crewed and available). Nor did it match the size of the twelve squadrons of Hurricanes and seven of Defiants also committed to nightfighter operations (145 and ninety-nine crewed and available aircraft, respectively).

Meanwhile the Battle squadrons originally scheduled to receive the Boston ended up re-equipping and returning to operations in 2 Group of Bomber Command with the British Bristol Blenheim light bomber, despite its known obsolescence.[12] Even though the Boston III had been ordered with the armament and defensive equipment the British regarded as essential, when they arrived in Britain in mid-1941, they were plagued by equipment and modification problems that caused political embarrassment to the MAP.

As Boston IIIs piled up in MAP maintenance and modification facilities, further diversions of Boston supplies took place. Delays in planned Baltimore deliveries led to Boston supplies being called on to help make up the shortfall in available light bombers overseas in 1941. This meant that deliveries of the Boston were to be split between the Middle East and 2 Group in the immediate future, with a reduced target of four out of ten squadrons in 2 Group to be equipped with the Boston by the end of 1941.[13] At this point, no Boston III had even begun operational service. Worse was to follow.

The German attack on the Soviet Union in June 1941 led to the British and United States governments promising substantial aircraft supply aid to the Soviet government. This included fighter supplies promised by Churchill in July and August, and which were followed by the negotiation of a combined Allied Supply Protocol by Beaverbrook and Averell Harriman in Moscow during September 1941. Roosevelt's supply promises to the Soviet Union were to prove a serious problem for British expectations of American aircraft supply deliveries, and the Boston was a case in point. The US commitment to the Soviets included an undertaking to supply a hundred bombers per month. The possible impact on bomber deliveries to the British represented by the American commitment to the Soviets was noted by Freeman at an ERP committee meeting in September 1941.

> . . . the present discussions with Mr Harriman made it almost impossible to make any firm decision about allocation of light bombers . . . [It] seemed inevitable that Hudsons would be diverted by the Americans from Lease/Lend production for this purpose. In view of this, it should be realised that in forming new squadrons overseas, we should be running the risk of the necessary aircraft being unobtainable from [the] USA.[14]

Freeman's initial fears were concentrated on light bomber units in Britain which were scheduled to re-equip with Hudsons before redeployment to the Middle or Far East as maritime reconnaissance bombers at the end of 1941, such as 139 Squadron in 2 Group (which used Blenheims throughout 1941). The primary focus of Soviet diversions turned out to be the Boston, however.

By the end of October 1941, the British had agreed to loan three hundred Bostons from their own cash-purchase contract deliveries to the USAAF to help them meet their Soviet quota. This figure quickly rose, with the addition of 515 Bostons due from Lend-Lease, many equipped with engines from British cash-purchase contracts. In total the USAAF intended to divert 815 Bostons from British contracts and previously agreed British allocations to meet the American commitment of nine hundred bombers due to be supplied to the Soviet Union between October 1941 and June 1942. More than 90 per cent of their Soviet supply commitment for bombers in this period would therefore be met from British allocations, and a third of it from British cash purchase aircraft. The USAAF now intended to retain 470 Bostons from their own contracts while supplying thirteen Bostons (and an additional seventy-two B-25 Mitchell bombers) to the Soviets in the same period. The British would be left with an allocation of fifty-two Bostons, thirty-three of which would later turn out to have been promised by the US administration to the Chinese government, too. This left the British with a firm allocation of nineteen Bostons out of 1,350 expected to be produced in that period. As Sinclair, the Secretary of State for Air, observed to Harold Balfour, his Undersecretary of State who was visiting Washington at that point: 'The American contribution of bombers to Russia appears almost negligible and the main burden falls on us.'[15]

This was a particular problem as the British were now concentrating on heavy bomber production which they did not want to divert away from their strategic bombing campaign, and their only prospect of a qualitatively equivalent domestic alternative to US light bombers was the de Havilland Mosquito which began delivery in small numbers at the end of the year. The only other alternative was a continued reliance on the obsolete Blenheim.

What made this worse from the British perspective was the change in procurement politics involved. Boston deliveries at the end of 1941 were scheduled to originate from contracts placed by the Office of Lend-Lease Administration, run by officials known to be relatively sympathetic to British demands. Future Lend-

Lease allocations, including repayment of earlier diverted aircraft, would come from War Department contracts for the USAAF, and would thus be under USAAF control. As a result, the British expected their remaining influence over the allocation of future Boston supply to decline further.[16]

By November 1941, disappointing production levels and the loss of deliveries to competition from the USAAF and the Soviets led to pessimism spreading in the Air Ministry about the prospects of American supply. One summary of the contribution of American supply to RAF expansion that month stated that the British were '. . . as far away as ever from any realistic approach to our aircraft requirements in the United States . . . so far as aircraft requirements are concerned, the outlook has never been worse.'[17]

The Boston problem, and the unilateral diversion of aircraft the British believed had been firmly allocated to them, dragged on throughout 1942. A shortage of Bostons to maintain the two bomber squadrons in the Middle East which had re-equipped from Blenheims dogged RAF supply policy throughout the year. At the beginning of 1942, the British were threatened by the complete elimination of Boston supplies for the rest of the year. After negotiation in the December 1941–January 1942 Washington conference, the British were promised 54 Bostons in the first six months of 1942. This was one component of the provisions of the first Arnold-Towers-Portal (ATP) agreement which established allocations of American aircraft for the following year (named after the signatories - the respective heads of the USAAF, General Arnold; the USN Bureau of Aeronautics, Admiral Jack Towers; and the RAF, Air Chief Marshal Sir Charles Portal). In the end the RAF received 46 Bostons in the first half of 1942, or 10% of production.[18]

In April 1942 the RAF delegation in Washington discovered that Bostons allocated to the British were again about to be reallocated to the Soviets 'without reference to us', and repayment of the similar earlier diversions in 1941 was being postponed. Whatever priority the British had received for Lend-Lease aircraft supply had clearly and consistently been reduced in favour of the Soviets. All this was taking place without any discussion by the relevant joint Allied bodies established under the Combined Chiefs of Staff since the Washington conference, making 'a farce' of the allocation machinery.[19]

These unilateral revisions of Anglo-American aircraft supply agreements generated resentment on the part of the senior RAF officers involved. An example illustrating this was revealed in May 1942 when Freeman responded to a request from Air Marshal Sir Philip Joubert, then C.-in-C. of Coastal Command. Joubert had received complaints from a Dutch squadron, under RAF command, equipped with Hudsons for maritime patrol duties over the North Sea. The Hudson was proving too slow and vulnerable to fighter interception for these operations, and Joubert passed on their request for faster Bostons to replace them. The Dutch had already bought forty Bostons from the United States but deliveries of these had been diverted to the Soviets. Freeman's response encapsulates the irritation the RAF felt with the diversion of their Boston supplies over the previous nine months: 'The Americans agreed to give a large number of Bostons to the Russians. They therefore pinched 600 of ours, and, in addition, some from the Dutch, and no doubt from other nations also. Like the Dutch, we had paid in hard cash for ours.'[20]

The April 1942 revision of supply allocations under discussion by the joint Anglo-American supply machinery in Washington left the British with a total of 199 Bostons in 1942, with the USAAF receiving 910, the Soviets 751, the Chinese fifty, and forty-eight for Dutch use in the Far East. A British request for an additional two hundred Bostons was rejected.[21] This left the British struggling to maintain their Boston squadrons in Britain and, more particularly, in the Middle East. The problem continued throughout the rest of 1942. Despite reaching a new allocation agreement during the Washington conference in June 1942 (the second ATP agreement) which further reduced British quotas of American aircraft supply, the RAF found that deliveries of light bombers still remained below these reduced expectations. This was to result in a rare instance of a specific aircraft type featuring in the diplomatic correspondence between Churchill and Roosevelt after 1940.

On 4 July 1942, Churchill appealed to Roosevelt directly for the diversion of the Bostons being supplied to the Soviets via the Persian Gulf port of Basra.[22] It is significant that the British chiefs of staff had previously felt unable to risk the refusal of such a request by the US and Soviet governments, and that the request was only made during the crisis the British faced in Egypt after the fall of Tobruk.[23] It was also entirely characteristic of the political dynamics involved that Portal felt obliged to warn Tedder (the intended recipient of the Bostons) that the aircraft must be seen to be used: 'It is most important to avoid keeping many of them idle in Egypt because of the effect on American opinion which is extremely sensitive on this point.'[24]

On the same date as Churchill's appeal for the Bostons at Basra, and to capitalise on the public relations dimensions of US Independence Day, the USAAF conducted their first raid from Britain against targets in German-occupied Europe. In both cases, the aircraft involved were American-built Bostons, but it is perhaps less well known that the aircraft involved were diverted from what were originally British allocations. In the case of the Bostons used by the USAAF, these were Boston IIIs borrowed from 226 Squadron in 2 Group and originated from cash purchase contracts.[25] Overall, between June and September 1942, the British received 50 per cent of their allocation of light bombers, with a deficiency of 107 Bostons alone.[26] This repeated the experience of the previous year, with a similar conclusion over the relatively favourable treatment given to the Soviet quota.[27]

The Boston problem lingered into 1943 when the three squadrons which had managed to become operational in 2 Group at the beginning of 1943 had their aircraft diverted to North Africa to replace the obsolete Blenheim V used by the RAF component of the force that had invaded North Africa in the previous November.[28] The 2 Group squadrons were slowly re-equipped with the Boston IIIA variant in early 1943. This is worthy of note because the Boston IIIA was the first Lend-Lease-procured Boston variant, and it entered operational service fully two years after the passage of Lend-Lease. This delay was typical of the earlier variants of the Boston ordered against cash purchase contracts; deliveries of the Boston III had begun in the spring of 1941 yet the first Boston missions were flown by 2 Group in February 1942, nearly two years after the aircraft had first been ordered. This was a clear indication that the aircraft supply problems, which had adversely affected American deliveries, were not immediately resolved by Lend-Lease.

In total, and ignoring earlier DB-7/A-20 variants, such as the Havoc, the RAF had ordered 781 Boston IIIs from a combination of French and British purchase orders. Out of this total, 246 were diverted to the USAAF (many of which were then supplied to the Soviets) and a further seventy-seven were shipped directly to the Soviet Union to meet American supply commitments, despite the aircraft involved being procured by cash purchase (rather than Lend-Lease).[29] In the end, the British received 458, or 59 per cent, of the aircraft they had paid for, aircraft that were replaced only after intensive negotiations with the USAAF up to a year later.

The British experience with other American light bombers was similar to this pattern. These bombers can be divided into two main groups: those like the Martin Maryland and its successor the Baltimore, which were supplied exclusively overseas; and those that were used to supplement the Boston in 2 Group in Britain. Taking the latter first, the failure to deliver sufficient Bostons, the need to divert them to replace Blenheims to the Middle East, and the problems the MAP faced in adapting them for RAF service left the RAF with barely enough available to equip four squadrons in 2 Group, or approximately half the total strength of the group.

What made this more significant was the conversion of factories involved in Blenheim production in Britain to heavy bomber production, leaving the flow of new and repaired Blenheims insufficient to maintain heavy operational losses in the existing squadrons. Coupled with this was the institutional conflict the RAF faced with the army over the provision of sufficient air forces to support military operations. These became particularly acrimonious in the spring of 1942 as the British Army reeled from defeats sustained in North Africa and the Far East, and the RAF's apparent obsession with the strategic bombing of Germany seemed to starve the army of support aircraft.[30]

The RAF was eventually able largely to meet this need by the evolution of fighter-bombers: Hurricanes and later Typhoons equipped with bombs or rockets conducting ground-attack missions. Fighter Command Hurricanes had already begun to supplant Blenheims in short-range anti-shipping operations conducted by 2 Group before the end of 1941, and this policy would later be developed with great success in the North African campaign. The use of fighter-bombers could reduce, but not eliminate, the requirement for light and medium bombers in short-range tactical operations in support of ground forces. This left the RAF facing a need to address the requirements for army-support light bombers without diverting heavy bombers away from the strategic bombing campaign.

One solution was the deployment of the de Havilland Mosquito, an unarmed bomber which had the performance to outrun contemporary fighters at certain altitudes and a range that permitted attacks deep into Germany. The Mosquito bomber would be slowly introduced into operations with 2 Group, equipping two squadrons before the end of the year. But the Mosquito was an unproven concept and then competition for other uses at which it was soon discovered to excel (strategic bombing, photographic reconnaissance and nightfighting) would mean that production would not be sufficient for it to equip the rest of the Group for a long time to come. This left two alternatives: other American light bombers and dive-bombers.

By the end of 1941, Boston supply was already overcommitted and Baltimore production was scheduled to be shipped directly overseas. There were three possible alternative American medium bombers to equip the remaining squadrons in 2 Group. These were the Lockheed Ventura, the North American B-25 Mitchell and the Martin B-26 Marauder. The last two aircraft types had originated with the USAAF rearmament orders in 1940 and had not been designed in time to feature in the Allied purchase contracts of 1940. Both promised a competitive performance (more so in the case of the Marauder) and a heavier bombload than the Boston. British access to them for Lend-Lease was restricted to Defence Aid releases from the USAAF which, based on the experience of American supply to date, would be contingent upon USAAF delivery targets being met before the British would receive any. RAF planning therefore devolved on the Ventura.

Essentially a larger version of the Hudson, the Ventura was considerably heavier with more powerful engines. This left it with a performance broadly equivalent to that of the Hudson except that it had a shorter range which ruled it out as a direct replacement for the Hudson in the GR role. In 1940 the British had ordered 675 Venturas. Deliveries had begun in March 1942, with 144 being delivered to Britain by the end of the year. In the end, these were to provide the available stock of aircraft for 2 Group, which used 134 of the aircraft, while most of the remaining production after 1942 was directed elsewhere. Aside from eighty-one which were sent to Canada as training aircraft, and 135 which were used by the South African government for maritime reconnaissance in southern Africa (rather than in the wider Middle East theatre), a further 280 out of the 675 produced to British purchase contracts were diverted to the US services after their entry into the war.[31] These figures reflected the limited use of the Ventura in 2 Group, which was governed by its inadequate performance and armament.

This factor, the qualitative issue, made the Ventura unpopular with 2 Group from the beginning of their operational service in November 1942. The commander of the group described the aircraft as 'thoroughly bad, being slow, heavy, unmanoeuvrable and lacking in good defensive armament', while their crews apparently referred to them as 'pigs'.[32] Slower than the Boston, and slower by far than the Mosquito, Venturas proved exceptionally vulnerable to interception if separated from their fighter escorts. The nadir of Ventura operations was experienced on 2 May 1943, when ten out of eleven Venturas were lost while attacking a power station in Amsterdam. Despite the presence of exceptional numbers of German fighters on this occasion, only one out of six Bostons engaged in a simultaneous attack on the nearby Ijmuiden power station was lost.[33] This can be taken as a crude but proportionate demonstration of the problem posed by the Ventura's performance. What threw this further into relief was the fact that, at the same time, the Mosquito squadrons in 2 Group had successfully begun small-scale but unescorted long-range daylight attacks on targets deep in Germany.[34]

After the transfer of the two operational Mosquito squadrons to Bomber Command's Pathfinder Force in June 1943, the Mosquito force in 2 Group was maintained and expanded by re-equipping the three Ventura squadrons. The use of the Ventura had attracted a considerable degree of attention from RAF planners who had considered it for other roles, such as a Hudson replacement as well as a light bomber in tactical operations. But, in the end, it barely repaid this attention, proving little real improvement on the Blenheim that it replaced.

The two USAAF-sponsored alternative twin-engined bombers, the Mitchell and the Marauder, appeared to escape the attention of the RAF planners in 1942, largely down to the fact that the British knew their deliveries were being scaled down as a result of USAAF requirements that year. Supplies of the B-26 Marauder proved as limited as expected, though its high speed and range allowed it to perform in a useful niche, being used by two squadrons in the Mediterranean as a low-altitude, medium-range maritime reconnaissance aircraft much as the Maryland had been in 1940–41.[35] More importantly for 2 Group, they began to receive supplies of the B-25 Mitchell. The Mitchell was a far more effective bomber, with better performance, more effective defensive armament and a considerably heavier bombload. The Mitchell was to equip three squadrons in 2 Group, and, alongside the three squadrons of Bostons, successfully maintained an operational presence of American bombers in service in 2 Group until the end of the war.

This situation took a long time to arrive, however, and was far below the expectations associated with British supply diplomacy in 1940–41. The impact of production delays and diversions on the contribution to overall RAF bomber strength can be seen in Table 5.1 below. This itemises the strength of RAF Bomber Command, responsible for the bombers based in Britain, and which included 2 Group until an administrative reorganisation in June 1943. The information is presented in the format of squadron–aircraft available from 1 October 1941 until 1 April 1943. Aside from four Bostons in use in trials during January 1941, and not in a formed squadron, there were no American bombers operational in Bomber Command until the first B-17 Flying Fortress heavy bombers entered service in July 1941.

Table 5.1 Aircraft strength in Bomber Command by type and squadron–aircraft available, 1 October 1941–1 April 1943[36]

Type	1 Oct 1941	1 Jan 1942	1 Apr 1942	1 Jul 1942	1 Oct 1942	1 Jan 1943	1 Apr 1943
Blenheim	10–148	6–96	3–69	4–65	3–72	3–72	0–0
Mosquito	0–0	1–5	1–7	1–11	1–19	2–25	3–53
Boston	1–9	2–33	3–58	3–63	3–44	3–48	4–31
Ventura	0–0	0–0	0–0	0–2	3–34	3–59	3–61
Mitchell	0–0	0–0	0–0	0–0	2–27	2–40	3–42
Fortress	1–9	1–11	0–0	0–0	0–0	0–0	0–0
Total (including all other types)	73–857	56–1,005	51–956	46–812	51–846	62–1,099	64–1,285

The overall decline in available squadrons after October 1941 was due to several causes, chiefly the diversion of squadrons to other roles, such as supporting Special Operations Executive, Coastal Command, the army airborne forces, and above all redeployment to overseas theatres. In terms of the presence of American aircraft in Bomber Command, the proportion rose from two out of seventy-three squadrons in October 1941, to three out of fifty-six in January 1942 and then ten out of sixty-four by April 1943. In the same period, the proportion of American aircraft involved would rise from eighteen out of 857 in October 1941 (or 2 per cent) to 105 out of 846 in October 1942 (or 12.4 per cent) and then fall to 134 out of 1,285 aircraft by April 1943 (or 10.4 per cent). This would prove the high-water mark beyond which American light and medium bomber supply would not rise, and no further squadrons were equipped with American types as the replacement of the Ventura by the Mosquito indicates.

The slow introduction of American types had seen them eventually entirely replace the Blenheim in Bomber Command but only after three years had passed since the aircraft involved had been ordered and after they became subject to extensive diversions elsewhere. Only by 1942 can American light and medium bomber supply be considered to have played any substantive part in air operations from Britain, and even those were short-range tactical raids against shipping and targets in occupied Europe designed to wear down German fighter resources in a battle of attrition more than to achieve any decisive result by themselves.

The problems of production delays and operational effectiveness were to be particularly significant in the supply of American dive bombers, and it is worth considering these aircraft in particular before examining the impact of American aircraft supply to overseas theatres. In the summer of 1943, the commander of 2 Group had emphatically rejected the prospect of using the Vultee Vengeance dive-bomber on operations.[37] The Vengeance was one of two dive-bomber types ordered in 1940, the other being the Brewster Bermuda, and the story of the procurement and deployment of both types provides perhaps the most extreme example of the problems of late delivery and qualitative inferiority that plagued American aircraft supply well into the mid-war period.

The BPC had ordered 750 A-35 Bermudas and seven hundred A-31 Vengeances in 1940. The Air Ministry had little or no interest in the dive bomber but Beaverbrook had proved responsive to army demands influenced by the impression made by the German Junkers Ju-87 Stuka dive bomber during the German blitzkrieg of 1940. The RAF was less impressed, believing, as indicated by experience in the Battle of Britain and in North Africa, that dive-bombers were effective only against minimal or light anti-aircraft defence and were exceptionally vulnerable to fighter interception. As Freeman explained to the cabinet in July 1941:

> In the autumn of 1940 the War Office asked the Air Staff to provide dive bombers. In spite of the doubts which the Air Staff felt of their ability to operate dive bombers in support of land operations, they agreed to provide them. Since it would have taken 2½ years to design and produce a British type, it was agreed to order in quantity two existing American types, the Vengeance and the Bermuda.[38]

Doubts about their operational quality were evident from the very first, as Slessor observed at the end of 1940. 'We are taking an absolute pig in a poke with these Brewster and Vultee dive-bombers – God knows what they will turn out like.'[39] Both aircraft were subjected to major design changes before they entered full production (at British request and also to rectify problems identified by the manufacturers), and this delayed the beginning of deliveries until 1942. A report on further delays in May 1942 indicated the increasing embarrassment involved because, though the first prototype aircraft had been dedicated by the British ambassador to Washington more than six months previously, production had only just begun in March 1942 in minute quantities. The factory at Nashville, Tennessee, represented '. . . a huge, well-equipped plant and some 4,000 workers contributing practically nothing to the war effort'.[40]

Nonetheless, the expectation of eventual Vengeance production had become integral to British planning for the reinforcement of India and the equipment of Dominion forces in Australia, and they initially objected to further production delays associated with the introduction of a new A-35 variant with a more powerful engine.[41] Despite diverting 352 Vengeances to themselves after Pearl Harbor, the USAAF had no further interest in the type, and wanted to use the Vultee factory to produce other aircraft.[42] The eventual delivery of Vengeances was further delayed by shipping and assembly problems, with the end result that the Vengeance did not enter operational service in India before the spring of 1943.[43] They were then able, alongside the use of the Hurricane fighter as a fighter-bomber, to replace the Blenheim light bombers that had been used by the RAF in the Burma campaign since 1941.[44]

The Vengeance had at least finally managed to overcome interminable production delays and to struggle into service despite the RAF's prejudice against dive-bombers, even if this was in the theatre which was known to represent the lowest priority for reinforcement. The qualitative problems it had, particularly its low speed, were not exposed in combat owing to the relative scale of RAF fighter strength on the Burma front by 1943 and the weakness of the Japanese opposition. This allowed it to provide useful and effective operational service, albeit three full years after the aircraft had first been ordered. This limited measure of success was to be entirely denied to its contemporary, the Brewster Bermuda.

The French had placed an order for 250 Bermuda dive-bombers which were expected to follow the completion of the firm's contracts for Buffalo fighters in January 1941. The BAC had added follow-on orders to a combined total of 750 aircraft by early 1941. Serious problems were encountered immediately, as the company struggled to complete the Buffalo order and begin production of the Bermuda.[45] Despite a management reorganisation, problems multiplied in the spring of 1941 after the British demanded a redesign of the aircraft, and the company formally announced its inability to begin supply in April when the delivery of the first former-French contract was scheduled to be completed.[46] The inability of Brewster to deliver any of their parallel contract for SB2A Buccaneer dive-bombers (similar to the Bermuda) to the US Navy culminated in the USN formally taking over the Brewster works in April 1942.[47] Interminable production problems were now followed by the revelation of severe qualitative problems. In November 1942, when able to test production versions of the

Bermuda for the first time, BAC officials concluded: 'This is definitely a pretty poor aeroplane . . . [We] have no alternative but to continue to accept the aircraft with such minor improvements as we can progressively get embodied without interfering with production.'[48]

The Air Ministry view was even less charitable, listing a series of major technical faults, such as faulty control rods, unreliable brakes, carbon dioxide contamination of the cockpit and '. . . a good many minor defects'. The report concluded; 'They are all in a very unsatisfactory condition, and it looks as if BAC have been forced to accept them by political pressure.'[49]

By May 1943, the BAC announced the British intention to cut their losses on the Bermuda contracts and refuse further deliveries, after spending over $84 million on aircraft which were practically unusable.[50] Potential legal claims for cancellation represented a difficulty that might have led to public criticism, a constant worry when Lend-Lease appropriations were repeatedly subject to Congressional scrutiny and public criticism.[51] This led to the bizarre situation where the BAC accepted 468 aircraft it had no interest in, over two hundred of which ended up in Britain being used as target tugs (for the lack of a better use), while ninety-eight were transferred to the US services as instructional airframes and 152 were broken up for scrap without ever being used.[52] The net contribution of this multimillion dollar contract from 1940 towards British air power was negligible, and the eventual production and delivery of the aircraft had nothing to do with British operational needs.

The Bermuda was obviously an extreme example of the problem of delivery delays and operational utility. These problems also existed in British domestic procurement; at the time the Bermuda fiasco was progressing towards a conclusion the British had already been through numerous problems of their own which would culminate in the MAP's failure to reach heavy bomber production targets in 1942. That failure would result in the adoption of 'realistic' programmes in contrast to Beaverbrook's exhortatory approach to planning, and also in the return of Freeman to the MAP as Chief Executive at the end of 1942 to strengthen the technical knowledge at the head of the Ministry.[53] But there remained a material difference in that the British programme was still producing and equipping substantial numbers of aircraft adequate for immediate operational use. This had placed American production in a supplemental position which was exacerbated by the particular quantitative and qualitative failures associated with it.

As the experience of the Vengeance indicates, the final arena to consider in this evaluation of American light bomber supply was the overseas theatres identified as the focus for RAF supplies of American aircraft in July 1940. These were the Far East, including British possessions such as India, Malaya and Singapore, but, more importantly, the Middle East. This consisted of British possessions and dependencies in the Near East ranging from Egypt, Aden, Palestine and Iraq as well as naval bases including Gibraltar, Malta, and Alexandria across the Mediterranean basin. These all came under the purview of RAF Middle East Command, based in Cairo.

Between 3 and 27 July 1940, the ERP firstly relegated French-contract 'windfalls' and 'off the shelf' American purchases, the immediate products of the 1940 supply diplomacy, to supplementing RAF trainer supplies. More capable American aircraft equipped at the factory with British equipment and defensive armament to British specifications were expected to follow. Except for heavy bombers, these aircraft were now to be used to reinforce overseas theatres. This deployment plan expressed a conviction that the German offensive against Britain would be defeated and that future attention would be directed to the Middle East. 'When the German attack on [the] U.K. has failed it is almost inevitable that there will be a combined German-Italian drive towards the Middle East.'[54]

This represents a remarkable and prescient commentary on RAF expectations immediately after the French collapse in 1940. It not only accurately predicted the successful defence of Britain and the consequent evolution of British strategy before the evolution of full-scale American supply aid, it contradicted the rhetoric of critical dependency being utilised by contemporary British supply diplomacy. Despite the early identification of this strategic need, the ability of American supply to meet it would prove limited.

Conscious of the need to build up British forces to defend

strategic bases in Egypt and Malta against the potential German, and the immediate Italian, threat, and warned of overriding British domestic requirements for aircraft, the British commander in the Middle East had inquired about the availability of American aircraft. The Air Ministry had responded that there was no chance of the early supply of suitable aircraft from the United States.[55] This left the British with no alternative in the short term but to supply aircraft from their own domestic production.

On 3 July 1940, the ERP committee had set out an agreed reinforcement policy for the Middle East which included a monthly quota of twelve Blenheim light bombers, twelve Hurricane fighters and six Lysander army co-operation and communication aircraft per month.[56] By the end of July the RAF had overcome opposition from Beaverbrook to the additional supply of twenty-four Hurricanes and seventy-five Maryland bombers from the United States for the South African government whose forces were participating in the fighting against the Italians in Ethiopia and Somalia.[57] By September, despite the climax in the air fighting then taking place in the Battle of Britain, the Air Ministry continued to resist Beaverbrook's attempts to divert the Middle East's quota of Hurricanes to reinforce Fighter Command training units.[58] At the end of that month Air Ministry policy was confirmed again by a cabinet committee.[59]

This still left the British with demand outstripping available supply as commitments mounted. In October, when considering what could be done to procure American aid for Greece as that country was attacked by Italian forces through Albania, Churchill acknowledged that '. . . nothing was available which would be likely to affect the immediate situation'.[60] When RAF units were dispatched from Middle East Command to assist the Greeks, they were equipped with British aircraft – Blenheim bombers and Gladiator (and later Hurricane) fighters. The RAF remained dependent upon British aircraft supply to reinforce the Middle East until suitable American aircraft were available. When American supply fell short of expectations over the longer term, this dependency, which had originated as a temporary stopgap, increased substantially.

Table 5.2 indicates the statistics involved by comparing deliver-

Table 5.2 British and US aircraft delivered overseas, 1940–3[61]

Year	American aircraft (including trainers)[62]	Exports from Britain to RAF overseas commands[63]	Exports from Britain to other destinations[64]	British trainer exports[65]	Total British exports	Combined US and British total	American deliveries as percentage of combined total
1940 (from April)	833	725	161	1,698	2,584	3,417	24.4
1941	2,830	3,687	1,015	4,408	9,110	11,940	23.7
1942	3,879	5,959	2,241	1,792	9,992	13,871	28.0
1943	4,867	8,713	2,300	1,143	12,156	17,023	28.6

ies of US aircraft exported to overseas destinations on British or Dominion government account to British deliveries to overseas commands and other destinations.

The overall statistics tell only part of the story, however. The ERP committee decisions to depend upon American fighter and bomber deliveries for their operational units overseas were affected by quantitative and qualitative problems further than the figures given above suggest. This becomes clear when the deliveries of aircraft types are taken into account.

American aircraft deliveries represented about a quarter of British exports to overseas destinations in 1940. But, breaking down the deliveries by aircraft type and particular destination reveals a very different picture. British exports to overseas commands in 1940 included 687 aircraft sent to the Mediterranean and Middle East, or about 90 per cent of the deliveries. At the same time, only thirty-seven American aircraft were exported to the Middle East, or 4 per cent of the total American exports in the same period. At this time, the delivery of trainer aircraft represented the mainstay of US exports, with 628 North American Harvards and eighty-nine Yales exported to Canada.[66]

The relative inability of American aircraft supply to meet the demand to reinforce operational combat units in the Middle East is revealed by the fact that in 1940 the British exported seventy-nine Wellington and 167 Blenheim bombers there, along with 215 Hurricane fighters. The American aircraft did not bear comparison, with only four P-36 Mohawk and two P-40 Tomahawk fighters being delivered. Fifteen Brewster Buffaloes, diverted from former Belgian contracts, will be dealt with elsewhere and it should be noted here that some were used briefly by a Royal Navy fighter squadron before their lack of spares and poor serviceability saw the last of them abandoned on Crete before the German assault of May 1941.[67]

There is one significant exception to the extremely limited role of American aircraft in 1940: this was the use of the Martin GM 167 Maryland. The Maryland originated from pre-war French purchase contracts. Many of those delivered before the fall of France remained in the service of the Vichy government in Algeria and Syria, in the latter case going into combat to defend Syria against the British invasion of April–May 1941.[68] The Maryland promised the earliest deliveries of any American bomber aside from the ex-French Douglas DB-7s. Though suffering from a similar lack of operational equipment and defensive armament to the DB-7, the Maryland had a similar high performance at low to medium altitudes and a significantly better range. This gave the aircraft considerable potential as a reconnaissance machine at a time when the RAF was converting unarmed Spitfire fighters with increased fuel capacity for photographic reconnaissance (PR) duties in Britain to exploit their high performance in this role.[69] Four Marylands were supplied to Malta to improve the strategic reconnaissance capacity for the RN in September 1940, and had an immediate impact which was reflected in the Churchill–Roosevelt correspondence: in November 1940 Churchill attributed the success of the attack on the Italian fleet at Taranto the previous month in part to Marylands based on Malta.[70]

This is one example of American aircraft successfully meeting a niche requirement in air operations which was contingent upon their performance, or perceived quality, and it deserves acknowledgement. This throws the experience of the rest of American aircraft supply into sharp relief, however. The Maryland was the only American aircraft supplied in 1940 to have been of any operational significance to the RAF, and the numbers involved were minimal. In total, twenty-three Marylands were exported to Malta and the Middle East in 1940 (eleven of them re-exported from Britain).

While American aircraft deliveries to the overseas theatres did increase, the relative proportion remained static as British deliveries increased at the same rate. This trend becomes even more marked when the delivery of types with adequate combat value is considered. Table 5.3 presents the statistics of aircraft deliveries to the Middle East and associated destinations (that is, to Gibraltar or South Africa, where the aircraft involved were normally available for operational use to RAF Middle East Command) broken down by types that were regarded as adequate for operational service in combat.

There are many features worthy of comment in these figures. The most obvious is that in 1941 and 1942, the RAF in the Middle East

Table 5.3 Deliveries of selected operational types to Middle East and associated destinations, 1941–3[71]

Type	1940	1941	1942	1943
Martin Maryland	23	132	3	0
Martin Baltimore	0	17	367	745
Martin Marauder	0	0	45	68
Douglas Boston	0	111	50	86
Bristol Blenheim	173	956	566	173
de Havilland Mosquito	0	0	2	115
Consolidated Liberator	0	0	48	55
Handley-Page Halifax	0	0	41	105
Vickers Wellington	79	331	708	879
Curtiss Mohawk	4	95	61	1
Curtiss Tomahawk	2	542	23	7
Curtiss Kittyhawk	0	197	828	592
Bristol Beaufighter	0	98	454	780
Hawker Hurricane	215	1,528	1,257	938
Vickers-Supermarine Spitfire	0	0	1,585	2,639

received 715 light and medium American bombers (135 Marylands, 384 Baltimores, forty-five Marauders and 151 Bostons) against 1,522 Blenheims. Clearly the expectations of the Air Staff had not been met, and the ability of American bombers to meet requirements in the Middle East was limited. The figures for Bostons in particular were contingent upon re-exports from Britain in 1941 and 1942 at the expense of 2 Group (130 out of 151 aircraft supplied that year) as well as exceptional diversions from deliveries to the Soviet Union made at the highest political level.

This bomber situation becomes more lopsided when the 1,039 Wellingtons delivered in the same period are considered. There was no comparable equivalent to the twin-engined Wellington (used as a night bomber against strategic targets) in the available American types. The closest equivalent would be the four-engined Liberator heavy bomber which was a more capable aircraft and eventually used to replace the Wellington in the Middle East from 1943. Deliveries of the Liberator in 1942–3 were, however, more than matched by those of the British Halifax four-engined heavy bomber used for the same purpose (103 Liberators being delivered against 146 Halifaxes). Deliveries of both types were still exceeded by continuing deliveries of the Wellington (a further 879 being delivered in 1943).

The totals involved indicate that, considering the aircraft the RAF actually used in combat, British-built bombers represented the following proportion of aircraft supplied to the Middle East. In 1940, they represented 252 out of 275 aircraft, or 92 per cent; in 1941, 1,287 out of 1,546 aircraft, or 83 per cent; in 1942, 1,317 out of 1,830 aircraft, or 72 per cent; and in 1943, 1,272 out of 1,853 aircraft, or 69 per cent. Overall, British bombers represented 75 per cent of the supply of those types actually used in combat in the Middle East between 1940 and 1943.

The situation was no better with the fighter aircraft involved, as Table 5.4 indicates. Including figures for deliveries of the former-French P-36 Mohawk, which was used only briefly in combat during 1941 by a South African squadron in East Africa, and excluding figures for the twin-engined British Beaufighter, American fighter supply in the period amounted to 2,352 aircraft between 1940 and 1943 (161 Mohawks, 574 Tomahawks, and 1,617 Kittyhawks) against 8,162 British fighters (3,938 Hurricanes and 4,224 Spitfires). American fighters made up only 22 per cent of the single-engined fighters supplied to the Middle East which the RAF used in combat between 1940 and 1943.

This meant that American aircraft supply played a minimal part in RAF strength in the Middle East and Mediterranean until mid-1941, and only a supplemental part thereafter. Table 5.4 indicates the composition of RAF front-line strength in Middle East Command by reference to the operational types mentioned above in the format of aircraft present in squadrons serviceable/unserviceable, exclusive of aircraft in reserves, maintenance and training units as well as assembling or in transit along the Takoradi air ferry route. It should be noted that, if anything, this increases the significance of the Maryland which was classified as a GR type while RAF GR types (apart from fourteen Wellingtons in October 1941) have been excluded. Obsolete British types, such as the Vickers Wellesley bomber and Gloster Gladiator fighter which saw combat in the first half of 1941, have also been excluded (both types together accounting for eighty-one serviceable aircraft in squadrons on 1 January, declining to thirty by 1 July).

Table 5.4 Middle East Command, operational aircraft in squadrons, January–October 1941[72]

Type	1 Jan 1941	1 Apr 1941	1 Jul 1941	1 Oct 1941
Maryland	0/0	9/0	52/6	71/2
Blenheim	102/9	121/26	109/15	99/3
Wellington	41/4	49/5	49/5	76/9
Tomahawk	0/0	0/0	51/14	85/5
Beaufighter	0/0	0/0	13/3	15/5
Hurricane	61/5	76/13	177/11	276/13
Total (including other types)	337/44	368/45	550/74	675/44
American types as percentage of serviceable aircraft	Nil	2.5	18.7	23.1

This indicates that it was not until October 1941 that the operational employment of American aircraft began to reflect the overall delivery statistics associated with them. The key factor affecting this was the difficulty of maintaining aircraft that the RAF was unfamiliar with, that arrived in irregular batches swamping available assembly and ferrying facilities, and that often lacked spares and vital equipment. To take one example, arrivals of the Curtiss P-40 Tomahawk fighter, which began in early 1941, did not translate into the first squadrons becoming operational until June, a delay of several months. These delays often reflected the particular problems encountered adapting aircraft for operation in the desert, such as the requirement for air filters to protect their engines from ingested sand and dirt. These affected all aircraft used in the desert but appear to have been particularly significant with American types.

Tedder complained frequently about the teething troubles of American types in his command. Examples included the Boston and Baltimore bombers.[73] Another was the Tomahawk fighter.[74] These problems can be quantified, and indicate that serviceability for some American aircraft types was lower than their British equivalents, qualifying the value of their delivery statistics. The serviceability of the two main fighters employed in the Middle East, the Hurricane and the Tomahawk, could vary significantly. Between the two specific dates 15 November and 15 December 1941, a period associated with the intensive fighting involved in

'Operation Crusader', which culminated in the successful relief of Tobruk, Hurricane serviceability varied from 80 to 72 per cent while Tomahawk serviceability varied from 63 to 60 per cent. Not only were more Hurricanes on hand (a total of 600 rising to 668) compared to the Tomahawks (322 rising to 365), more of them were available for operations.[75]

These figures reflect the situation several months after the Tomahawk had first entered service and after the RAF had been able to address initial spares and equipment issues. Considerable effort was expended to resolve these problems, involving the despatch of USAAF staff and American civilian technicians to the Middle East to improve the maintenance situation with American types. These gained added impetus with Harriman's visit to the Middle East in June 1941 to improve the reception and assembly of American aircraft.[76] At this point, many aircraft being delivered to the Middle East were being ferried along the trans-African air-ferry route the RAF had established from Takoradi on the coast of western Africa to Egypt. This had been established in 1940 when the Mediterranean was closed to shipping by the Italian declaration of war, and saved ten weeks' shipping time when compared with the longer route around South Africa and along the eastern coast of Africa to Suez.

While the RAF welcomed American assistance with maintenance and ferrying, this did not prevent irritation at the tone or content of American advice which often came along with it. American criticism of RAF organisation and morale in Egypt, arising during the Harriman mission, was brought before the cabinet in June 1941. This was indirectly blamed by Portal on Harriman and the US ambassador in Cairo and, in an interesting perspective on the diplomacy of critical dependency, it was attributed to 'misdirected enthusiasm' to 'hasten and increase American help'.[77] Portal's response gave short shrift to Harriman's criticism of the conditions at Takoradi, with the observation that a hastily developed route across 3,000 miles of Africa could not compare to a trans-American civil air line.[78]

One outcome of the Harriman mission had been the suggestion that Pan American Airways (PAA) assume some of the responsibilities for passenger services along the Takoradi route, increasing the circulation of ferry pilots along the route and thereby increasing capacity. Despite being the primary beneficiary of such aid, Tedder was, in fact, strongly critical of what he took to be PAA's encroachment on British air routes, with dangerous implications for the position of British post-war aviation.[79]

Within months of the start of Pan American's operations in Africa, Tedder observed: 'The cloven hoof of Pan American [is] now well to [the] fore'. Tedder and other British commentators were justly suspicious of PAA's utilisation of short-term wartime agreements to penetrate British-controlled areas in civil aviation for post-war advantage. In February 1941 one PAA official

> proclaimed openly that it was his company's intention to operate commercially east of Cairo on the grounds that '. . . naturally Uncle Sam must try to get some return on the expenditure he is currently incurring in operating an air service to the Far East for military purposes'.

Though subsequent negotiations leading to the Halifax agreement in 1942 deferred commercial exploitation of the Takoradi service (and subsequently established wartime air supply routes) until after the war, it was clear that US investment in air routes to support British theatres of operation came with implications for post-war commercial competition; they could be, and were, used for American penetration of what had been British-controlled areas on the heels of wartime supply assistance.[80]

While this was a minor incident, it is worthy of note that the driving force behind the initiative was – as Tedder rightly suspected – the RAF officials in Washington making wide-ranging concessions to PAA at the behest of Whitehall.[81] Tedder's contemporary opinion indicates that this was another example of how American aid policy was driven by political and diplomatic considerations beyond the issue of local aircraft reinforcement. Despite his admitted need for American aid, Tedder had clear differences with Whitehall over the interests which should be sacrificed to achieve it.

Tedder was left with a dependence upon American aircraft supply that disappointed quantitative expectations, involving delivery delays, diversions and reduced scales of delivery. The Bostons were a good example. They offered Tedder a qualitative improvement over the Blenheim which, thanks to problems with the Baltimore, was his only available alternative at the end of 1941. In November 1941 he criticised the decision to divert to the Soviet Union forty out of the hundred Bostons he expected to receive between November 1941 and June 1942 to Freeman. Far from being able to replace the painfully outclassed Blenheim, the delay in Baltimore deliveries and the diversion of Bostons, originally allocated to substitute for them, meant that he would be forced to re-equip Boston and Maryland squadrons with Blenheims, with consequent damage to unit morale and to the results of the campaign.[82]

This exposes the RAF's qualitative deployment policy which, until the arrival of the Mosquito, recognised American bombers to be qualitatively superior to their available British equivalents. As will be seen subsequently, this policy did not always operate in favour of American types. But, even when it did, as in the case of the Boston and Baltimore in 1941–2, securing adequate supplies of them was a major and chronic problem. In Tedder's case, being the primary focus of the British strategic dependency on American aircraft supply was a cause of particular frustration.

> . . . I was doing everything possible to build up our air strength in the Desert, a task rendered no easier by our dependence upon American supplies and the apparent inability of the Americans to deliver anything like the promised quantity of goods anywhere near the promised time.[83]

The final example of the practical outcome of the dependency on American aircraft supply was the Far East where a need to substitute British types for disappointing American deliveries was equally evident. British planning had relegated the defences of Malaya and Singapore far below the requirements of the RAF in Britain, the Middle East and the requirement to assist the Soviets. To compensate for the absence of the fleet required to defend Singapore in 1940, the British had been forced to rely upon air power.[84] To this end, a target of 336 first-line aircraft had been established for the defence of Malaya, involving the re-equipment of obsolete types and the provision of fighter and bomber squadrons.

Setting a date for completion of this programme proved to be a difficult problem. By January 1941, the Dominions Office had to admit to the Australian government that the target remained subject to '. . . the general situation and the supply of aircraft'.[85] This was the situation that the ERP committee hoped could be addressed by American supply. These did, indeed, become slowly available in 1941, with sufficient Brewster Buffalo fighters to equip four fighter squadrons before the expected Japanese invasion materialised in December 1941. The situation with regard to other types scheduled for the Far East was considerably worse, however.

Five Catalina flying boats originating from British orders were flown out across the Pacific to reinforce the RAF in Singapore during April 1941. Though they were vital for the long-range maritime reconnaissance required to detect any prospective Japanese attack, the Air Ministry dismissed demands for more Catalinas on the basis of the unreliable delivery schedules associated with American supply.[86] This was amplified in the supply of bombers. The ERP committee had originally allocated future Baltimore deliveries to be shared by the Middle East and Far East in November 1940.[87] The impact of delivery failures and delays meant that, when Baltimores did begin to appear, re-equipping operational squadrons in the Middle East had priority. Owing to production and delivery falling badly behind schedule by August 1941, at the same time as Boston supply was begun to the Middle East, the supply of American dive-bombers was resorted to, all before being rendered irrelevant by the Japanese offensive that December.[88] All this was affected by the failure to produce and deliver the relevant aircraft on schedule which left the British, yet again, being compelled to substitute the supply of British aircraft to compensate.

In this case, reinforcement was achieved by the supply of Blenheim bombers and Hurricane fighters drawn from the Middle East, with the additional export of 810 Hurricanes to India from Britain in 1942. While some Kittyhawks were delivered from

British contracts to the Australian and New Zealand air forces for use in the south-west Pacific area in 1942, the situation in the Far East repeated the experience of the Middle East. Plans to depend upon American supply to meet the needs of both theatres had demonstrably failed by the end of 1941, to the extent that the majority of aircraft supplied to these theatres came from British production. This problem can be clearly measured by looking at the outcome of the relevant high-level aircraft allocation agreements.

In January 1942, the Americans had agreed a delivery schedule that allocated the British a total of 4,272 light and dive-bomber aircraft for the following year. In the event, by the end of 1942, the RAF had accepted a total of 1,189 aircraft or 27.8 per cent of their expectations.[89] Renegotiation of supply allocations in June 1942 involved a downward revision of the expectations of American aircraft supply but even these revised schedules could not be met. In the autumn of 1942, as the British fought the decisive desert battles at El Alamein, Tedder was still complaining about the failure of American supply to meet expectations, with Portal admitting to him that this was a further and 'seriously embarrassing' failure of the Americans to meet their obligations under the existing second ATP agreement.[90]

The delivery delays and qualitative shortcomings associated with American aircraft supplies left the British with the problem of reconciling the diplomatic importance of American aircraft with their marginal value. As Michael Bowyer has pointed out: 'Political considerations surrounding these deliveries were considerable, for Britain needed as much backing from the USA as possible, moral as well as material. That made it imperative to use what America was providing.'[91]

The British understood this political importance, yet were unwilling to compromise on what they considered to be an irreducible qualitative requirement. This meant that most of the aircraft secured by the 'emergency' British supply diplomacy of 1940, such as the Northrop A-17 dive-bomber, were never used operationally. Even the most mature supply contracts, such as the P-40 Tomahawk and the DB-7/A-20 Boston, took nearly a year in gestation after deliveries began before the aircraft involved were committed to combat. By the end of 1941 the MAP recorded that 203 Boston IIIs had been delivered, or were in the process of delivery, but none had yet flown a bombing mission.[92] While this generated considerable criticism of the MAP's record in modifying American aircraft for operational use, it remains undeniable that the British were not prepared to use these aircraft without such modification. Meanwhile, and despite the considerable overcommitment involved, they were willing and able to use their own aircraft supply to substitute for the quantitative shortcomings of American supply.

The primary factors in explaining this were the relative success of domestic British aircraft production and the problems involved in expanding the American aircraft industry from a later start to rearmament. The success of the former provided the British with the means to meet their defensive needs while permitting the marginalisation and eventual diversion of American aircraft to secondary theatres and roles. As American production rose, so did the diversions away from supply to the British, leaving deployment policy set in the pattern established in 1940–1.

Far from ending British supply problems, the nature and complexity of the problems involved in aircraft supply persisted long after Lend-Lease. Delivery delays and supply diversions ensured that aircraft actually procured under Lend-Lease legislation took up to a year to arrive in British units. The case of the Boston IIIA has already been mentioned. Other examples include the P-40E Kittyhawk where all previous Tomahawk deliveries, as well as the first 560 P-40D Kittyhawks, were procured under British cash purchase contracts. The first Lend-Lease P-40E/Kittyhawk IAs entered RAF combat service in Egypt in mid-1942 while only twenty-seven Baltimore IIIAs from Lend-Lease contracts were delivered to the Middle East by the end of that year – all the previous Baltimores (Marks I, II and III) supplied in 1941–42 originated from cash purchase contracts.[93] Partly as a result of this, British supply was to remain the mainstay of RAF air strength both in Britain and in the overseas theatres originally selected to become dependent upon American supply.

This conclusion provides substantial problems for the uncritical acceptance of the assertions of 'critical dependency' made by British diplomacy at the time, and any assumption that British supply needs were automatically met as a result of the aircraft supply diplomacy of 1940–42. The picture of late and inadequate deliveries, the constant competition for allocations of American aircraft, and the resulting need to substitute British aircraft for American presented here indicates that a considerable divergence remains between the assertions of Allied supply diplomacy and the operational reality. This divergence would become even more pronounced when the British would attempt to reorient US aircraft production towards the heavy bombers required to wage the strategic air offensive against Germany

Notes

1. Kimball, *Forged in War*, p. 130.
2. Tedder, p. 271.
3. Hallion, p. 85.
4. ERP committee minutes, 25 and 27 July; AIR 20/3461.
5. K. J. Meekcoms, *The British Air Commission and Lend-Lease* (Tunbridge Wells: Air Britain, 2000), pp. 93–4, 96.
6. ERP committee draft minutes, 29 March 1940; AIR 20/3461.
7. ERP committee minutes, 25 and 27 July; ibid.
8. ERP committee draft minutes, 29 March 1940; ibid.
9. ERP committee minutes, 13 September, 4 and 12 October 1940; ibid.
10. Michael Allan, *Pursuit Through Darkened Skies* (Shrewsbury: Airlife, 1999), pp. 56-8.
11. Fighter Command daily strength return, 31 December 1941. AIR 22/38.
12. Michael J. Bowyer, *2 Group RAF* (Somerton: Crécy, 1992), p. 175.
13. ERP committee meeting minutes, 4 July and 31 July 1941; AIR 20/3461.
14. ERP committee meeting minutes, 18 September 1941; ibid.
15. Sinclair to Balfour, Air Ministry to RAF Delegation, Washington, Webber W.396, 31 October 1941; AIR 9/436.
16. Self to Scott, BAC to MAP, Briny 11,004 MOSSY, 19 November 1941; ibid.
17. 'American Supply and the Royal Air Force Expansion programme',

anonymous Air Ministry memorandum, 27 November 1941; AIR 19/275.

18. 'Execution of Arnold/Portal agreement January–March 1942', AIR 8/637. 462 Bostons were produced in the first quarter of 1942.
19. RAFDEL to Air Ministry, Signair 39, WX.4424, 18 April 1942; AIR 9/165.
20. Freeman to Joubert, 22 May 1942; AIR 20/2779.
21. M.B.W. fifteenth meeting, '2. Change in Allocation of A-20A, B & C Airplanes', 23 April 1942, Box 194, Harry L. Hopkins Papers, FDR Library, Hyde Park. Hereafter Hopkins Papers.
22. Churchill to Roosevelt, C-105, 4 July 1942; Kimball, *Complete Correspondence*, p. 518.
23. Lieutenant Colonel Hollis to prime minister, 30 June 1942; AIR 8/865.
24. CAS to AOC-in-C, AX.174, 15 July 1942; ibid.
25. The serials of the aircraft involved are given in the Z and AL serial ranges. These were produced against British (A-87) and French cash purchase contracts (F-219). Stephen W. Pope, 'Combined Ops', in *Flypast* magazine, June 2002, p. 45.
26. 'Non-fulfilment of the Arnold–Towers–Portal Air Agreement, initialled by the President and the Prime Minister in Washington on June 22, 1942', Annex 1 to memorandum 'The Working of the Combined Boards' by the Minister of Production, War Cabinet 434 (42), 29 September 1942; AIR 19/204. Deficiencies listed in this report include sixty Hudsons and 164 Baltimores as well as sixty-nine Vengeance and 176 Bermuda dive-bombers.
27. Ibid.
28. Bowyer, *2 Group*, p. 291.
29. Meekcoms, pp. 93-94.
30. Alanbrooke diary entry, 11 March 1942; Danchev and Todman, p. 238.
31. Bowyer, *2 Group*, pp. 254–5; Meekcoms, 90–1.
32. Bowyer, *2 Group*, pp. 324–5.
33. Ibid., pp. 308–14.
34. These included daylight raids on targets as distant as Berlin on 30 January 1943 and Jena on 27 May 1943. Bowyer, *2 Group*, p. 287–9; Stuart R. Scott, *Mosquito Thunder: No. 105 Squadron RAF at War 1942–5* (Stroud: Sutton Publishing, 2001), pp. 89–92, 114–20.
35. Operations began in December 1942. Vincent Orange et al., *Winged*

Promises: A History of No. 14 Squadron RAF 1915–1945 (Fairford: RAF Benevolent Fund, 1996), pp. 180–2.

36. Figures from AIR 20/2016.
37. Bowyer, *2 Group*, p. 320.
38. Air Staff memorandum, 'The Dive Bomber', War Cabinet 182 (42), 16 July 1941; CAB 66/18/5.
39. Slessor to CAS, undated; AIR 8/446.
40. 'Airplane Production at Vultee Plant in Nashville', Memorandum by Isador Lubin to Harry Hopkins, 14 May 1942; Hopkins Papers.
41. 'Dive Bombers: A-31 (Vengeance),', Air Marshall Hill, BAC, to Major General Echols, Material Division, War Department, 28 May 1942; papers of Robert Lovett, Assistant Secretary of War, Records Group 107, Entry 210, National Archives and Records Administration, College Park, Maryland. Hereafter Lovett papers.
42. Figures from Meekcoms, pp. 103–4; 'Dive Bomber Production', record of discussion in the War Department, 5 April 1943; Lovett papers.
43. 'Allocation of Vengeance Aircraft to Australia, Far East, Middle East, and West Africa', Air Ministry memorandum L.M. 52/O.7, 15 November 1941; AIR 23/1722.
44. 82 Squadron, a Blenheim unit originally transferred from 2 Group, re-equipped with the Vengeance in February–March 1943, followed by three more RAF and two Indian Air Force squadrons. Christopher Shores, *Air War for Burma: The Allied Air Forces Fight Back in South-East Asia* (London: Grub Street, 2005), pp. 56, 64–5.
45. Sir Henry Self to Beaverbrook, 30 December 1940; AVIA 38/797.
46. L. C. Ord, BAC, to F. William Zelcer, Brewster Aeronautical Corporation, 11 March 1941; L. C. Ord to C. R. Fairey, BAC, 22 March 1941; C. R. Fairey to T. B. Stabbinge, 11 April 1941; AVIA 38/797.
47. Memorandum by A. C Boddis, BAC, 21 April 1942; ibid.
48. Air Vice Marshal Jones to Director General, BAC, 30 November 1942; ibid.
49. Air Ministry memorandum, 4 December 1942; AIR 20/2915.
50. 'Brewster Bermuda', undated BAC memorandum, February 1943; AVIA 38/797.
51. Discussion between USN and BAC representatives, 28 May 1943; ibid.
52. Meekcoms, p. 102.
53. Cairncross, pp. 21–2.
54. ERP 19, 23 July 1940; AIR 20/5777.

55. Air Ministry to Wavell, 25 May 1940; AIR 2/7244.
56. ERP committee minutes, 3 July 1940; AIR 20/3461.
57. War Cabinet 210 (40), 23 July 1940; CAB 65/8/22.
58. War Cabinet 240 (40), 3 September 1940; CAB 65/9/2.
59. 'Despatch of Aircraft to the Middle East', memorandum by Anthony Eden, Ministerial Committee on Military Policy in the Middle East, War Cabinet 387 (40); CAB 66/12/17.
60. War Cabinet 278 (40), 28 October 1940; CAB 65/9/40. As it turned out, the British did benefit from the diversion of thirty F4F-3A Grumman Wildcat naval fighters intended for Lend-Lease supply to Greece and then transferred after the fall of Greece in April 1941.
61. Figures compiled from quarterly summaries, 'Deliveries of American Aircraft to Overseas Commands and Dominion Governments by Destination', annual summaries, 'Exports from the United Kingdom to Overseas Commands', and annual summaries, 'Exports from the United Kingdom to other destinations'; AIR 20/2039
62. Including American aircraft imported to Britain and then exported overseas. Adjustments include the following additional aircraft: 101 in 1940, 651 in 1941, 748 in 1942 and 597 in 1943.
63. Excluding American aircraft imported to Britain and then exported overseas. Adjustments include the following reductions: thirty-seven in 1940, 178 in 1941, 467 in 1942 and 284 in 1943.
64. Excluding American aircraft imported to Britain and then exported overseas. Adjustments include the following reductions: one in 1940, 242 in 1941, 281 in 1942, and 313 in 1943.
65. Excluding American aircraft imported to Britain and then exported overseas. Adjustments include the following reductions: sixty-three in 1940 and 231 in 1941, with none thereafter.
66. Unless otherwise stated, all figures from AIR 20/2039.
67. Christopher Shores, Brian Cull and Nicola Malizia, *Air War for Yugoslavia, Greece and Crete 1940–41* (London: Grub Street, 1999), pp. 139–41, 304.
68. Haight, *American Aid*, p. 244; Christopher Shores, *Dust Clouds in the Middle East: The Air War for East Africa, Iraq, Syria, Iran and Madagascar, 1940–42* (London: Grub Street, 1996), pp. 199–269.
69. Aside from difficulties in maintaining aircraft without spares, and operating without self-sealing fuel tanks, opinions on the Marylands were positive. Christopher Shores, Brian Cull and Nicola Malizia, *Malta: The Hurricane Years 1940–1941* (London: Grub Street, 1987), pp. 404–5, 410–18.
70. Churchill to Roosevelt, C-40x, 21 November 1940; Kimball,

Complete Correspondence, p. 85; Churchill, *Finest Hour*, p. 482.

71. Figures distilled from AIR 20/2039. Associated destinations include Gibraltar, North Africa and Iraq. West Africa has been excluded; aircraft based here did not participate in combat under RAF Middle East Command or successor commands, such as Mediterranean Allied Air Forces, while aircraft ferried along the Takoradi air reinforcement route are counted under destination commands.
72. Figures from AIR 20/1892. Serviceable and unserviceable aircraft not in squadrons (in reserve, training and miscellaneous non-combat units) have been excluded.
73. Tedder, pp. 226, 234.
74. Tedder, pp. 73, 77.
75. Figures from AIR 20/1980.
76. Harriman and Abel, pp. 64–70.
77. Minute by CAS, War Cabinet (41) 133, 16 June 1941; CAB 66/17/6.
78. Minute by CAS, 16 June 1941; ibid.
79. Tedder, pp. 156–8, 218–24.
80. Alan P. Dobson, *FDR and Civil Aviation: Flying Strong Flying Free*, (New York: Palgrave, 2011), pp. 146–7.
81. 'Air Marshall Harris said it would be O.K. with them for PAA to take over the entire service, pilots, mechanics, installations, radio and everything else.' Item h); memorandum for General Arnold, minutes of meeting, 26 June 1941, Box 305, Hopkins papers. For Tedder's suspicions, Tedder, p. 158.
82. Tedder to Freeman, AOC 397, 30 November 1941; AIR 23/1722.
83. Tedder, p. 280.
84. Notes from Chiefs of Staff, paper C.O.S. 40, 23 July 1940; AIR 20/2113.
85. Dominions Office to High Commissions of Australia and New Zealand, G.5600, 30 January 1941; AIR 20/2113.
86. Air Ministry to C.-in-C. Far East, X.6942, 20 November 1941; ibid.
87. ERP committee, 8 November 1940; AIR 20/3461.
88. 'Allocation of Aircraft to the end of 1942', ERP committee, 21 August 1941; ibid. Actual deliveries from quarterly returns in AIR 20/2039.
89. In the first ATP Agreement, 'Allocations of American Aircraft during 1942', 4 January 1942; AIR 8/413.
90. Tedder, p. 343.
91. Bowyer, *Aircraft for the Few*, p. 241.
92. MAP memorandum, 18 December 1941; AIR 20/1834.

93. Aircraft serials for cash purchase Kittyhawk Is in the AK and AL range give way to Lend-Lease Kittyhawk IAs in the ET and EV range in June 1942. The 112 squadron serials are recorded in Robin Brown, *Shark Squadron: The History of 112 Squadron 1917–1975* (Cornwall: Crécy, 1994), p. 250. Baltimore IIIA deliveries from AIR 22/280.

6 Heavy Bomber Supply Diplomacy, 1941–2

> The Fighters are our salvation, but the bombers alone provide the means of victory.
>
> *Winston Churchill*[1]

The critical Allied defeats of 1940 had left the British geographically isolated and confined to a traditional strategy of naval blockade and peripheral ground campaigns, such as that developing in North Africa, designed to wear down a Continental enemy. By 1941, the aircraft involved in the 1940 purchase programme and the consequent '3,000 per month' plans behind Lend-Lease had been clearly directed towards relieving British aircraft production from this peripheral commitment. Yet that commitment was becoming increasingly marginal to British plans for the future. The strategic bombing offensive waged against Germany now became central to British strategy, and obtaining the heavy bombers necessary for expanding this campaign became a new focus of Anglo-American aircraft supply diplomacy after 1940.[2]

Intensifying the strategic bombing campaign required the dedication of enormous production resources. In the first place, wastage, or the loss of aircraft on operations, was substantial. As an example, between July and November 1941, Bomber Command lost 526 aircraft on operations – the equivalent of its entire front-line strength.[3] The most efficient policy to secure the quantity of replacement aircraft needed was to expand further the production of existing types. But this conflicted with the RAF's desire to improve aircraft quality, most notably by the introduction of heavy bombers to replace the medium bombers in service in 1940.

The Short Stirling, Handley-Page Halifax and Avro Manchester (and later Lancaster) were designed to have greater range and up to three times the bombloads of contemporary medium bombers, offering major economies in crewing, servicing and support at the same time as increasing the striking power of the bomber force.

All these new bomber types were entering production in 1940–1 but these were relatively complex aircraft and they all encountered the extensive teething problems associated with the introduction of new types to production and then service. This meant that deliveries had fallen behind schedule and operational serviceability remained low. Between September 1939 and June 1941, the RAF had expected to receive 243 Stirlings, 117 Halifaxes, and 194 Manchesters. In fact they received fifty-nine Stirlings, fifty-eight Halifaxes, and 103 Manchesters, or 40 per cent of their expectations.[4]

The end result of these problems was that heavy bombers were a marginal presence in RAF front-line strength by mid-1941. On 30 June 1941, Bomber Command returns reveal a strength of 45½ squadrons with 532 serviceable aircraft. The heavy bombers provided 6½ squadrons from this total but with only sixteen serviceable aircraft present (five Stirlings and eleven Halifaxes, and no Manchesters). Bomber Command's main strength consisted of older types, with seven squadrons of Blenheim light bombers, six squadrons of Hampden and Whitley medium bombers respectively, and twenty squadrons of Wellington medium bombers. The heavy bombers represented only 3 per cent of the aircraft available. This clearly demanded an increased production of heavy bombers, and Lend-Lease appeared to provide the means to do this beyond existing British resources.

Although two types of four-engined heavy bombers had entered production in the United States by 1941 (the Boeing B-17 Flying Fortress and the Consolidated B-24 Liberator), production figures were lower than for associated light and medium bombers. Lend-Lease production plans had initially been based on the so-called '3,000 per month' plan of July 1940, designed to increase the production of American military aircraft to three thousand per month by mid-1942. Only 250 heavy bombers were expected to be produced every month compared to six hundred light and medium bombers and four hundred dive-bombers.[5] These aircraft would have negligible potential for strategic bombing, lacking the range and bombload required. On the basis of RAF plans current with Lend-Lease, Bomber Command would have ninety-five bomber squadrons by the end of March 1942 but only thirty-nine of them would be heavy bombers and only five of these would be equipped with American aircraft.[6]

On this basis the British would be presented with large numbers of aircraft that could not fulfil the main strategic task facing the RAF. Reflecting the views of the RAF Air Staff that April, Sinclair regarded this as 'unacceptable':[7]

> . . . much of the American air effort now being mobilised will be in a form which will be almost valueless; and in saying that I referred to the huge mass of American light and medium bombers which is looming up on the American horizon.[8]

This problem of operational utility had direct implications for the prospects of continuing access to American supplies. As Sinclair observed:

> The Americans themselves continually express anxiety that we should be able to employ usefully the aircraft we get from them. These aircraft are certainly of very limited utility. The political consequences of failure to use possibly some thousands of aircraft might well be very serious.[9]

What made this more critical was the vast increase in British plans that followed Lend-Lease. These aimed to increase the size of the front-line heavy bomber strength of Bomber Command to four thousand operational aircraft by the spring of 1943, known to RAF planners as 'Target Force E'.[10] Even after the plan was revised in June 1941 to include medium bombers (mainly the Wellington) in the total, the interim targets remained extremely ambitious, with heavy bomber strength expected to rise to thirty-two squadrons of 512 aircraft by the end of the year, 172 squadrons by the end of 1942 and 252 squadrons by the target date of 1 April 1943, when Bomber Command would reach a strength of 4,176 aircraft, 96.6 per cent of which would be heavy bombers.[11]

This required the production of one thousand heavy bombers per month to be achieved by June 1942. Existing plans were estimated to reach five hundred heavy bombers per month from British factories at that point, with two hundred per month from the United States, leaving a deficiency of three hundred aircraft per month. In total the British now required seven thousand heavy bombers in 1942 and twelve thousand in 1943. British output in 1941 was expected to be 4,500, leaving a deficiency of 2,500 in that year alone.

At this point, the first appropriations for Lend-Lease supply were going forward, and the scope for any alteration of this programme would quickly diminish over time as the production lines involved were tooled up. Without a substantial diplomatic effort, the British might lose their only chance of influencing American aircraft production in favour of the types of aircraft their strategy required. Sinclair advised Churchill to take the issue up directly with Roosevelt while American plans for the creation of new production capacity were crystallising.[12] Portal had already prepared the ground by attempting to influence the USAAC in favour of heavy bomber production during the ABC negotiations.[13]

The message was then reinforced during Arnold's visit to Britain in April when Sinclair advised Beaverbrook that 'extreme pressure' and 'immediate action' would be necessary to divert US industry into the production of the required types.[14] Already wedded to the concept of strategic bombing for doctrinal reasons to justify USAAC independence from the US Army, Arnold proved receptive and reproduced British opinions almost verbatim to the US War Department.[15]

> The number of heavy type bombers needed from America is greatly in excess of our present production plant. Portal and the rest of the chiefs in the Air Ministry very emphatically stress the need for more heavy bombers from us . . . To get 4,000 bombers by the spring of 1943, a big step-up in production is necessary and the deficit must come from the US . . . Light bombers are of secondary importance and do not in any way make up for our failure to deliver heavy bombers.[16]

By early May, Hopkins and Harriman confirmed a planned production figure of five hundred four-engined bombers per month (to be reached in 1943) and an overall acceleration of the production schedule.[17] But this still lagged behind British plans, with 205 heavy bombers per month expected by June 1942 when the British wanted five hundred. The only way to achieve this increase was to reallocate production away from light and medium bombers to the heavy bomber types. The stage was set for a renewed effort to recast both American production plans and allocations to the British in favour of the heavy bomber.

What made this far more politically sensitive was the experience the British had accumulated to date with the American heavy bombers. As early as September 1940, evaluations of early variants of the B-17 and B-24 had been pessimistic, with both being regarded as unsuited to operational use. Aside from having smaller bombloads than the equivalent British types, the American bombers suffered from what the RAF considered to be a lack of essential operational equipment, such as defensive armour, power-operated gun turrets, self-sealing fuel tanks and flame-damped exhausts for night operations. The British had tried and failed to introduce their own heavy bomber designs into American production plans which left them with no alternative but to accept US types while deploying them in roles other than bombing operations, at the same time pressing for the addition of the equipment they deemed necessary. Early delivery models of the Liberator were a case in point. '. . . [we] regard the B-24 as an insurance or as an aircraft for use on less arduous fronts and in conditions which favour its less desirable features'.[18]

This qualitative appreciation led to the employment of the first Liberators to be received from cash purchase contract deliveries as transport aircraft on the transatlantic air ferry then being established, with subsequent deliveries being used for long-range anti-submarine warfare (ASW) duties in the Battle of the Atlantic. This tension, evident between British supply objectives and their operational deployment policy, became particularly controversial in the case of the B-17 Fortress.

First ordered in 1935 for coastal defence, and equipped with the gyroscopically stabilised Norden bombsight, the B-17 offered the potential capacity as a strategic bomber needed to vindicate USAAC ambitions for service independence from the US Army. As such, B-17s represented the most politically valuable aircraft in the USAAC inventory. As Arnold put it in his memoir; '. . . our whole fight for an Air Force had come to center more and more around bombardment, precision bombardment by daylight, all the things summed up by the great word "B-17".'[19]

Originally rejected on the grounds of cost by pre-war British purchase missions, the supply of B-17s had become an issue in 1940 when the RAF had agreed to a proposal to request twenty B-17s from the United States. Though interested in securing as many American aircraft as possible, the Air Ministry doubted the value of the B-17s, with their interest being largely to test their potential and to demonstrate to the USAAC the need for any equipment improvements.[20] Initial opposition from the US services was overcome, in part, by replacement of the top-secret Norden bombsight with a Sperry model.

After three months delay caused by the need to fit the aircraft with self-sealing fuel tanks, the first B-17 was ferried across the Atlantic by a USAAC crew on 14 April 1941. Subsequent ferrying operations, handled by civilian crews attached to the British Ministry of Aircraft Production (MAP), attracted War Department criticism for the delays involved and the behaviour of the crews.[21] The MAP took the point. 'We cannot do too much to impress upon the United States authorities with our high opinions of the B-17.'[22]

This was to become increasingly difficult as the Fortress entered RAF service with 90 Squadron. With RAF bombers compelled to operate by night to avoid interception, it was intended to exploit the high-altitude performance provided by the B-17s' turbo-charged engines to launch extremely high-altitude daylight raids. The evident lack of success which followed was to cause serious political controversy with a direct impact on supply diplomacy.

The first instance of this arose during the lengthy period during which the B-17s were modified and re-equipped for operations, leaving only four serviceable out of the fourteen delivered by 24 May.[23] The serviceability problems involved were detailed in a critical report by General Harmon of the US observer group in Britain. The arrival of this report in Washington led to Air Commodore George Pirie, the British Air Attaché, being summoned by General Brett who was temporarily in charge of USAAC headquarters during Arnold's absence in Britain. By this account Harmon's report had come as a 'bombshell' which had stirred up 'a hornet's nest' with the USAAC staff being extremely bitter about the RAF's 'apparent gross slight on their pet aeroplane'. As he informed Portal:

> Slessor has no doubt told you of the inordinate regard Air Corps has for B.17, and how bitterly they resent criticism of it . . . we must mollify them and assure them we so appreciate their efforts. This is particularly important as BAC are now negotiating with Army for additional B.17s and situation reported above has made their task most difficult.[24]

Portal's hasty response on 5 May assured Arnold that the British 'were delighted' with the B-17 and 'longing to have more as soon as possible'.[25] Nonetheless, by the end of the month, Harriman warned the British that the B-17's operational use '. . . had become a political question of some importance'.[26] This clearly demanded the management of critical USAAC reports from Britain, and it is significant that, while Harmon's report of 3 May was never seen by anybody in the RAF until the Air Attaché was carpeted in Washington, his next report on 24 May was copied by Harriman directly to Portal.[27]

The RAF was not to be rushed by this pressure, however, and continued the slow process of training for high-altitude operations, leading to further USAAF complaints (the USAAC became the US Army Air Force in June 1941).[28] By July, operational missions had begun but these were plagued with technical problems, notably engine oil loss at high altitude. One of the reasons for persevering was the political dimension involved, as the Air Staff notified the C.-in-C. of Bomber Command that month:

> You know, of course, how large a part the use and success we make of the 'Fortress' plays in our relations with the United States. We fully

> realise the difficulties which the continued focussing of the political spotlight on the 'Fortress' may cause you, but I am afraid this is the price we have to pay for obtaining all the aircraft we so badly need from America now that this has become increasingly dependent on their good-will and on their estimate of our use of what they send us under the operation of the lease and lend policy.[29]

Partly as a consequence, 90 Squadron struggled to conduct missions throughout July and into September 1941. The human and technical difficulties of flying at over 32,000 feet in unpressurised aircraft remained intense, and sorties were frequently aborted because of problems such as the breakdown of heating or oxygen supplies. Interceptions by German fighters began to mount, and it became apparent that the defensive protection and armament were inadequate. British tests indicated that the Fortress was difficult, but not impossible, to intercept and the crew stood little hope of evading or outfighting their attackers if a successful interception was achieved.[30]

A further problem, even closer to the heart of USAAF ambitions than the self-defensive potential of the Fortress, was the level of bombing accuracy actually achievable under operational conditions. After criticism from a Sperry technician of the level of accuracy obtained by the RAF, the technician involved was permitted to fly as a bomb-aimer on an operational mission to Bremen. To the ill-concealed satisfaction of the Air Staff, he missed the target by over 3 miles.[31]

Air Staff opinion concluded that the Fortress was unable to do more than make harassing raids in good weather, and it would be more economical to use the pressurised Wellington then under development or the new de Havilland Mosquito for that purpose. Meanwhile, the nadir of the B-17's fortunes in RAF service was reached elsewhere. As the arrival of winter weather further affected high-altitude operations in Britain, a detachment of four B-17s was sent to the Middle East in October to conduct 'experimental' efforts in high-altitude bombing.[32] The results were poor and, by early 1942, the two surviving B-17s were unserviceable in India from where they were eventually transferred back to the USAAF.[33] Arnold's verdict on all this was unsympathetic: '. . . in the RAF's hands in 1941, the long-awaited combat showing of the B-17's was a fiasco'.[34]

The remaining Fortresses in Britain were tested and rejected as night bombers owing to the problems of flame-damping their exhausts, and, by the end of January 1942, the aircraft and crews had been transferred to Coastal Command for long-range ASW patrols.[35] The situation with the early variants of the B-24 Liberator was similar.

In June, the Air Staff attempted to accelerate the entry of the first Liberator squadron into service with Coastal Command on the grounds that '. . . we do not want to repeat the hold-up which has been experienced with the Boeing B-17'.[36] But the same issues of modification and equipment obtained, particularly because of the need to fit Coastal Command Liberators with Anti-Surface Vessel radar. By 24 September, a survey of the Liberator aircraft available listed only three out of the total of fifteen aircraft fully modified and fit for use.[37] This state of affairs did not pass uncriticised by the USAAF, precisely as the RAF had feared.

> The inability of the British Government to properly employ these aircraft in the theatre of operations gives rise to the conclusion that further deliveries of B-24 aircraft covered on British Lend-Lease requisition #65 should be deferred until the RAF demonstrates the capability of employing these aircraft in actual tactical conditions.[38]

These complaints were passed on to Churchill by Hopkins when he visited Britain in July 1941 to prepare the ground for the Atlantic conference. Churchill, in turn, passed the criticism of American heavy bombers 'lying idle' on to Portal with the recommendation that they be used in the strategic bombing of Germany.[39] Portal's response established the reality that the RAF was labouring under. The Fortress was afflicted with serious technical problems while the defensive armament and state of equipment of the first Liberators delivered made them 'unsuitable for bombing Germany either by night or by day'. Using them for ASW patrols freed British bombers for strategic bombing.[40] This was the situation behind the scenes as the British pressed their heavy bomber supply agenda but, clearly, this could not be revealed in public.

Instead, Hopkins's visit was used to extol American aircraft supply for morale purposes. During a radio broadcast on 27 July, he referred to twenty US bombers which had flown across the Atlantic with him.[41] Only one B-17 had been ferried across the Atlantic in July, and no Liberators. Hopkins was almost certainly referring to Lockheed Hudsons which were, at this point, being ferried by air across the Atlantic: nine were imported in the week ending 19 July, with a further twenty-five in the week after (some of them by sea).[42] These represented the great majority of the 168 aircraft delivered by the Atlantic air ferry that month.[43] Hopkins was, understandably, eliding over the fact that these aircraft were not front-line bombers and that they were all (including the single B-17) products of British cash purchase contracts. The aircraft involved were certainly not dropping bombs over Germany or occupied Europe as Hopkins's script suggested.[44]

The British wanted the American heavy bombers to be improved as a result of their experience and then supplied on a massive scale while, at the same time, deflecting USAAF attempts to divert them for their own use. Reconciling this with the RAF's deployment policy required a sustained campaign to contain the potential damage caused by the USAAF reaction to the RAF's initial experience with American heavy bombers. The prompt reaction of the RAF to Harmon's criticisms in early May 1941 was a case in point, with regular subsequent attempts being made to explain the technical problems involved.[45]

By July the British had already detected the chill hand of hostile USAAF influence on their allocations as a result of the promises made by Churchill and Roosevelt to supply the Soviet Union.[46] During this period the US service departments were drawing up the 'Victory Plan', a comprehensive schedule of the American production required to meet all US and Allied munitions demands for the defeat of the Axis powers; it would shape US industrial strategy for the rest of the war. They continued to press for an increase in heavy bomber production in June and July in the runup to the Atlantic conference which was held off the coast of Newfoundland between 9 and 12 August 1941.[47]

The British had several aims at this conference, not least the coordination of British and US foreign policy in the Far East where a stiffening American diplomatic resistance to Japanese expansion, without any undertaking towards defensive collaboration with the British, was believed to be dangerously exposing British possessions to attack. A further objective was the establishment of personal contact between the British and US chiefs of staff. This carried the implicit hope that such direct personal contact might overcome American resistance to British strategy, such as the commitment to the Middle East, which was believed to conflict with the 'Germany first' priority agreed in the ABC discussions of the previous spring.

At the conference itself, the British hoped to convince the US service chiefs of the importance of strategic bombing, as a corollary of which Air Marshal Sir Wilfred Freeman, Vice Chief of the Air Staff, had been sent to galvanise American heavy bomber production. Freeman had been warned that, as British deliveries from cash purchase contracts were completed, future aircraft allocation under Lend-Lease would be increasingly in the hands of the US services.[48] He had been warned that the progress of the US towards more active involvement in the war would make defending British allocations more difficult as US requirements rose but he was nonetheless expected to 'rescue what he could' from the Slessor agreement.[49]

Arnold's co-operation was therefore central to the achievement of British plans, and this was contingent upon his acceptance of the British use of the aircraft involved. As he stated in his diary before the conference began, he wanted to restrict the aid supplied to competitors such as the British, the Soviets and the Chinese to items which they could 'use effectively'.[50] Arnold's position in their early talks at the conference confirmed Freeman's fears that the British were unlikely to get any increase in heavy bomber supply and that the US services did not regard the Slessor agreement as binding.[51]

Freeman's objectives to increase heavy bomber supply to the RAF therefore had serious hurdles to overcome. He opened with deliberately high stakes presented on the basis of a revised '4,000 bomber' plan.[52]

Freeman's production figures were conservative, pushing American delivery estimates back by three months but, even if US

Table 6.1 'Heavy Bombers'; Freeman memorandum, 9 August 1941[53]

	1 Aug '41 to 31 Dec '42	1 Jan '43 to 31 Mar '43	1 Apr '43 to 30 June '43	Total
Total requirements	6,520	3,000	3,000	12,520
British production	3,620	1,404	1,508	6,532
US production	1,395	723	1,039	3,157
Deficiencies	−1,505	−873	−453	−2,831

production matched expectations, this would still leave the British with a deficiency of almost 1,400 bombers. Freeman's figures – as he admitted – assumed that the whole of US heavy bomber production would be made available to the British.

The scale of the demand shocked Arnold who saw it as 'wishful thinking'.[54] In response, he presented Freeman with the latest USAAF supply forecasts, and these made grim reading. Only 113 Liberators were expected to be produced against British orders in the period August–December 1941. The British would get no further heavy bombers at all until deliveries of B-17s would resume in August 1942 (five months after the British had expected them) and those of B-24s would resume in October 1942 (when the British had been expecting a constant supply from Lend-Lease to follow their own orders).[55] Arnold's forecasts allocated a total of 290 B-17s and 165 B-24s to Britain, or 455 aircraft in total, 85 per cent of which would be delivered in the last quarter of 1942.[56] This gave the British 568 heavy bombers from the United States at a time when Freeman's figures indicated that they had been expecting 1,395 and when they were demanding an increase to 1,900.

Freeman's negotiations were not fruitless, however, as Arnold welcomed an increase in heavy bomber production, even if he was resistant to this benefiting the RAF at the expense of USAAF expansion plans. Under pressure, he moved from denying the British any releases from USAAF contracts to accepting a continuing allocation of 50 per cent of production once American needs had been met.[57] This pressure almost certainly originated from the access the administration's civilian officials had to the president, as Freeman had admitted beforehand: 'Our hope is therefore in extent to which Harriman and Hopkins are willing to and can influence President in our favour'.[58]

Freeman understood that Arnold himself was subject to the hostility of the United States Army hierarchy and the United States Navy towards the prioritisation of heavy bombers in the US rearmament programme. This confirmed the paramount importance of civilian officials, such as Hopkins and Harriman, with their direct link to Roosevelt for British attempts to change US production strategy.[59] The influence of these agents on US procurement and allocation policy, while real, was limited. The resistance of the other US services to the whole concept of a major increase in heavy bomber production for an unproven strategy of strategic bombing also remained an unresolved problem. As Freeman said, 'There is immense good will but that is all and we want more.'[60]

The extent to which American aircraft supply to Britain was undergoing a crisis, and one which was confirmed rather than resolved by the Atlantic conference, has tended to be ignored. Even when they question the concrete strategic outcomes of the conference, historians have tended to assume that the developing diplomatic relationship between Britain and the United States was reflected in a growing impact of US supply on the British war effort. One example is Theodore Wilson's reference to British bombers accompanied by American-made Liberators returning to their bases on 11 August after conducting raids on Germany during the conference.[61]

The reality was considerably different from this assumption. That night, Bomber Command despatched ninety-three bombers to attack Rotterdam, Krefeld and Mönchengladbach; none of the aircraft involved was American. The following day, the RAF launched a rare large-scale deep-penetration daylight raid by fifty-four Blenheim light bombers against power stations near Cologne. Out of the seventy-eight bombers involved, including diversion and supporting raids, the only American aircraft were four Fortresses from 90 Squadron.[62] The first RAF Liberator operations were flown by Coastal Command a month after the conference.

A sense of failure was evident at the time, as Freeman expressed to Hopkins:

> When I left England I had hoped that it might be possible to get some more heavy bombers from America than we had been led to expect, but it was made clear to me at my first meeting with Arnold that, far from getting more, we were going to get very considerably less.[63]

On his return to London, despite talking up the achievements of the conference, Churchill admitted that American production was 'somewhat disappointing'.[64] This was amplified by the details of chiefs of staff's report which observed the failure to honour the Slessor agreement and to reach the targets associated with the '4,000 plan'.[65] Characteristically, Beaverbrook, now Minister of Supply, had a more intemperate response, demanding that British procurement officials in Washington be replaced by 'toughs'. 'Plans, papers and programmes were always produced – but never the goods. Promises were useless.'[66]

Those officials took a longer and more sanguine view. Achieving the relevant production increases would require the adoption of a war economy, redirecting US civilian production towards military needs. Without such measures in the next three months, there was no prospect of production being dramatically improved before the end of 1942.[67] Despite their failure at the Atlantic conference, the British continued their pressure for '500 bombers per month' after the conference on this basis.[68]

One encouraging straw in the wind from the British perspective was the conclusion of the first Moscow protocol in October 1941 which established a monthly quota of fighters and light bombers to be supplied to the Soviet Union by Britain and the US for the next nine months. The British initially regarded the protocol agreement as a success, specifically because it deflected the Soviets away from British bomber requirements and increased their chances of receiving a larger allotment from the US.[69] These hopes were not borne out, however, and by the end of September the British were informed that they would receive a grand total of 7,534 combat aircraft from US production in the period September 1941 to June 1942 instead of the 12,748 expected under the Slessor agreement, and only 188 out of the 513 heavy bombers expected.[70]

The British response was to renew their diplomatic offensive with Hopkins and the president. Again, there were some minor grounds for encouragement as, despite favouring further USAAF heavy bomber reinforcement of the Philippines, Roosevelt over-ruled War Department desires to establish a heavy bomber unit in Newfoundland to allocate a further 100 to 150 heavy bombers to the British between February and June 1942, with further bombers to follow in the second quarter of 1942 if war had not broken out with Japan by then.[71] This would amount to half of US heavy bomber production, or up to 389 aircraft, in a period where Arnold had proposed at the Atlantic conference that the British receive none. Hopkins also leaked figures which suggested that Arnold now appeared willing to maintain his commitment at the Atlantic conference, with 674 out of 1,383 heavy bombers produced in the second half of 1942 being allocated to Lend-Lease, and thereby potentially to the British.[72] This at least was a marginal improvement on the 568 aircraft Arnold had promised at the Atlantic conference though a long way short of the 1,900 Freeman had asked for in the same period.

The post-conference situation was summed up by Sinclair on 2 September. This detailed Air Ministry returns on 1 September which indicated that the RAF was lagging about sixteen squadrons behind the current '4,000 plan' even when the target date was extended to the end of 1943. The production figures for the first eight months of 1941 demonstrated the continuing problem.

MAP returns that August confirmed that the British had received: fifty heavy bombers from domestic production and two from the United States and Canada; 237 medium bombers against fourteen; and 100 light bombers against 137. Though British

Table 6.2 Bomber deliveries for January–August 1941[73]

	UK deliveries			US deliveries		
	Planned	Actual	Deficiency	Planned	Actual	Deficiency
Heavy bombers	502	257	−235 (46 per cent)	91	21	−70 (77 per cent)
Medium and light bombers	3,428	2,896	−532 (15 per cent)	580	344	−236 (49 per cent)

production was finally beginning to rise, American bomber deliveries were expected to be disappointing.[74] This brought into question the value of American industrial capacity and, indeed, the whole 'Arsenal of Democracy' thesis central to Lend-Lease. As Portal put it:

> It is an astonishing fact that according to the latest forecast the British production of heavy bombers remains very much ahead of that of the United States throughout the whole of 1942. Remembering the vast resources of the United States, their freedom from enemy action and their virtually untapped manpower, it is all too clear how wide is the gap between American potentialities and American performance and how much remains to be done if they are to redeem their promise to be the arsenal of the democracies and give effect to their determination 'to devote their entire industrial effort to the prosecution of the war'.[75]

One unwelcome aspect of this reality was that the RAF had to consider relaxing the rigidity of their quality agenda by extending production of the Wellington and even equipping as many squadrons as possible with the British twin-engined Albemarle medium bomber despite its 'miserable performance'.[76] That Portal was willing to consider them as operational bombers, albeit with severe limitations, indicates the pressure for numbers involved in British expansion plans by the end of 1941. But the significance of the Albemarle should not be overstated – only five hundred were due to be produced, with perhaps one squadron equipped by the end of 1941.

A more significant aspect of the quality agenda was expressed in the British desire to see the Lancaster bomber – which was recognised by the British to have the best performance of all the available heavy bombers at this point, with a bombload of over twice that of the American types – begin manufacture in the United States. This led to a short but illuminating return to the 'battle of the types' conducted the previous year when the British had attempted to convince the Americans to build British aircraft types.[77] The concept of getting the Lancaster into American production plans was broached with Hopkins in September but met a predictable response from the USAAF. Arnold rejected the suggestion on the legitimate grounds of the delayed production associated with the introduction of a new type which would require extensive retooling of existing production lines. He further doubted that the Lancaster could outperform the Liberator, as the British claimed.[78] Arnold's rejection of the Lancaster left the British unable to balance an improvement in individual bombload against a decline in the numbers of bombers supplied.

A further attempt to settle both the heavy bomber supply dilemma and the question of aircraft allocations as a whole was at the 'Arcadia' conference held between Churchill, Roosevelt and their chiefs of staff in Washington between 22 December 1941 and 14 January 1942 immediately after Pearl Harbor and US entry into the war. The strategic discussions largely confirmed the 'Germany first' strategy established by the ABC talks, and established joint Anglo-American staff machinery in the form of the Combined Chiefs of Staff and their subordinate committees in Washington. Munitions procurement and distribution were also among the most important aspects of the conference. 'In fact, no issue provoked more heated debate during Arcadia than that of war production and allocation. It was political to the core.'[79]

Aircraft allocation was no exception as the British sought a binding replacement for the defunct Slessor Agreement. Arnold and Portal now had the opportunity to go into American aircraft allocation in a series of direct personal meetings. One of Portal's aims was to defend against any diversion of heavy bombers to the Pacific theatre; the RAF's objective was to continue the focus of American heavy bomber supply against Germany whether crewed by the RAF or by the USAAF.[80] At this point, Arnold seemed to be more optimistic about production capacity under the stimulus of war, eventually agreeing with Portal that the British would receive a monthly quota of B-17s and B-24s throughout 1942.[81] In the resulting first ATP agreement, Arnold was willing to allocate 275 B-17s and 314 B-24s to the RAF in 1942.[82] Nonetheless, the outcome allocated the British few more American heavy bombers in the whole of 1942 than they had been previously expecting to receive every month that year.

The sense of optimism surrounding the first ATP agreement would not last and the same pressures that were evident in 1941 soon reasserted themselves. The first problem was the continuation of the British diversion of American heavy bombers to roles other than the bombing of Germany. At the beginning of February, Harris, just before he left Washington to assume his new post as C.-in-C. of Bomber Command, warned of the possible repercussions of using the promised Fortresses for long-range ASW patrols in Coastal Command.

> I cannot impress upon you too strongly the extremely bad impression created by the proposed diversion of 275 B-17s this year to Coastal Command. Their ewe lambs, the finest bombers in the world, etc etc. It is my personal view that apart from other ill-effects on inter-service relations persistence in this diversion may well result in the total loss to us of these aircraft on [the] score [that] if we don't use them for their proper function the US Air Forces can and will. Of course I appreciate your reasons but in such matters US are not disposed to reason.[83]

Portal believed that '. . . we must take serious note of this warning', and asked the Air Staff to consider the use of the Martin B-26 Marauder medium bomber promised in 1942 as an alternative, observing that: 'I feel that the political consequences of persisting in our original intention may be so-far reaching that I must at least examine this proposed alternative'.[84] The Marauder was a non-starter, however, at that point enduring a high accident rate in development and training that eventually demanded a modified wing profile to resolve, as well as lacking the range required by Coastal Command. Portal then attempted to defend the RAF's deployment policy to Arnold, observing that only forty-five B-17s were destined for Coastal Command, and that the B-17 had a lower bombload than the B-24 which involved the minimum reduction in striking power by diverting any of the existing heavy bomber types away from the bombing offensive.[85]

Arnold was not convinced. At the beginning of February 1942, he was already having second thoughts about the British allocations in the first ATP agreement.[86] By April he had raised the issue of renegotiating the ATP agreement in Washington and, by the end of May, Arnold had visited Britain to conduct the negotiations that led up to the second ATP agreement of June 1942. The British had been informed by Hopkins of the political significance attached to increasing USAAF allocations. Hopkins had referred to the administration 'facing an uprising' if aircraft were delivered to the British while USAAF crews stood idle; in addition, there was the USAAF's belief in the superiority of American crews for American aircraft on the grounds of national exceptionalism.[87] This political dimension was a primary reason for the eventual acceptance by the British of allocations revised in USAAF favour. But Balfour did gain a revealing response about the perception of the ATP agreement when he questioned Hopkins about why it could have been made in the first place if it needed to be revised so quickly.

> Hopkins reply was that this agreement was probably entered into by Arnold before he appreciated public feeling and USA Army feeling described above. At any rate the President and the White House knew nothing of Arnold/Portal agreement . . . so far as President is concerned Arnold/Portal agreement ranks something like the Slessor agreement did.[88]

While Arnold's negotiations, which lead up to the second ATP agreement, will be examined in detail subsequently, it is instructive to note that the same concern about the British misuse of American heavy bombers was evident from the beginning. Arnold had flown in to Britain via the transatlantic ferry route and had landed at Prestwick in Scotland. Observing the number of Liberators being modified for Coastal Command there, he noted, '. . . from my point of view, too many of the planes were just standing there when they were badly needed elsewhere'.[89] Arnold raised the problem when Portal attempted to secure enough Fortress and Liberator replacements to maintain the five squadrons of VLR aircraft required in Coastal Command. 'The Army Air Force [USAAF] are definitely opposed to utilising heavy bombardment planes for anything but heavy bombardment missions.'[90]

This was not unexpected. In April, Freeman had even gone as far as suggesting that it was 'undesirable' that the Americans should learn of the renewed supply of Liberators to Coastal Command (due to delays in the planned receipt of B-17s originally allotted to them in 1942), and had to be corrected by a subordinate who pointed out that this would violate agreed procedure for aircraft allocation by the Combined Boards in Washington.[91]

Arnold continued negotiations with the British, including a visit to Chequers to see Churchill on 30 May when Harris, appointed the new Bomber Command C.-in-C. that February, staged the first of a short series of spectacular raids on German cities involving one thousand RAF bombers.[92] Meanwhile, apparently as a response to his observations at Prestwick, Arnold assigned Colonel Eugene Beebe, his aide and personal pilot, to perform a survey of British maintenance procedures to investigate the delay involved between delivery and deployment of American aircraft in British service.[93] Beebe's report was predictably critical of British practice which, though it may have satisfied Arnold's prejudices, was dismissed as 'superficial' by General Chaney, the USAAF commanding general in Britain.

What annoyed the British was that they had addressed similar criticisms made in a report by General Brett in 1941 by pointing out the long modification times required to install in Britain operational equipment, such as armour, self-sealing fuel tanks and improved oxygen systems. The obvious conclusion had been to install this equipment at the factory in later production aircraft. The extent to which the USAAF consented to such modifications on production aircraft had a clear impact on their suitability for operations in RAF hands. For example, the USAAF did not dispute the necessity, revealed by British experience, for armour, improved armament and the installation of self-sealing fuel tanks in the B-17. But the USAAF's rejection of night bombing, and the parallel rejection of the American heavy bombers for daylight bombing by the RAF, left the British struggling well into 1942 to convince the Americans to adopt the flame-damped exhausts needed on night bombers.[94]

In this particular case, Brett's report and the British response had apparently disappeared into the ether on Brett's reassignment to the Middle East, leaving the British to face a repeat of what they considered to be ill-founded criticisms a year later at another sensitive point in Anglo-American aircraft supply diplomacy.[95] The end result of all this was predictable enough: British allocations of American heavy bombers were reduced to a total of fifty-four Liberators to be received between June and December 1942.[96]

Throughout 1941 and 1942 disappointing levels of production had increased the competition from the USAAF for heavy bomber output. This had been intensified by USAAF suspicions of the RAF's qualitative deployment policy which relegated American heavy bombers to roles other than that of strategic bombing. As a result, the British were unable to secure their objectives in heavy bomber supply before the entry of the United States into the war and the deployment of American heavy bombers to the USAAF's own strategic bombing effort. Ironically, this in itself was subject to similar problems of serviceability, equipment and German opposition, which left Arnold directing his suspicions over the effective employment of American heavy bombers to his subordinate commanders of the USAAF strategic bombing force in Britain. In the event, the first strategic bombing raid conducted against German targets by USAAF B-17s took place in January 1943.

The cumulative disappointment the British faced with American supply in this area was one issue; the impact this had on their strategic planning was another and perhaps more interesting outcome. Churchill's summary after the Atlantic conference was indicative. 'He would certainly be prepared to press the United States to increase their production but no reliance should be placed on a successful outcome. We must rely on our own efforts.'[97]

British plans in September 1941 stuck to the modified Target Force E plan which required twenty-two thousand bombers to be delivered between July 1941 and July 1943, only 5,500 of which could now be expected from the United States. British production targets were then raised from eleven thousand to 14,500 to make up most of the difference.[98] This required an exhaustive and detailed process to prepare the ground for a substantial modification of existing British production priorities in an economy that was now approaching full mobilisation.[99] This represented a significant change in the way American aircraft supply was viewed. No longer were the British considering using American production to make up the deficiency in their plans; now they were considering increasing British production to make up the deficiency in American deliveries.

A month before Pearl Harbor, Churchill defended in cabinet government policy towards the United States in rhetoric that would be echoed by the conventional understanding of the evolution of the Anglo-American supply relationship and Roosevelt's own personal influence in particular.

> In the last twelve months American opinion had moved under his leadership to an extent which nobody could have anticipated. They had made immense credits available to us; they had made immense resources available to us under the Lend-Lease Act; their Navy was escorting the Atlantic convoys; and finally they were taking a firm line with the Japanese.[100]

This was not quite how matters were perceived at the coalface of the British aircraft procurement machinery where it was observed a few days after Churchill's statements that '. . . money under Lease Lend appropriation is critically tight', with hopes being invested in a third Congressional appropriation (due in early 1942) involving a request for $2 billion to fund the supply of an additional two thousand heavy bombers.[101] The same month the RAF criticised the wider reality of American aircraft supply, noting how their plans had depended on a large supply of American aircraft since the collapse of France and how Lend-Lease seemed to set the seal on those expectations.[102] The following period had seen those hopes dashed to the point where American supply could be described as a failure.

Ultimately, British aviation supply diplomacy had failed to alter the low priority afforded to heavy bombers by the USN and War Department in time to have any impact on British allocations. Although they had won Arnold's support on the matter of creating new capacity, production from this capacity would not materialise in time to alleviate the present competition for allocations; a competition in which they could sense their position declining. In the meantime, aircraft supply diplomacy had been marked by the unilateral abrogation by the USAAF of the Slessor Agreement which the British had believed to be the basis of their plans for American aircraft supply.[103]

Accounts of the bomber supply issue in 1941 tend to gloss over the reality of British disappointment and celebrate the role of agents like Hopkins, Harriman and even Freeman while obscuring the role actually played by Arnold.[104] As Hopkins observed to Slessor, in what can only have been a pointed reference to Arnold and his staff, 'You are liable to find that, even when it's all signed up, the boys muscle in.'[105] This illustrated the limits to which British supply diplomacy could function, regardless of the sympathy of Roosevelt and his civilian appointees charged with expediting supply to the British. In September 1941 the head of the RAF Delegation in Washington observed:

> It is a mistake to imagine that contact and discussion with individuals such as Arnold, Lovett, Stimson and even Hopkins and the President is the path to accomplishment here . . . their promises often peter out to nothing in practice through material lack or departmental opposition . . .[106]

The ambitious plans associated with American supply mattered little beside the deliveries which actually took place and which governed the actual war effort that resulted. The delivery figures tell their own story. Between January 1941 and the end of 1943 the RAF received 7,421 heavy bombers; 7,017 of them (95 per cent) came from domestic production.[107] The quantitative and qualitative limitations on American heavy bomber supply ensured that Bomber Command's operational effort would remain contingent upon British aircraft production. It is significant that this was clearly understood at the time. Even at the very beginning of the British campaign for increased heavy bomber supply, Air Ministry planners were admitting a sense of realistic caution. 'The consensus of opinion was that it was useless to hope for the production of heavy bombers in the USA to reach a rate of 500 per month by June 1942.'[108]

This was even more marked in the opinion of Slessor himself. With the jaundiced eye born of his experience as a group commander in Bomber Command in mid-1941, waiting for the obsolete Hampdens in his squadrons to be replaced by chronically unreliable Manchesters and the uncertain prospect of eventual Lancaster deliveries, he regarded the '4,000-plan' as 'an opium-smoker's dream'.[109]

In view of this, British aircraft supply diplomacy must be understood to have operated in an exhortatory manner. Deliberately ambitious plans were presented to stimulate future heavy bomber production expansion against considerable opposition from the other US services hostile to the idea of strategic bombing. Increasing supply would then help overcome USAAF resistance and secure a reliable allocation to supplement their own production of heavy bombers which they continued to regard as qualitatively most effective.

The British reaction to the failure of these plans in the heavy bomber supply diplomacy of 1941 is instructive. Instead of abandoning their plans, they responded by increasing their own production of heavy bombers to a level sufficient for the RAF to wage the historical strategic bombing campaign against Germany in 1941–3. That this campaign was waged by fewer bombers than planned, or that it was based on wild overestimates of the effectiveness of the strategy involved, are less important from this perspective than the demonstration of the enduring constraints on American aircraft supply to Britain and the British reaction to the operation of those constraints.

The quantitative and qualitative limitations on heavy bomber supply had compelled the British to adopt greater dependence upon domestic production to fulfil their strategic plans; the same dynamic would be present in the supply of fighter aircraft which would culminate in a crisis during 1942. This would feature a reversal of the usual direction of dependency when the British supplied their own fighter aircraft to the United States to secure both a minimum quantity of American aircraft supply at the same time as successfully imposing their qualitative agenda on the USAAF.

Notes

1. 'The Munitions Situation', 3 September 1940; Churchill, *Finest Hour*, p. 405; Richards, *Fight at Odds*, p. 229.
2. This chapter is drawn largelyl from Gavin Bailey, 'An Opium Smoker's Dream: Anglo-American Heavy Bomber Diplomacy at the Atlantic Conference 1941', in the *Journal of Transatlantic Studies*, Vol. 11, No. 4 (2013).
3. Martin Middlebrook and Chris Everitt, *The Bomber Command War Diaries: An Operational Reference Book 1939–1945* (Leicester: Midland, 1996), p. 220.
4. Production and programme figures from AIR 20/2039.
5. William S. Knudsen to Arthur Purvis, '3,000 Planes per Month Program', 31 July 1940; AVIA 38/14.
6. Air Marshal Sir Christopher Courtney, Air Member for Supply and Organisation (AMSO), to Portal, 22 March 1941; AIR 8/404. Squadron establishment at this time was sixteen aircraft.
7. Sinclair to Churchill, 2 April 1941; AIR 8/404.
8. Sinclair to Beaverbrook, 24 April 1941; ibid.
9. Sinclair to Churchill, 2 April 1941; ibid.
10. 'Production of Heavy Bombers', memorandum from Sinclair to War Cabinet, 8 May 1941; ibid.
11. Target Force 'E' figures from 'Expansion of the Metropolitan Air Force, July 1941 to March 1943'; ibid.
12. Sinclair to Churchill, 1 May 1941; ibid.
13. Portal to Slessor, X.482, 3 April 1941; AIR 20/2868.
14. Sinclair to Beaverbrook, 22 April 1941; AIR 8/404.
15. Arnold diary entries, 13 and 16 April 1941; Huston, pp. 140, 144; Furse, pp. 215, 216–17
16. Arnold to War Department, Secret Cable from London No. 1027, 18 April 1941; Box 306, Hopkins papers.
17. Hopkins to Harriman, 6 May 1941; Box 305, Hopkins papers, 'Production of Heavy Bombers'; AIR8/404.
18. Air Commodore G. B. A Baker to Freeman, 13 September 1940; AVIA 10/124.
19. Arnold, p. 259. As one of his biographers observes, Arnold's personal credibility was also tied into the success of the B-17; Thomas Coffey, *Hap* (New York: Viking Press, 1982), pp. 239, 251.
20. Note to Sir Arthur Salter, 18 August 1940; CAB 115/83; Llewellyn to Wilson, 1 October 1940; AVIA 38/1245.
21. Stimson quoted to Portal by Brigadier General Raymond E. Lee,

AM 2708/REL, 12 May 1941; AIR 8/563; Sinclair to Moore-Brabazon, 12 May 1941; ibid.
22. Moore-Brabazon to Sinclair, 14 May 1941; ibid.
23. 'Memorandum for Mr Harriman: Organisation of 90 Squadron B-17', AM 2746/MFM, 24 May 1941; ibid.
24. Air Attaché, Washington, to Portal, X.2924, 3 May 1941; ibid .
25. Air Commodore G. Pirie, Air Attaché, to Arnold, 5 May 1941; Lovett papers.
26. Freeman to Portal, 27 May 1941; AIR 8/563.
27. 'Memorandum for Mr Harriman: Organisation of 90 Squadron B-17'; Ibid.
28. Memorandum for Major General Arnold by Major E. R. Reynolds, 2 July 1941: comments on 'British Air Activity over the Continent, 7 August 1941'; Lovett papers.
29. Air Marshal Sir Norman Bottomley, Deputy Chief of the Air Staff (DCAS) to Air Marshal Sir Richard Peirse, C.-in-C. of Bomber Command, 15 July 1941; AIR 20/880.
30. 'Report on High Altitude Interception Practice on 2/10/41', 10 Group, 9 October 1941; AIR 14/629.
31. Director of Bomber Operations to Freeman, 24 September 1941; AIR 20/880.
32. Portal to Churchill, undated memorandum, October 1941; ibid.
33. AHQ to Air Ministry, A.336, 29 August 1941; Air Ministry to AHQ India, AX.965, 2 September 1942; ibid. Further details in Roger Freeman, *B-17 Fortress at War* (London: Ian Allen, 1977), pp. 24–5.
34. Arnold, p. 261.
35. DCAS to DGO, 27 January 1942; AIR 20/880. Further details in Bowyer, *2 Group*, pp. 195–206.
36. Air Vice Marshal Sir Ralph Sorley, Assistant Chief of the Air Staff (ACAS) to Deputy Chief of the Air Staff (DCAS), 15 June 1941; AIR 20/1774.
37. Wing Commander Calder to ACAS (T), 24 September 1941; AIR 20/5519.
38. 'Deferred delivery of B-24 aircraft on British Lend-Lease requisition #65'; memorandum for General Arnold by Brigadier General H. A. Dargue, 11 July 1941; Lovett papers.
39. Churchill to Portal, 21 July 1941; AIR 9/436.
40. Portal to Churchill, 23 July 1941. CAB 120/352.
41. Sherwood, *Hopkins*, p. 321.
42. Figures from 'Imports Weekly'; AIR 20/2039.

43. Carl A. Christie, *Ocean Bridge* (Toronto: University of Toronto Press, 1995), p. 88.
44. Theodore Wilson, *The First Summit: Churchill and Roosevelt at Placentia Bay 1941* (London: Macdonald, 1969), p. 41.
45. Harris to Lovett, A.20,576/41, 4 October 1941; Lovett papers.
46. Dallek, pp. 278–9; Harris to Portal, Britman, Washington, to Air Ministry, X.8455, 1 July 1941; AIR 8/414.
47. Portal to Harris, 25 June and 21 July 1941; Lovett papers.
48. Portal to Freeman, Sloane No. 15, 10 August 1941; AIR 8/591.
49. Furse, p. 218; Portal to Freeman, Sloane No. 5, 8 August 1941; ibid.
50. Arnold diary entry, 6 August 1941; Huston, p. 220.
51. Freeman to Portal, Avenue No. 21, 11 August 1941; AIR 8/591.
52. Furse, p. 221.
53. AIR 8/591.
54. Arnold diary entry, 10 August 1941; Huston, p. 227.
55. British B-17 and B-24 expectations from memorandum RD/DO/76 by Wing Commander Sturgis, August 1941; AIR 14/340.
56. Figures from Freeman's draft notes from the Atlantic conference, 'Summary of Principal Points Affecting RAF', August 1941; AIR 8/591.
57. Freeman to Harris, 12 August; ibid; Huston, p. 240.
58. Freeman to Portal, Avenue No. 21, 11 August 1941; AIR 8/591.
59. Freeman to Harris, 12 August 1941; ibid.
60. Furse, p. 222.
61. Wilson, p. 155.
62. Middlebrook and Everitt, pp. 190–1.
63. Freeman to Hopkins, 11 August 1941. AIR 8/591.
64. War Cabinet WM (41) 84, 'Discussions between the Prime Minister and President Roosevelt', 19 August 1941; CAB 65/19/20.
65. War Cabinet Memorandum, Annexe III – British–American Chiefs of Staff Discussions, WP (41) 202, 20 August 1941, CAB 66/18/25.
66. 'Note for Air Marshal Harris of a meeting of heads of missions with Lord Beaverbrook', by Air Commodore Fiddament, 16 August 1941; AIR 8/591.
67. Washington Embassy to Admiralty, Gleam No. 104, 9 August 1941; AIR 8/414.
68. Note from CAS to Winant, 'The Production of Heavy Bombers in the United States of America', 15 August 1941; AIR 8/404.
69. Balfour to Sinclair, No. 31 Linen, 2 October 1941; AIR 19/287.
70. 'Note on the Slessor Agreement in relation to releases to Britain of

US Army Air Corps Contracts', Harris to Hopkins, A.21, 255/41, 29 September 1941; Box 125, Hopkins papers.

71. Roosevelt to Stimson, 14 October 1941; Lovett papers.
72. Balfour to Sinclair and Beaverbrook, Caesar 970, WX.4535, 10 November 1941, AIR 9/436.
73. 'Bomber Production and the Expansion of the Bomber Force', memorandum by Sinclair, 2 September 1941; AIR 20/2689.
74. J. Eaton Griffith, MAP, to Lt. Col. Jacob, War Cabinet Offices, 2 September 1941; ibid.
75. Portal to Churchill, undated, September 1941; ibid.
76. Portal to Courtney, AMSO, 27 November 1941; ibid .
77. Confidential Annexe, DC (S) (41), 4 September 1941; AIR 19/274.
78. Memorandum for Mr Lovett, 'Introduction of a British 4 Engine Bomber into American Production', 29 September 1941; Lovett papers.
79. David J. Bercuson and Holger H. Herwig, *One Christmas in Washington. Churchill and Roosevelt Forge the Grand Alliance* (London: Weidenfeld and Nicolson, 2005), p. 209.
80. Richards, *Portal*, p. 250.
81. Arnold, p. 285; Portal to Air Ministry, Caesar 610 WX.3964 part 2, 4 January 1942; AIR 8/413.
82. 'Allocations of American Aircraft during 1942', Caesar 610 WX.3964 part 2, 4 January 1942; ibid .
83. Harris to Portal, Caesar 612 WX.4884, 6 February 1942; ibid.
84. Portal to AMSO, 6 February 1942; ibid.
85. Portal to Arnold, 19 February 1942; ibid.
86. Huston, p. 268.
87. Air Marshal Evill, RAF Delegation in Washington, to Portal, Marcus 252 WX.3591, 14 May 1942; AIR 9/165.
88. Air Marshal Evill to Portal, 14 May 1942; ibid..
89. Arnold, p. 309.
90. Arnold to Portal, Memorandum for CAS, 30 May 1942; AIR 19/349.
91. ERP 35 report, 'Heavy Bombers. B. American Production (Aircraft in the UK)', 6 April 1942; AIR 20/3461.
92. A total of 1,047 aircraft were despatched, 379 of them from training units. Some 417 heavy bombers were involved. No American aircraft were used. Middlebrook and Everitt, p. 272.
93. Huston, p. 315.
94. Churchill to Roosevelt, 16 October 1942; Hopkins papers.
95. Courtney, AMSO, to Portal, 6 June 1942; AIR 20/1834.

96. Text of the second ATP agreement, 'Memorandum of Agreement between Lt. Gen. Arnold, Rear Admiral Towers and Air Chief Marshal Portal', 21 June 1942; 'Annex A. Allocations of Aircraft Other than Fleet Air Arm Types to Great Britain'; Box 164, Map Room Files, FDR Library.
97. Confidential Annexe, DC (S) (41), 4 September 1941; AIR 19/274
98. Churchill to Anderson, M 678/1, 7 September 1941; AIR 20/2689.
99. War Cabinet WM (41) 90, 5 September 1941; CAB 65/19/26.
100. War Cabinet WM (41) 112, Confidential Annexe, 12 November 1941; CAB 65/24/4.
101. Self to Scott, MAP, Briny 11004 MOSSY, 19 November 1941; AIR 9/436.
102. Anonymous Air Ministry memorandum, 'American Supply and the Royal Air Force Expansion Programme', 27 November 1941; AIR 19/275.
103. 'Allocation of US production', Sinclair to Churchill, 8 November 1941; ibid.
104. This is at least an improvement over one biography of Arnold which ignores his role in aircraft supply diplomacy almost entirely. Dik Alan Dasso, *Hap Arnold and the Evolution of American Airpower* (Washington, DC: Smithsonian, 2000).
105. Slessor, p. 330.
106. Probert, *Harris*, pp. 119–20.
107. US aircraft delivered to UK only; figures from AIR 20/2039.
108. 'Production of Heavy Bombers', 8 May 1941; AIR 8/404.
109. Slessor, p. 385.

7 The Problem of Quality: the Fighter Supply Crisis of 1942

> . . . quality is more important than quantity in the production of fighters.
>
> *Air Marshal Sir Sholto Douglas,*
> *C.-in-C. of Fighter Command, 1942*[1]

The problems experienced in the heavy bomber supply diplomacy of 1941 indicated that the British ability to overcome resistance from the USAAF to their supply objectives was already strongly limited before the American entry into the war. Another factor involved in that diplomacy was the dominant influence of quality in terms of aircraft performance by type and in their operational equipment. Both these features were to come together in an unexpected fashion in the fighter supply diplomacy of 1941–2 which culminated in the negotiations to conclude the second Arnold–Towers–Portal agreement of June 1942.

Though the first ATP agreement of January 1942 had appeared to confirm a reduced British position in aircraft supply allocations, the pressure the USAAF faced in the following six months led to a further renegotiation at British expense and against British protest. This pressure was due to demands of equipping and deploying USAAF combatant units alongside the continuing demands of Allied supply, and against a continuing background of insufficient production. This was a familiar enough story but what made the situation particularly interesting, with regard to the supply of fighter aircraft in 1942, was the extent of this pressure and the British response to it.

To begin with, in the spring of 1942, the British were threatened with the complete termination of American fighter supplies.

The second significant aspect of this period was that, despite this pressure, the RAF was able to mount a successful defence of their claim on continuing supplies of American aircraft in the second ATP agreement in June. Further than this, they were able to influence American aircraft deployment policy and to improve the future quality of American aircraft at the same time: areas where they had enjoyed minimal success previously. This involved a complex series of exchange deals revolving around two key elements: the supply of British Spitfire fighters to USAAF units deploying to Britain in Operation 'Bolero', the build-up of American forces for the eventual invasion of Europe; and the supply of Mustang fighters together with the development of it with the Rolls-Royce Merlin engine. This Spitfire–Mustang deal was at the heart of the fighter supply diplomacy involved in the second ATP agreement which evolved when a crisis had become evident in the quality of American fighter aircraft.

All this sprang from the performance differential between the fighters involved: the American Lockheed P-38 Lightning, Bell P-39 Airacobra and Curtiss P-40 Kittyhawk, on one hand, and the Spitfire on the other. The ultimate explanation for the existence of this differential was technical: the inferior performance at high altitude of the American Allison V-1710 compared to the British Rolls-Royce Merlin engine.

The Allison and the Merlin were liquid-cooled engines of similar capacity but the Merlin had an advantage in supercharger efficiency which, as a result, increased the power produced at high altitude.[2] The three main American fighter types produced in 1942 – the P-40 Kittyhawk, the P-39 Airacobra and the P-38 Lightning – all used the Allison. They had all been evaluated by the RAF by the end of 1941 and serious shortcomings had been identified. These American aircraft formed the core of British fighter purchasing plans in the United States, representing nearly three thousand of the total of four thousand fighter aircraft recorded against British purchase contracts in 1940–1.[3] Production of these types represented almost the entire USAAF-controlled American fighter production both for the USAAF and for supply to the Allies in 1942, with obvious implications for the qualitative value of American fighter supply as a whole.[4] Exploring the deployment history of each of these aircraft, beginning with the P-40 as the first to be supplied and enter combat, demonstrates how the issue of quality could have significant military and diplomatic implications.

The P-40 Tomahawk Is originally ordered by France had been specially prominent in Allied supply diplomacy in 1940 but were used by the RAF to replace the Westland Lysander in Army Co-operation Command to perform low-level fighter reconnaissance missions. Army Co-operation Command was acknowledged to be the Cinderella command of the RAF and, by the end of 1941, the five squadrons eventually equipped with Tomahawks were admitted to be in a 'parlous' state because of spares shortages and critical generator drive failures.[5] Shortages of replacement aircraft and spares, because of allocations to the Middle East and the Soviet Union, led to demands for units to be re-equipped with Hurricanes in mid-1941.[6] At the end of the 1941, the Tomahawks provided only sixty-six out of the 143 serviceable aircraft available in the command, and the RAF admitted the '. . . great necessity to meet our moral obligations about these squadrons in a better way than we are doing at present.'.[7]

The position of the Tomahawks in Britain had been adversely affected by the decision to allocate them to overseas theatres, and primarily to the Middle East. In that theatre, the value of American supply against technically inferior Italian aircraft was higher but still limited. The precursor of the Tomahawk indicated the pattern to be followed. Former French Curtiss P-36 Mohawks, shipped to South Africa, had been used in the conclusion of the East African campaign against the Italians but the squadron involved reverted to training status by the end of 1941.[8] P-40C Tomahawk IIs, ordered from the joint Anglo-French purchase programme and equipped to British specifications, had been scheduled for delivery direct to the Middle East since January 1941. Five squadrons equipped with the Tomahawk had seen extensive combat service from June 1941 onwards but production shortfalls, delivery delays and serviceability problems saw it outnumbered two to one by Hurricanes in the same theatre. The altitude limitations of the engine also saw the Tomahawk outclassed by the Luftwaffe's Bf 109s that were deployed in Libya at the same time as the Tomahawks entered service.

The P-40D and E Kittyhawk variants, produced at the end of 1941, and the succeeding P-40K and M variants, produced throughout 1942, were Tomahawks re-engined with a marginally more powerful Allison V-1710-F engine. Unfortunately, the increased power was offset by increased weight while the limitation on power output at altitude, dictated by the existing supercharger design, remained.[9]

One solution was the installation of a Packard-built Merlin engine, and this was tested in June 1941.[10] Packard had contracted to build Merlin engines in the United States in 1940, and the British planned to use their output to supplement production of the widely used Merlin 20 series engine.[11] The USAAF was scheduled to receive three thousand of the initial production of nine thousand engines, and had earmarked them for improving their P-40 deliveries. The P-40F Kittyhawk was delivered with the Packard-built Merlin in mid-1942, alongside the equivalent Allison-engined P-40K model. In July 1942 the RAF in the Middle East expressed a preference on performance grounds for the F over the K variant.[12] The USAAF had already beaten them to it, however. In January 1942 Arnold had rejected a British attempt to increase their allocations of future Packard-Merlin production which would have come at the expense of P-40F deliveries to the USAAF. The grounds for this rejection were clearly performance based, as the aircraft involved were allocated to equip some of the first USAAF units scheduled to be deployed in combat. As Arnold said; '. . . I cannot see my way clear to go back to the P-40Es once we start in with the P-40Fs, since the P-40Fs will have such a greatly superior performance.'[13]

As a result of this, Merlin-engined variants were used to equip all five of the USAAF P-40 groups deployed to North Africa in 1942–43. USAAF requirements for Merlin-engined P-40s ensured deliveries to the British were a fraction of the American usage of the type, and the RAF was consequently denied substantial supplies of the variant it preferred.[14]

This left the British dependent upon continuing production of Allison-engined variants. They had originally ordered 560 Allison-engined P-40D Kittyhawks as part of the Anglo-French purchase programme. These had been expected to supplant the

Tomahawk on the Curtiss production lines in February 1941 and complete delivery in the following June. Successive delays in the production of the new V-1710-F engine delayed anticipated deliveries to June–December 1941, requiring further orders for Tomahawks to ensure continuing production output in the Curtiss plant in the meantime.[15] In June 1941 British planners had anticipated sending 480 Kittyhawks to the Middle East by the end of the year but further production delays reduced this to a total of 197.[16] Despite the delays involved, by October 1941 the RAF planned eventually to equip all thirty-two of the planned single-engined fighter squadrons in the Middle East with Kittyhawks from the British purchase contract and, following Lend-Lease orders, allowing them to phase out the supply of Hurricanes entirely.[17] This left Middle East Command particularly vulnerable to any fluctuations in Kittyhawk supply: 'Unless we can count upon every Kittyhawk in the present programme from the U.S.A. to the Middle East, there will be a complete breakdown in fighter organisation there during the summer of 1942.'[18]

This threat materialised as a result of USAAF supply diplomacy after Pearl Harbor. One of the first reactions to the Japanese offensive in the Far East was the diversion of British Kittyhawk allocations to south-east Asia and the Soviets in favour of the USAAF.[19] As a result, by February 1942, original plans for Kittyhawk equipment for the Middle East were reduced by 75 per cent from a target of thirty-two squadrons to eight.[20] Even this proved difficult to achieve during the climax of fighting in Libya and Egypt that year, with Tedder complaining about 'Kittyhawk starvation' in April 1942 when deliveries fell from an initially planned 330 in the two-month period February–March to a quota of just 123.[21] He reiterated the problem in September:

> My ability to maintain vital battle now going on in this theatre depends to a very great extent on promises of delivery from America being kept. We have never even approached such conditions. Between April and August I was promised 513 Kittyhawks and I received 251 . . . Can nothing be done to ensure that the Americans meet their bond?[22]

In the first ATP agreement, the British had been allocated 629 P-40s over the following six months, almost all destined for the Middle East, but in the event they received only 387.[23] Overall, the British had received approximately half of their scheduled deliveries, even after these had been scaled down from the expectations of 1941 by the first ATP agreement. The lack of Kittyhawks forced Tedder to consider re-equipping his last two Tomahawk squadrons with Hurricanes instead.[24] There was little prospect of this picture being improved when, in May 1942, Arnold proposed reallocating 100 per cent of the existing British quota of American fighters for that theatre to the USAAF after August 1942.[25]

Faced with the chronic shortage of Kittyhawks, Tedder's preferred alternative was to increase his allocation of Spitfires to compensate.[26] In August 1941, Freeman had approved the deployment of two squadrons of Spitfire Vs to the Middle East to respond to the performance inferiority experienced by the Hurricane and Tomahawk against the Messerschmitt Bf 109F.[27] The numbers involved were small because the Spitfires were intended as a qualitative supplement for the Kittyhawks which were still planned to remain the mainstay of the fighter supply for the Middle East.[28] The requirement for Spitfires then rose when Kittyhawk supply failed to meet those expectations in 1942.

The Kittyhawk situation illustrated the full range of problems British supply policy faced during 1942. The first of these was quantitative: production and delivery shortcomings of the Tomahawk in 1941 were followed by diversions from agreed RAF Kittyhawk allocations in 1942. These ensured that the numbers supplied were insufficient to meet RAF objectives. The second problem was qualitative: operational performance of the type involved was regarded as inadequate, demanding improvement with the Merlin engine and supplementation with Spitfires.

The relationship between qualitative shortcomings and diplomatic importance was particularly significant in the British deployment of the Bell P-39 Airacobra, the next of the three main US fighters evaluated by the RAF. The Airacobra was an unconventional design, using an Allison engine mounted in the mid-section of the aircraft, driving the propeller by a shaft which passed through the cockpit. The Airacobra had originally featured a turbocharger to improve engine output at high altitudes but this had been removed to resolve installation problems during development, leaving it with poor high-altitude performance.[29] Bell resorted to airframe modifications of the first aircraft on the RAF contract to improve performance during acceptance tests but these were entirely unrepresentative of later production aircraft. Testing of early production USAAF P-39C models in Britain, rushed across the Atlantic before the first British-contracted Airacobras were delivered, duly revealed substantial performance shortcomings at high altitude when compared to the contemporary Spitfire V.[30] The first Airacobras originating from the April 1940 Anglo-French purchase contract were eventually delivered to 601 Squadron, a Hurricane unit in Fighter Command, in August 1941.[31] 601 Squadron began operations with the Airacobra in November, and these revealed some important equipment problems.[32] But the decision had already been made to phase the Airacobra out of British service before it flew its first operational mission.

In September 1941, Freeman investigated the possibility of using Airacobra supplies to meet the British quota of the Soviet supply protocol.[33] This built upon Churchill's promise to supply two hundred Tomahawks to the Soviets alongside a short detachment of two Hurricane squadrons to Murmansk in northern Russia in July 1941. These undertakings had been quickly followed by another to supply a further two hundred Hurricanes to the Soviets in August.[34] This had been followed by the Moscow Supply Protocol, at the end of September 1941, which promised the Soviets two hundred British-supplied fighters every month until June 1942. Even given the conversion of Fighter Command Hurricane squadrons to Spitfires throughout 1941, which reduced RAF requirements for Hurricanes, this remained a substantial commitment given that production averaged 270 Hurricanes per month in the last quarter of 1941. Fighter Command was still scheduled to operate twelve squadrons with the type, and 150 per month were required to supply the Middle and Far East by the end of the year.[35] The initial commitment had already come at the expense of Fighter Command's reserves.[36]

The Airacobra – just starting delivery but already regarded

as obsolete – offered a ready alternative source of supply when Freeman's attempt to have the Soviet protocol quota temporarily reduced was rejected in December 1941.[37] This was entirely due to the RAF's qualitative appreciation of the Airacobra which was contingent upon its altitude performance. In response to Freeman's enquiries on the operational utility of the Airacobra with 601 Squadron, Douglas identified the main problem with the aircraft:

> Up to a point it is a promising and attractive job, and if only the high altitude performance could be improved, I think that we should find them very useful. I have asked that the question of either fitting a turbo-supercharger to the Airacobra, or alternatively of putting a bigger blower [supercharger] on the Allison engine should be investigated as a matter of urgency.[38]

Freeman's response was uncompromising. 'I spoke to C.-in-C. [Douglas] and asked him to choose between Spitfire and Airacobra – he didn't hesitate in selecting Spitfire.'[39]

Shipments of Airacobras from Britain to the Soviets began in mid-November 1941.[40] This was not without problems, however, as the MAP complained about 'lamentable' quality-control problems with Airacobra deliveries including crossed control cables, leaking fuel tanks, short fuel connections, as well as 'swarf, and hand-tools and odd bits and pieces left lying about inside the aeroplane . . .'[41] Bell satisfied an on-the-spot inspection of its plant and attributed the problems to the British facility at Colerne which assembled the aircraft after shipment across the Atlantic. Nonetheless, to monitor the problem, the MAP initially instructed the BAC to ship Airacobras directly to Britain before re-export to the Soviet Union.[42]

Douglas later admitted that the British experience with the Airacobra was 'dismal', and he expressed an interest in equipping 601 Squadron with Hawker Typhoons before Freeman's offer of Spitfires materialised in March 1942.[43] While Typhoons were in chronically short supply at this point, owing to interminable problems with their Napier Sabre engines, the rationale for the delayed re-equipment of the squadron was political:

> . . . it was not on supply considerations that the ERP Committee at its meeting on 9 January [1942] decided to continue to maintain one Airacobra flight in this squadron. The reason was the diplomatic one that we are hoping to meet a substantial part of our commitments to Russia with the Airacobras, and it would be disastrous if the market for this type were spoiled by the Russians being able to say that they were fully justified in not accepting it because we, ourselves, had completely rejected it.[44]

Fortunately for the British, and in a reversal of the RAF's opinion, the Soviets were to prefer the Airacobra over the Hurricane, largely because of the Airacobra's better low-altitude performance, and they also favoured it over the P-40 because of the Airacobra's powerful main armament of a 20- or a 37-millimetre cannon.[45] Despite eventual Soviet approval for supplies of the aircraft, the policy of using the Airacobra for the Soviet quota was almost immediately jeopardised by the revision of aircraft allocations in the first ATP agreement in January 1942. Between April and July 1942, 375 out of the 674 British purchase contract Airacobras were diverted to the USAAF and a further 494 P-39D-1s, originally scheduled for Lend-Lease supply to Britain when the cash purchase contract was completed, were also diverted to the USAAF during the same period. Though the British had been promised 394 Airacobras from Lend-Lease supply, from August–December 1942, there was a clear danger that these would materialise too late to meet the Soviet quota, even if they were not also diverted to USAAF use first.[46]

A tactic, which swiftly emerged to limit the diversion of types the British wanted, was to trade them in exchange for aircraft the USAAF wanted more than the British did. The first demonstration of this involved the last of the three USAAF-sponsored fighters to reach the RAF in 1941, the Lockheed P-38 Lightning. The Lightning was an advanced twin-engined design, using turbocharging to improve the power output of the Allison engines at altitude, and it had the clear potential to overcome the known shortcomings of the Airacobra and Tomahawk.[47] Some confusion exists in aviation sources over the British procurement of the

Lightning, which was abandoned in 1942 after an Anglo-French contract for 667 aircraft had been placed in 1940.[48] Contrary to much speculation on the matter, the decision to terminate the Lightning contract was driven entirely by perceived qualitative problems with the aircraft.

Testing of the initial production aircraft in the United States between April and October 1941 had revealed serious aerodynamic problems, including elevator buffeting and compressibility in high-speed dives, as well as engine-power output restrictions owing to coolant-system limitations.[49] The first two aerodynamic problems threatened the pilot with the possible loss of control, and limited the manoeuvrability of the aircraft, while the last reduced its full power output and thereby its maximum speed and rate of climb. In November 1941, the BAC rejected Lightning deliveries until the problems were resolved:

> . . . the aircraft has not completed with the specification requirements sufficiently to make it incumbent on us to accept delivery. The technical limitations on speed which must be imposed on flight operation are such as to make the aircraft useless for operational employment until the trouble is cured.[50]

The continuing faith the USAAF placed in the Lightning as a capable high-altitude fighter, despite these early problems, made it an obvious choice to trade in exchange for aircraft the British wanted. In January 1942, the British traded 160 of the Lightnings expected from their cash purchase order for a further 160 Kittyhawks for the Middle East to make up in part for previous Kittyhawk diversions.[51]

Technical problems with the Lightning continued into 1942. The USAAF believed the elevator buffeting problem had been overcome by June 1942 but this still left it with engine output and diving speed limitations that remained unacceptable to the RAF.[52] The British wrote off the Lightning because of these shortcomings and turned over twenty-three completed aircraft, and their remaining contracts for 644 undelivered aircraft, to the USAAF.[53] In the end, the compressibility problem was only partially resolved with the provision of dive flaps to limit diving speed in the P-38L variant in May 1944, more than two years after the problem was first identified.[54]

The British rejection of the Lightning, alongside the parallel testing and rejection of the Airacobra and the previous relegation of the Tomahawk, raised qualitative doubts over the entire USAAF fighter production programme and its contribution to RAF strength. As the development of the Kittyhawk supply crisis indicates, the quantitative problems experienced with the slow build-up of American production in 1941 worsened after the first ATP agreement with the exponential growth of American service requirements which followed Pearl Harbor.[55] By the spring of 1942 Arnold had convinced Roosevelt that strategic and political imperatives demanded a comprehensive revision of the ATP allocations in favour of the American services to accelerate the formation, training and deployment of USAAF units for reinforcement of the Pacific, Middle East and Europe.[56] The RAF could clearly see the implications of this unilateral initiative in the 'Kittyhawk starvation' Tedder had already started to experience, and this situation was apparently going to be repeated across the full spectrum of American aircraft supply.

At a time when American industrial output was finally rising to meet the hopes of 1940–1, the prospects of realising ambitious RAF expansion plans using extensive supplies of aircraft from USAAF-controlled Lend-Lease procurement were now dimming.[57] This represented a decisive watershed for British expectations of American supply, as the post-Pearl Harbor claims of all the United States services were set to incorporate the whole of future American production. Whatever allocation policy was decided at this point would be likely to govern the respective British and American war efforts for the rest of the war. As Field Marshal Sir John Dill, the British representative on the Combined Chiefs of Staff, warned Portal: 'I feel sure that [the] tendency is to edge us off the US platform.'[58]

The British were now forced to continue production of the Hurricane, originally scheduled to finish in 1942, to meet the continuing need for British fighters for the Soviets, the Middle East and Far East.[59] Arnold's proposals would terminate British deliveries of the Kittyhawk, with obvious repercussions for the

Middle East, and also the Airacobra, leaving Portal to claim that the British had no other way of meeting their Soviet quota.[60]

Arnold returned to Britain in May 1942 to secure British agreement to the reduction in their allocations. British objections to Arnold's plans were manifold. His stated intention to maximise the use of American-produced aircraft by American crews contradicted previous assurances that this would not prejudice existing British allocations. The force targets being used by Arnold were 'manifestly impossible' to achieve in the near future; as an example, the diversion of the entire upcoming single-engined fighter production of the United States would equal only 64 per cent of the planned expansion by the end of the year. Finally, the RAF claimed that diverting British allocations to the USAAF would involve a four- to six-month delay in using the aircraft operationally.[61]

Arnold's proposals were estimated to cost the RAF a total of 123 out of 196 squadrons which had been expected to be equipped with American aircraft by 1 April 1943.[62] While the actual reduction in potential RAF strength might have been less – RAF planners estimated that 105 out of those 123 squadrons could be equipped with British aircraft instead – this could be achieved only by abandoning their existing qualitative deployment agenda which entailed concentrating their most effective (British) fighters and heavy bombers in their preferred theatres.[63] Eventual British consent to Arnold's revision was based on the political impossibility of opposing the early build-up of American forces after the United States's entry into the war but also on a compromise that allowed sufficient supplies of aircraft to maintain existing RAF units equipped with American aircraft, a so-called 'maintenance clause'.

Slessor returned to Washington with Arnold to settle the details of the new allocations at the beginning of June. The final result of this renegotiation of the first ATP agreement left the British allocated half their previously agreed total requirements from American supply in the second half of 1942, with an even greater cutback in their allocation of American fighters, which dropped from 2,360 to 770 aircraft.[64] But, at this moment of apparent weakness in the competition for American aircraft allocations, the British were able to overcome USAAF resistance to defend a claim to continuing American fighter supply, and also to improve the quality of those fighters.

The decisive factor behind this lay in the final acceptance by the USAAF of the qualitative shortcomings of their contemporary fighters. The RAF's judgement on this had not initially been acceptable; indeed, one USAAF observer attributed the RAF's rejection of the Airacobra to the chauvinism of British aircraft companies.[65] This all changed with the dramatic success of the Japanese offensives in the Pacific which followed Pearl Harbor. Allied defeats were largely attributed to the superior performance of Japanese fighters, and specifically the Japanese navy's A6M Type 0, or 'Zero'.[66] Though this Japanese qualitative superiority had probably been most pronounced against the Brewster Buffaloes used by the RAF in Malaya and Singapore, and evident against Hurricanes rushed to Singapore and Java in January 1942, internal American criticism was concentrated on the P-39 and P-40 fighters deployed to the Philippines and New Guinea by the USAAF. General MacArthur summarised the problem to Arnold:

> In order to meet 0 ['Zero' fighter] on more equal terms, I consider it essential that a more suitable type of fighter be allocated to this theatre. As both Jap fighters and bombers operate above rated performance altitude of P-39s and P-40s, altitude is an absolute necessity.[67]

This appreciation was echoed by General Chennault, the former USAAF officer commanding the Chinese air force. Chennault had formed a unit of American volunteers for the Chinese air force to fly the Tomahawks diverted from British contracts in 1941, and he added his opinion to the chorus of disenchantment with the Allison-engined fighters in July 1942.[68] Criticism of the Airacobra was repeated by General Harmon, the USAAF commander in the Solomon Islands, as the Guadalcanal campaign began in August. Arnold directly confronted the failure of the Airacobra to achieve the necessary high-altitude performance after a visit in September to the Solomons to investigate. As a result of this visit, he confirmed the local commander's reliance on the USN's Grumman

F-4F Wildcat in preference to the Airacobra by inviting the USN to take over responsibility for high-altitude interceptions.[69]

At the southern edge of the same theatre, the issue of American fighter performance expanded into Anglo-Australian relations after the disastrous defence of the northern Australian port of Darwin by USAAF Kittyhawks that February.[70] Faced with the acrimonious collapse of the pre-war Imperial Defence consensus after the fall of Singapore, Churchill made the promise of a Spitfire wing of three squadrons to defend Australia in May 1942 as a symbolic political gesture at a time when the Australian government was publicly appealing for assistance from the United States.[71] As a result of the British defeats in Libya in June 1942, Churchill then requested that the first shipment of Spitfires for Australia be diverted along the Takoradi air reinforcement route from West Africa to reinforce the British position in Egypt.[72] The Australian government initially rejected Churchill's request on the grounds of fighter performance: 'These [Spitfires] are most urgently needed against the Japanese [Zero fighter which can] out fight the American Kittyhawk at higher altitudes'.[73]

Even when the Australians finally accepted the diversion of the Spitfires at the end of June, the perceived comparative inferiority of the American fighters was reiterated:

> We wish to emphasise that the air strength of Australia without the Spitfire squadrons represents a great wastage of personnel and equipment because of the superiority of the Japanese fighter aircraft over the American types that are at present being used against them.[74]

The British shared this perception which they could observe extending to the American public as a result of the Japanese victories in the Pacific. The head of the RAF delegation in Washington that September outlined the public perception of the fighter quality problem that was a matter of concern not just in 1942 but also for the year ahead:

> The question of fighter production [in 1943] is causing great concern here. The main hope is the P47 [Thunderbolt] which is clearly not quite right yet, and later the Merlin Mustang. Arnold is coming in

> for a great deal of criticism in the press and there are open suggestions that the Spitfire be put into production here. There are awkward comparisons with British equipment to which I'm afraid remarks or articles in the U.K. occasionally contribute. But, in the main, criticism is based on reported opinions of U.S. pilots and it is getting very sharp indeed.[75]

The Republic P-47 Thunderbolt had begun delivery in mid-1942 but experienced technical problems into the spring of 1943. This was the last of the USAAF-sponsored fighter designs to enter production, using a turbocharged Pratt & Whitney R-2800 radial engine to improve high-altitude performance. In the negotiations for the first ATP agreement, the British had previously tried and failed to win an allocation of Thunderbolts, which would have been used to meet the need for high-altitude interceptors in the Middle East, leaving them dependent upon Spitfires.[76] The Merlin Mustang was the P-51 Mustang with the Merlin engine, an initiative that sprang from the evidently public crisis of confidence that the USAAF was experiencing with the American fighters available in 1942.

Arnold later complained about 'uneducated' press comparisons, '. . . disparaging our airplanes in favour of the enemy's . . .'[77] This was confirmed by Dwight D. Eisenhower, recently appointed to command United States forces in Europe, after unfavourable comparisons were made against US fighter aircraft to *Time* magazine by American former RAF pilots under his command; a final vindication of the RAF's 1940 decision, for publicity purposes, to equip the 'Eagle' squadrons with British fighters.[78] Possibly the most influential critic was Alexander Seversky, the air power pundit and original chairman of the Republic Aviation Company that designed and produced the Thunderbolt. Despite being confronted by Arnold, Seversky confirmed many of the press criticisms of the Allison engine and USAAF fighter procurement, and later went on to link the supply of Spitfires to the USAAF with the perceived qualitative inferiority of American fighters.[79] Unable to silence criticisms from commentators like Seversky, the USAAF tried to address the problem through a public relations campaign. This openly admitted the problem:

> . . . appraisal of our older fighter types – the Bell P-39 and the Curtis P-40 – compels the conclusion that they are not right for operation under today's high altitude tactics in England. Admitted deficiencies in their performance make them unsuitable. Both are outclassed in the high-altitude field by the British Spitfire and the German Messerschmitt 109 and Focke Wulf 190.[80]

Despite these admissions, press criticism remained widespread with even Harry Truman, then heading a Senate investigation into military procurement, criticising the USAAF's defensiveness on the issue.[81] Combat experience had led to the perception of a crisis in confidence in US fighter performance spreading from the RAF to the American public. The RAF noted this and came up with a response. This involved two initiatives: the supply of Merlin-engined Mustangs and the supply of Spitfires to the USAAF.

The qualitative problems evident in American fighters left the RAF in 1941 dependent upon the Spitfire which retained a central position in British procurement because of the quality issue. By the summer of 1942, that position had come under threat as the RAF encountered the German Focke-Wulf 190 fighter which outclassed the contemporary Spitfire V.[82] As Douglas stated when questioning the apparent complacency of the MAP on the issue of fighter quality that July, 'There is however no doubt in my mind, nor in the minds of my fighter pilots, that the F.W. 190 is the best all round fighter in the world today.'[83]

This had prompted the British to develop the Spitfire IX, a Spitfire V modified to accept the more powerful Merlin 61 engine. That June, Freeman defined the RAF's conventional wisdom on the issue of fighter quality to Portal, and established the position of the Spitfire within that context: '. . . supposing the Spitfire IX is the best fighter in the world at the present time, then we should equip American squadrons with the Spitfire IX, while obsolescent types like the Airacobra (which of course is really obsolete) should go out of production.'[84]

Confronting the Luftwaffe in western Europe – as the 'Bolero' units were planned to do – presented them with the most qualitatively formidable opposition in the form of the FW 190, and placed them at a further tactical disadvantage performing high-altitude operations where their aircraft were already known to be inferior. As the staff at Fighter Command commented with regard to a visit by General Chaney, Eisenhower's predecessor, in May,

> Unless the American fighters are better than we believe at present they will soon find their daylight escort work very expensive. I understand we are to give them some Spitfires which will help, but I imagine only practical experience will show them that the F.W. 190 is an aeroplane to be treated with respect.[85]

The suggestion of supplying Spitfires to the USAAF units deploying to Britain, in exchange for continued allocations of Kittyhawks to maintain the existing RAF force in the Middle East, represented a potential temporary solution to several aspects of the problems faced by the RAF and the USAAF in early 1942. It would overcome the qualitative problem with American fighters facing the FW 190 in bomber escort operations from Britain, and also meet the RAF's desire to avoid having to substitute larger numbers of Spitfires in place of Kittyhawks for their units in the Middle East. In April 1942, Portal first raised the idea with Arnold, emphasising the saving of shipping involved. USAAF units could be shipped to Britain without their aircraft and then be equipped with Spitfires on arrival, at the same time avoiding the need to ship further Spitfires from Britain to the Middle East.[86] After the rejection of this initial British proposal to exchange Spitfires for a stable Kittyhawk allocation for the Middle East at the end of that month, the British resumed the attack through Chaney in the runup to Arnold's visit to Britain later in May.[87] They did so partly by emphasising the savings on shipping space this would provide but also on the issue of comparative fighter quality.

In a series of telegrams to Arnold in April and early May, Chaney adopted the British position on the qualitative problems with both the Lightning and Airacobra, and recommended the re-equipment of 'Bolero' fighter units with Spitfires in exchange for Kittyhawks for the RAF in the Middle East. He questioned the use of the Lightning, on the basis of its known aerodynamic problems, and advocated using the Spitfire, '. . . which has been proven [the] outstanding fighter of this war . . .', on the grounds of simplifying supply requirements on one fighter type, its better firepower and manoeuvrability, and the savings on shipping tonnage.[88] On 26 April, Arnold rejected Chaney's evaluation of the Lightning while accepting the proposition to replace the Airacobras in the 52nd Fighter Group, the second of the 'Bolero' Airacobra units to deploy, with Spitfires.[89] Chaney repeated his arguments again after further consultation with the RAF in early May but Arnold resisted the re-equipment of the 31st Fighter Group, the first Airacobra unit scheduled to deploy to Britain, until his arrival in Britain later in the month.[90]

During Arnold's preliminary discussions with the British in London, which followed, over the plan to revise their allocations, Chaney and the US ambassador, John Winant, raised the issue of American fighter quality again while Arnold stuck to his belief that they should see a trial in combat.[91] It was at this point that the issue of the supply of Spitfires to the USAAF in exchange for Kittyhawks for the Middle East became entangled with the supply of Airacobras and Mustangs and also the development of the Mustang with the Merlin engine.

The Mustang did not originally feature in discussions of Lend-Lease allocations because, despite being an American aircraft, it had evolved without any direct input from the USAAF. In 1940, the North American Aircraft Corporation, the firm responsible for the design and production of the Harvard trainer which had featured in the first British pre-war purchase mission, had responded to a British request to build P-40s under licence from Curtiss-Wright by designing a new fighter, the P-51 Mustang. This was ordered and began production in late 1941. The Mustang shared the same Allison V-1710-F engine as the Kittyhawk but, because it had a more efficient airframe and a reduction in drag associated with the engine cooling system, it proved to be the best-performing American fighter tested by the British.[92] The USAAF secured two Mustangs for testing in 1941 but expressed no interest in the aircraft. With the completion of British orders, production continued only with the conversion of the Mustang into the A-36 dive-bomber to secure a USAAF contract.[93] In his memoirs, Arnold was later to admit the error involved in the

USAAF's disinterest in the Mustang, while the USAAF's failure to recognise its potential has been identified as '. . . close to the costliest mistake made by the USAAF in the war'.[94]

The RAF had originally planned to use the Mustang to replace the Tomahawk in Army Co-operation Command.[95] The 620 Mustangs expected from British purchase orders and 150 from a single Lend-Lease contract were anticipated to equip the seventeen RAF fighter-reconnaissance squadrons demanded by 'Bolero' plans. The end of Mustang deliveries from British-sponsored procurement orders, the disinterest of the USAAF in the type, and the threatened termination of all American fighter supplies to the British left them with the problem of maintaining those squadrons. As Portal put it to Arnold:

> . . . for this I am almost entirely dependent on our expectations of Mustangs. The Spitfire is not suitable for Fighter Reconnaissance, and I therefore propose that you should restore the cut in Mustangs, and that in return I should provide for U.S. Pursuit squadrons in this country an equivalent number of Spitfires.[96]

Portal had now linked three separate British requirements for the second half of 1942 – Kittyhawks for the Middle East, Airacobras for the British quota to the Soviets and Mustangs for Army Co-operation Command – with the supply of Spitfires to the USAAF which he privately referred to as a 'bargaining counter'.[97] The last of the British requirements was secured by Portal's offer of Spitfires for the first P-39 group to deploy to Britain. In negotiations with Slessor on 6 June, Arnold accepted a commitment to allocate two hundred Mustangs in the second half of 1942. As Slessor summarised to Portal, 'He [Arnold] confirmed that the arrangement to send over the P.39 Group without aircraft to take over Spitfires means the Mustang deal will go through.'[98]

With the two hundred Mustangs promised in exchange, and the acceptance of a requirement for continuing production of 125 aircraft per month to maintain seventeen British and twelve US squadrons in 1943, this apparently dealt with British Mustang requirements.[99] Alongside the acceptance of a continuing allocation of fifty Kittyhawks per month to maintain existing British squadrons in the Middle East, this left the British with two out of three objectives achieved. Slessor, however, had since discovered that USAAF planning for the allocation of Airacobras had ignored the British and American commitments to supply the Soviets.[100] All three requirements were reconciled on the final draft of the second ATP agreement prepared by Arnold and Slessor; the British offer of Spitfires was consolidated into two allocations totalling 350 Spitfires to equip two USAAF fighter groups in exchange for six hundred Kittyhawks, 250 Airacobras and two hundred Mustangs for the British.[101] Included in the draft agreement and then the agreed text was a reduction to zero Mustangs in the British quota in the period January–March 1943. This carried a significant qualification, however: 'Subject to revision if additional production of Mustang is created using Merlin LXI engine'.[102] The introduction of the concept of the Merlin 61-engined Mustang to American procurement policy was the final, and in many respects, most important element of the Spitfire–Mustang deal.

In the spring of 1942 testing of the first Mustangs to arrive in Britain indicated that it had the best performance of all the existing American fighters. As one official at the MAP put it, the Mustang was recognised as '. . . the one American fighter that we regarded as equal (or superior) to our own'.[103] In May 1942 an immediate effort was made by Rolls-Royce, with Freeman's encouragement, to adapt a couple of Mustangs to utilise the improved Merlin 61 engine about to be used in the Spitfire IX.[104] The RAF had no interest in the Mustang as a long-range escort fighter, the role it was later to excel in with the USAAF. The British concern was simply to develop an American fighter that was competitive with the performance of contemporary German fighters. On those grounds, the RAF mounted an additional diplomatic effort to persuade the USAAF to procure Merlin Mustangs, using Merlin 60-series engines, to be produced in America by Packard.

Portal's instructions to Slessor on the issue, sent together with Rolls-Royce's projected performance data on a Merlin 61-engined Mustang on 5 June, arrived during the Spitfire–Mustang deal negotiations and exposed the RAF's perception of USAAF resistance:

> It is understood that Arnold does not favour the continuation of Mustang orders possibly because it was not built to U.S. Air Force specification and he is banking everything on the P.47 [Thunderbolt]. To force the continuation of the Mustang fitted with [a] British engine would probably meet with strong opposition from Arnold even though Americans in this country are, as we know, strongly in favour of it. At suitable opportunity you should discuss with Arnold and if possible arrange with him to put forward the proposition as his own.

Portal (or Freeman who almost certainly drafted the message to Slessor) went on to reveal how he expected the impact of the Merlin-engined Mustang's performance on public opinion to help overcome this resistance:

> We are fitting the Mustang with [the] Merlin 61 and there is no doubt that when it is tried out the results will be most impressive and the continuation of Mustang production with the Merlin 61 engine will be forced, repeat forced, on Arnold by American and British opinion.[105]

The Americans in Britain who were 'strongly in favour of it' included Winant who had been brought on board the British project by Freeman and Portal. Winant had apparently outlined the British intention to fit the Mustang airframe with the Merlin 61 engine during Arnold's visit and requested that Arnold approve a parallel test with a Packard Merlin 28 engine which was then in production in the United States.[106] Even with the Packard Merlin 28 installed (equivalent to the engine used in the Merlin-engined P-40F and L variants) instead of the superior Merlin 61, the performance of the Mustang was expected to outclass the Spitfire V and '. . . be far better than that of the Airacobra at all altitudes'.[107] Winant was simultaneously advocating the development of the Merlin-engined Mustang with Hopkins while Slessor did the same in his negotiations with Arnold in Washington, both using arguments derived directly from Freeman.[108] In Winant's words:

> I am concerned about the superior performance of the Focke-Wulfe 190 as compared to any Brit combat plane with the exception of the Spitfire 9 equipped with the Merlin 61 engine. The battle of Britain

was won over larger numbers because of the superior quality of the British fighter.[109]

By 9 June, Winant was encouraging Rolls-Royce and the MAP to produce a prototype Merlin-engined Mustang conversion before North American could.[110] In the event, the Rolls-Royce Mustang conversion flew first, on 13 October 1942, but the North American prototype, first flown on 30 November 1942, proved superior and was selected for production as the P-51B. While the USAAF's subsequent commitment to the Merlin-engined Mustang, and the part played by Rolls-Royce in starting development, have been questioned, it is clear that the Merlin-engined Mustang was initiated by Rolls-Royce and then pushed by the RAF as a priority in their aircraft supply diplomacy in early June 1942.[111] Slessor approached Arnold over the issue via General Carl Spaatz, an acquaintance of his as an American observer in Britain in 1940, and then the designated commander of the 8th Air Force forming in Britain.[112] Arnold issued instructions for North American to begin their Merlin-installation project on 12 June 1942, nine days after MAP's similar instructions to Rolls-Royce, and clearly in response to British pressure.[113] As a result, the provision for extending Mustang production using the Merlin 61 engine was written into the draft second ATP agreement of 13 June.

Realising that option was implemented after the promised review demanded further diplomacy from the British in October–November 1942. This included supplying performance figures from the tests of Rolls-Royce's first prototype and even a message from Churchill to Roosevelt, repeating the qualitative argument: 'This [the Merlin-engined Mustang] in Portal's view would be far ahead of anything in the fighter line you have in hand'.[114]

But even before this, at the end of September, the USAAF had included four hundred Merlin-engined P-51Bs in the USAAF procurement programme, separate from any further Allison-engined orders and pre-dating the first flights of the Rolls-Royce and North American prototypes.[115] The terms established by the Spitfire–Mustang deal of June 1942 shaped American fighter supply in the following year. The third ATP agreement of December 1942, which established aircraft supply quotas for the first six months of

1943, continued the British-inspired policy of 1942; six hundred Spitfires were to be supplied to the USAAF in exchange for the same number of Airacobras for the British quota to the Soviets and Mustangs for the RAF, respectively.[116] Although Merlin-engined Mustangs did not begin delivery until mid-1943 or enter service until the end of that year, the facts that they existed at all and that the British had retained a claim on production output, were direct consequences of the Spitfire–Mustang deal of 1942 and the qualitative agenda that had inspired it.

Towards the end of 1941 the RAF had evaluated its approach to American fighter supply:

> The American fighters arriving in the UK during the period October to April [1942] comprise Lightnings, Airacobras and Mustangs. These again are as yet untried types which we are not yet able to say will prove themselves during the period in question as adequate substitutes for the well tried Hurricane and Spitfire.[117]

This qualitative appreciation dominated RAF fighter procurement and deployment policy. The Tomahawk had been marginalised in Army Co-operation Command and used in the Middle East; the Kittyhawk had also been relegated to the Middle East and re-engined with the Packard Merlin; the operational deployment of the Airacobra was manipulated to ensure that it could be passed on to the Soviets; and the Lightning was rejected entirely. Even the Mustang was limited to secondary roles while the development of it with the two-stage Merlin engine was pushed as a matter of high priority in British aviation supply diplomacy.

Overall, American fighters had varied from the ineffectual, such as the Brewster Buffalo, to the relative usefulness of the Kittyhawk which was an effective fighter-bomber with significant performance advantages over the Hurricane at lower altitudes. In the end, the Lightning exceeded British expectations in American service with a long operational range that showed considerable value in the Mediterranean and Pacific theatres. Nevertheless, a perceived qualitative crisis, springing from the respective performances of the Allison V-1710 and Merlin engines at high altitude, existed in mid-1942 and has not been fully explored before. Even aviation historians have missed the true nature of the technical issue involved.[118] The Merlin's greater power output at height was complemented by the lighter weight and aerodynamic qualities of the Spitfire which resulted in the Kittyhawk being unable to equal the performance of the Spitfire V at altitude even when it was equipped with a similar Merlin engine.[119] This differential increased with the introduction of the Merlin 61 in the Spitfire IX. The power of the V-1710 engine at high altitude was increased by the use of a turbocharger in the P-38 Lightning but aerodynamic and engine problems still undermined the capability of the aircraft and it was replaced by the Mustang in the US 8th Air Force in 1944.[120]

The USAAF was certainly aware of the need for high-altitude fighter performance which had been demonstrated by British experience in the Battle of Britain and identified by American observers, including Arnold himself during his visit to Britain in April 1941.[121] Yet, by 1942, the problems evident in the British experience of American fighters of 1940–1 remained unresolved, and the extent of this problem has often been played down.[122] Given the enormous literature inspired by the development of the Mustang as one of the decisive weapons of World War II, this is surprising, and some of the misconceptions involved demand exploration.

For example, the official USAAF historians, Craven and Cate, assert that the problems experienced with the Airacobra in the Solomons were attributable to the P-400, or USAAF designation for the British cash purchase variant of the P-39, which 'lacked proper superchargers'.[123] In fact, the P-400 used the same engine as the equivalent USAAF P-39D variant with the same power output at altitude.[124] Substantial modifications were made to the Airacobra and to the Kittyhawk to improve their performance as interceptors – including the adoption of the Packard Merlin in the P-40, changed supercharger gearing in the P-39, and attempts to remove excess weight in both aircraft. There can be no doubt that their poor altitude performance was evident to military commanders and to the American public by mid-1942, and this was a factor exploited by British aircraft supply diplomacy.

These shortcomings are reflected elsewhere in the relevant

historiography when it comes to the role of British aircraft supply diplomacy in 1942. The connection between the acceptance of the Spitfire by the USAAF and the RAF's initiative to develop the Merlin-engined Mustang in the second ATP agreement has escaped detailed examination.[125] It has been stated that the British attempt to hold the USAAF to the existing first ATP agreement was 'self-serving' while their argument for Arnold visiting Britain for negotiations for the second ATP agreement was 'hollow'.[126] This discounts Arnold's partial agreement with British objectives which then followed. The official USAAF historians mention the British proposal to link Kittyhawk supplies to the Middle East in exchange for Spitfires for the USAAF only to note its rejection in April 1942.[127] The reversal of the USAAF position in the Spitfire–Mustang deal which followed is not investigated, despite the acknowledged shortcomings of the Airacobra and Kittyhawk and the admission of the USAAF's failure to recognise the potential of the Mustang.[128]

The further implication in Craven and Cate that the British initiative would relieve RAF fighter supply requirements is also partially mistaken. The background context for the initial British offer in March–April 1942 was set by an examination of British fighter resources and commitments that revealed a surplus of Spitfires which would be available in 1942 if supplies of Kittyhawks and Airacobras could be relied upon to meet, in part, the Soviet quota and the Middle East commitment.[129]

In the event, British Spitfire commitments were, in fact, increased by the undertaking to equip the 'Bolero' Airacobra units. This was then compounded by the transfer of the three 'Eagle' squadrons to the USAAF 4th Fighter Group in September 1942. This involved the supply of a further fifty-four Spitfires to the USAAF over and above the agreed second ATP quota.[130] Most of these aircraft were already available in the form of the reserve being built up to sustain the intensive combat expected as a result of the cross-Channel attack that the RAF was planning to support in mid-1942.[131] Though the British would successfully deflect American plans for what they considered a premature cross-Channel invasion attempt in mid-1942, RAF planning did not assume that result beforehand.

In any case, Spitfire production and availability were not necessarily the quantitative problems that have been implied. The peak monthly allocation of 120 Spitfires to the USAAF in July 1942 established in the Spitfire–Mustang deal amounted to 40 per cent of the current monthly wastage replacement allocation to Fighter Command alone, regardless of other Spitfire supply commitments, such as the Middle East or Australia.[132] Any pressure on Spitfire supply, caused by the need to expand Spitfire supplies to the USAAF and overseas theatres while building up a large reserve, was relieved by temporarily reducing Fighter Command's offensive operations and the consequent attritional replacement required.[133] The full explanation for the RAF's policy lies elsewhere – in the unexplored interaction between quality, quantity and theatre of deployment. As the RAF delegation in Washington noted with regard to the USAAF's initial reaction to their offer to exchange Spitfires in April 1942, 'Refusal [is] based on arguments derived from figures of our total resources without regard to operational purpose and suitability of types'.[134]

Supplying Spitfires to the USAAF in exchange for more than double the number of Kittyhawks and Airacobras did little to relieve RAF commitments in total but it did enable the RAF to maintain their preferred qualitative deployment policy. This utilised less-effective types such as the Hurricane, Kittyhawk and Airacobra to meet the demands of political commitments and secondary theatres where the main opposition, whether Japanese or Italian, was supposed to be of a lower quality than the Luftwaffe. Confronting the potential main strength of the Luftwaffe, equipped with superior fighters, such as the Bf109G and the FW 190, whether in the process of defending Britain, escorting bombing attacks over Europe, or in support of a possible invasion of the Continent, demanded the use of the best available fighters. This remained RAF policy even if the Spitfires involved happened to be flown by the USAAF.

The overall qualitative problems evident with American fighters in 1942 have previously been acknowledged but the full implications have not been fully explored. It has been observed that the Roosevelt administration's priority of supplying the Allies before the USAAF in 1940–1 prevented American combat units from being equipped with '. . . a surplus of obsolescent planes'.[135] Even disregarding the contemporary USAAF disagreement with that thesis, the necessary but unarticulated corollary is that the Allies received those obsolescent planes. It also provides an interesting sidelight on the clichéd perception of Allied (and particularly American) military effectiveness which is thought to be exclusively based upon materiel superiority when Allied air operations could be successful in 1942 despite quantitative and qualitative aircraft inferiority. Whatever material superiority would ultimately be secured by American mass production, this was not evident in RAF fighter deployment policy nor in the experience of the USAAF units deployed into early combat in places like Guadalcanal.

While Arnold was confronted by the apparently insatiable demands of Allied supply alongside the expanding worldwide commitment of American forces, his problems were not unique. That year Spitfires were required on all battlefronts from Britain to Africa to Australia. By October, Spitfires had even been requested by the Soviets.[136] This global deployment sprang from the identification of the qualitative problem with US fighter aircraft in high-altitude combat, the perceived ability of the Spitfire to meet it, and the British willingness to supply them for political, as much as military, reasons. As Chaney's commentary indicated, the USAAF decision to accept the Spitfire was based in part upon qualitative arguments, and the Spitfire was used to supplement the requirement for capable high-altitude fighters in a similar manner to Arnold's subsequent acceptance of the USN's Wildcats for the same role on Guadalcanal.

The supply of Spitfires to the USAAF and the development of the Merlin-engined Mustang were contingent upon British success in persuading American officers and officials to overcome their institutional resistance to the British agenda and accept the qualitative policy involved. The British qualitative aircraft deployment policy was perceived to misuse American aircraft, and it threatened to restrict British access to American supplies as a result. The British were aware of this; in November 1941 the RAF officer responsible for rejecting the Lightning would even refer to the possible impact it could have on the Anglo-American relationship.[137] The fact that the British could achieve their qualitative agenda in the fighter supply diplomacy in mid-1942 was due to such resistance being undercut by the widening exposure of the USAAF to the shortcomings of American aircraft in combat.

Arnold's apparent success in recalibrating American aircraft allocation policy in the second ATP agreement has been seen as demonstrating his status as 'the primary Allied arbiter of American-produced aircraft distribution'.[138] Freeman made it clear to Slessor that the British initiative to replace the Airacobra and develop the Mustang had to convince Arnold if it was to overcome the vested interests involved.[139] It did, despite originating from the suspect judgement of the British who had, from his perspective, consistently misused American aircraft, and even when it was communicated by Chaney whom Arnold distrusted and replaced shortly afterwards.[140] The crisis in American fighter quality evident from the USAAF's own experience by mid-1942 made that possible.

The second ATP agreement represented a culmination of Anglo-American aircraft supply. By mid-1942 the British had successfully defended their existing claim on American aircraft allocation but the level of this had already been established by the reality of actual deliveries in 1940–1. From now on, British allocations would generally be limited to maintaining the units that had already been equipped with American aircraft. American aircraft supply had therefore reached a ceiling that fell far below the hopes of 'mobilisation procurement' in 1940–1, and which would remain in place for much of the rest of the war. At the same time, this level of supply had required a reversal of the direction of dependency, as the USAAF demonstrated itself to be – in however limited a fashion – dependent upon the supply of British aircraft.

The fighter supply diplomacy surrounding the second ATP agreement demonstrates several key factors in the Anglo-American supply relationship: the continuing problems the British had maintaining previous supply agreements; the impact of the institutional resistance embodied by Arnold on British supply expectations; the fact that the British had something to offer the USAAF in exchange for continuing American supplies; and the indivisibility of supply and procurement issues from diplomatic and political considerations. But, most of all, it indicates how supply diplomacy and the military deployment which resulted from that diplomacy cannot be sufficiently explained without an understanding of the qualitative values involved.

Notes

1. Douglas and Wright, p. 160.
2. Superchargers compressed air inducted into the engine to counter the reduction in ambient air density and consequent power output as altitude increased. The supercharger governed the full-throttle height (FTH) of the engine, above which the ability of the supercharger to compress air decreased with a corresponding decrease in engine power output. The Allison V-1710-C15 engine in the P-40B Tomahawk had a FTH of 13,000 feet (3,962 m); the Allison V-1710-F3 engine used in the P-40D Kittyhawk had an FTH of 15,000 feet (4,572 m), and the V-1710-E4 engine used in the P-39D had an FTH of 12,000 feet (3,658 m); Table 1.11 and Table 3.12, Daniel Whitney, *Vees for Victory!* (Atglen: Schiffer, 1998), pp. 45, 104. The Merlin 46 engine used in the contemporary Spitfire V had an FTH of 19,000 feet (5,791 m); Sir Stanley Hooker, *Not Much of an Engineer* (Marlborough: Airlife, 2002), p. 52.
3. The following British contract totals are recorded outside Lend-Lease contracts: 667 Lightnings; 674 Airacobras; 1,080 Tomahawks; 560 Kittyhawks ; 620 Mustangs; 204 P-36 Mohawks; and 203 Brewster Buffaloes; or 4008 aircraft in total: Meekcoms, pp. 105–6, 108, 112, 117.
4. In the first quarter of 1942, 433 Airacobras and 960 Kittyhawks were produced. This represented 23.6 per cent and 52.2 per cent of the production of the four main fighter types in the United States at the time. Of the other two types, 225 Lightnings (12.2 per cent) were produced exclusively for the USAAF while the 220 Mustangs produced (12 per cent) were British cash purchase aircraft. Table 76, USAAF, *Army Air Forces Statistical Digest World War Two* (Washington, DC: War Department, 1945), p. 119.
5. Director of Plans to Acting VCAS, 17 December 1941; AIR 20/2068. Correspondence between Army Co-operation Command and Air Ministry, July & December 1941, January 1942. AIR 39/25.

6. Air Marshall Barrett, C.-in-C. Army Co-operation Command, to Undersecretary of State for Air, ACC/S.31/Air 3 July 1941; ibid.
7. Army Co-operation Command strength return from 31 December 1941; AIR 22/38. Director of War Operations (DWO) memorandum, 'Notes of Survey of Fighter Resources', 5 December 1941. AIR 8/411.
8. Shores, *Dust Clouds*, pp. 157–62.
9. The Tomahawk's V-1710-C15 engine was rated at 1,090 brake horsepower (bhp) at 13,200 feet (4,023 m) and the V-1710-F3R used in the P-40D 1,150 bhp at 15,000 feet (4,572 m); Table 4.3 and Table 3.12, Whitney, pp. 123, 104.
10. Peter M. Bowers, *Curtiss Aircraft, 1907–1947* (Annapolis: Naval Institute Press, 1979), p. 485. The Packard V-1650-1 used was practically identical to the Packard Merlin 28 used in British aircraft; Alex Harvey-Bailey, *The Merlin in Perspective – The Combat Years* (Derby: Rolls-Royce Heritage Trust, 1995) , p. 77.
11. Packard contracted to build nine thousand engines, three thousand of which were allocated to the USAAF for the P-40; Hall, p. 191; Ian Lloyd, *Rolls-Royce: The Merlin at War* (London: Macmillan, 1978), pp. 52–6. The Merlin 20 featured the improved supercharger of the Merlin 45/46 and a second, lower supercharger gear to increase medium-altitude performance below the FTH of the full supercharger gear.
12. Tedder's response to a summary of the differences between the P-40F and the Allison-engined equivalent P-40K, 27 July 1942; AIR 2/7498.
13. 'Memorandum for Air Marshal Portal. Subject: Availability of Additional Packard Merlins', D.S.D. (41) 34, 12 January 1942; AIR 20/4092.
14. 1,300 P-40Fs and another seven hundred Packard Merlin-engined P-40Ls were built between the spring of 1942 and the end of production a year later; Bowers, pp. 481–5. British allocations of 150 P-40Fs and a hundred P-40Ls were reduced by transfers from the RAF to the USAAF in the Mediterranean and ultimately to the French Air Force; Meekcoms, p. 110. Tedder was able to operate one squadron of Merlin-engined Kittyhawks, though with difficulty; Tedder, p. 355.
15. Maurice Wilson to Colonel Llewellyn, MAP, 20 September 1940; CAB 115/78. Memorandum 104A, January 1941. AIR 2/7244.
16. Memorandum, 12 April 1941; BAC to MAP, X5658 4/10, 4 October 1941; AIR 2/7498.

17. A planned total of thirty-two fighter squadrons. Item 14, 'Review of Fighter Resources – Commitment Within RAF', October 1941; AIR 19/302.
18. Director of War Operations to VCAS, 18 September 1941; ibid.
19. Air Vice Marshal MacNeese Foster's complaint, sixteenth MBW Meeting minutes, 19 May 1942, p. 2; Hopkins papers.
20. Memorandum 43A; AIR 2/7498.
21. Tedder to Air Ministry, 8 April 1942; ibid.
22. Tedder to Air Vice Marshal Evill, RAFDEL and Freeman; Memorandum 101A; AIR 23/1315.
23. Expected delivery figures from Director of War Operations memorandum, 10 July 1941; AIR 2/7498. January 1942 allocations from Arnold–Towers–Portal agreement details of 14 January 1942; AIR 8/637. Kittyhawk export totals 2 January–2 July 1942 from AIR 22/280.
24. Tedder to Air Ministry, 11 July 1942; AIR 2/7789.
25. Memorandum to Chief of Air Staff, 30 May 1942; Hopkins papers.
26. '. . . only alternative as regards fighters would be increased allotment of Spitfires this far preferable in view of great superiority of Spitfire over Kittyhawk [which] is already verging on obsolescence'; Tedder to VCAS, 11 July 1942; ibid.
27. Tedder, p.202. Tedder's views are confirmed by Sir Kenneth Cross, *Straight and Level* (London: Grub Street, 1993), p. 151. CAS to Douglas, 5 October 1941; AIR 2/3133. Freeman to Tedder, 14 December 1941; AIR 20/2791.
28. An initial delivery of fifty and then a monthly quota of seventy Spitfires per month. Memorandum, 30 December 1941; AIR 2/7272.
29. Matthews, p. 101. Turbochargers utilised engine exhaust gases to drive the supercharger compressor, in contrast to a mechanical supercharger which diverted some of the engine power output at the crankshaft.
30. Twenty P-39Cs were made in the first quarter of 1941. The P-39C lacked the armour and self-sealing fuel tanks installed in the British Airacobra and the USAAC P-39D produced subsequently. Birch Matthews, *Cobra! Bell Aircraft Corporation 1934–1946* (Atglen: Schiffer, 1996), pp. 119–20, 264–5.
31. 601 Squadron ORB, 1941; AIR 27/2069.
32. FC/S 23903, 'Compass Deviation – Airacobra Aircraft', 7 November 1941; AIR 20/2999.

33. VCAS to C.-in-C. Fighter Command, 28 September 1941; ibid.
34. Churchill, *Grand Alliance*, pp. 345, 403.
35. Hurricane production from AIR 20/2039. Supply quotas from Director of War Operations to CAS, 31 December 1941; AIR 8/411.
36. Reduced from 622 to 416 Hurricanes. CAS to prime minister, 9 November 1941; AIR 2/3133.
37. 'Fighter Resources', VCAS to Chiefs of Staff Committee, 23 December 1941; AIR 8/411.
38. Douglas to VCAS, FC/S 26102, 29 September 1941; AIR 20/2999.
39. Freeman's note, 30 September 1941; ibid.
40. Weekly exports in AIR 20/1904.
41. MAP to BAC, MAP 12063, 1 December 1941; AVIA 38/735.
42. 'Report on Visit to Bell Aircraft Corp, Buffalo, December 5th and 6th 1941', A. E. Marsden, 8 December 1941; AVIA 38/793; MAP to BAC, MAP 1040, 1 February 1942; AIR 9/436.
43. Douglas, p. 158; note to VCAS, 19 November 1941. AIR 20/2999; 601 Squadron ORB. AIR 27/2070.
44. 'Re-equipment of 601 Squadron'; AMSO to VCAS, 28 February 1942; AIR 2/3133.
45. Stalin to Roosevelt, No. 41, 7 October 1942; USSR Ministry of Foreign Affairs; *Stalin's Correspondence with Roosevelt and Truman, 1941–1945* (New York: Capricorn, 1965), p. 35; Meekcoms, pp. 105–6.
46. Delivery schedules from the first ATP agreement, 'Allocations of Airplanes – 1942'; AIR 8/637.
47. The turbocharged V-1710-F series engines used in the P-38 Lightning typically had an FTH of 25,000 feet (7,620 m), or 10,000 feet (3,000 m) more than the same engine without a turbocharger; Table 5.5, Whitney, p. 145.
48. The use of the V-1710-C15 engine in the Lightning I in place of the turbocharged V-1710-F used in the USAAF P-38 and the British Lightning II has contributed to this. Whitney attributes the British rejection of the Lightning to lack of funds and inadequate altitude performance; Whitney, p. 141. Bodie repeats the importance of funding; Warren M. Bodie, *The Lockheed P-38 Lightning* (Hayesville: Widewing, 1991), pp. 46–7, 64. In fact, the British ordered the Lightning I with the same engine as the Tomahawk to ensure against delivery delays with both the F engine and the complicated turbocharger used in USAAF P-38s and the British Lightning II. Correspondence between Sir Henry Tizard and ACAS, May 1941; AVIA 15/1025.

49. Report by Wing Commander Addam, Director of Technical Development (DTD), MAP, to BAC, 9 October 1941; AVIA 15/1025. The compressibility problems stemmed from disruptive high-speed airflow over the control surfaces on the wing and tail.
50. Air Marshal Roderic Hill to C. R. Fairey, BAC, 29 November 1941; AVIA 38/861.
51. Portal to Freeman and Air Marshall Sir Christopher Courtney (AMSO), Caesar Arcadia 679 WX.4566, 6 January 1942; AIR 8/413. The figure appears to specify the total cash purchase order for 667 Lightnings in total minus the twenty aircraft completed by Lockheed at the end of 1941.
52. RAFDEL WX.9017, 9 June 1942; AIR 19/349. Elevator buffeting had been resolved by the addition of fillets to the wing leading edges where they met the fuselage; Bodie, p. 58. 'I cannot recommend the Lightning II be considered as a type satisfactory to introduce, in its present stage, as a fighter into the RAF.', Controller of Research and Development (CRD) at MAP to DTD, 17 June 1942; AVIA 15/1025.
53. BAC to MAP, BRINY 3194, 20 May 1942; ibid. For the formal handover, Amendment 77 to Contract A-242, 14 August 1942; AVIA 15/652.
54. Colonel Ben Kelsey, the original P-38 project development officer, admitted the severity of the P-38's compressibility problems; Benjamin S. Kelsey, *The Dragon's Teeth?* (Washington, DC: Smithsonian, 1982), p. 117. Dive flaps were rushed to units in Britain to modify earlier models in May 1944; Arnold to Eisenhower, No. WAR-42694, 27 May 1944; General Arnold's Message Logs. Hereafter Arnold's Logs. Record Group 18, Entry 6, National Archive and Records Administration, College Park Maryland. Hereafter NACP.
55. J. M. A. Gwyer, *Grand Strategy*, Vol. III, Part 1, *June 1941–August 1942*, (London: HMSO, 1964), pp. 129, 151; Butler, *Grand Strategy* III, Part 2, p. 556.
56. Wesley F. Craven and James L. Cate (eds), *The Army Air Forces in World War Two*, Vol. I, *Plans and Early Operations January 1939 to August 1942* (Washington, DC: Office of Air Force History, 1983), p. 566; Huston, pp. 267–75.
57. Slessor, p. 406.
58. Sir John Dill to CAS, 8 April 1942; AIR 8/637.
59. Freeman to AMSO, 14 January 1942; AIR 8/411.
60. 'Memorandum to Chief of Air Staff, RAF', 30 May 1942.

'Memorandum to Commanding General US Army Air Force' from CAS, 31 May 1942; AIR 19/349.

61. Craven and Cate, Vol. I, p. 248. Part 6, Minutes of CAS meeting 'to discuss Material Required for Arnold/Towers conference', 17 May 1942; AIR 19/348. Slessor, p. 405. Slessor was by then ACAS (Policy).
62. AT/42/8, 'Effect of Revised Allocations Proposed in Marcus 38 of 8/5', 16 May 1942; AIR 19/348.
63. 'Effect of Revised Allocations Proposed in Marcus 38 of 8/5'; ibid.
64. Butler, *Grand Strategy*, III, Part 2, p. 557; Richard M. Leighton and Robert W. Coakley, *Global Logistics and Strategy 1940–43* (Washington, DC: War Department, 1955), p. 283. Figures from Craven and Cate, I, pp. 248–9, 568.
65. Colonel deFreest Larner to John Scott, 19 August 1942; Hopkins papers.
66. Much of the combat experienced by Allied air forces in south-west Asia had been against Japanese army air force fighters, such as the Nakajima Ki 27 and Ki 43, rather than the Japanese navy's Mitsubishi A6M 'Zero'. All these fighters demonstrated outstanding range, manoeuvrability and good high-altitude performance, however. Japanese aircrew were also highly trained and experienced, in contrast to most of the Allied forces that could be spared in Asia in 1941.
67. MacArthur HQ SWPA No. AG 730, 14 May 1942; Arnold's Logs.
68. 'It is urgently recommended that reconsideration be given to supplementing our present P-40 Fighters with a new and improved type . . .', New Delhi, Naiden, No. Aquila 3331B, 25 July 1942; Arnold's Logs.
69. Chief of Staff to C.-in-C., United States Fleet and Chief of Naval Operations, 'Aircraft Situation in Solomon Islands', 26 September 1942; Lovett papers.
70. Christopher Shores, Brian Cull and Yasuho Izawa, *Bloody Shambles*, Vol. 2, (London: Grub Street, 2000), pp. 176–82. The resulting Australian inquiry revealed critical problems with early warning and ground control, Appendix 3, 'The RAAF and the Darwin raids'; Douglas Gillison, *Australia in the War of 1939–1945*. Series 3 – *Air*, Vol. I (Canberra: Australian War Memorial, 1962), pp. 714-16.
71. Christopher Thorne, *Allies of a Kind: The United States, Britain and the War Against Japan 1941–1945* (Oxford: Oxford University Press, 1979), pp. 252–7. For the offer of a Spitfire wing, Butler,

Grand Strategy, III, Part 2, p. 496. The Australian Minister of Foreign Affairs described the Spitfires as '. . . the best fighters in the world' and Churchill's initiative as '. . . an expression of mutual support which should bind together the countries of the Empire and will go some way towards repaying the sacrifices made by Australia in [the] Imperial cause.' Cablegram ET33, Evatt to Curtin, 28 May 1942; Document 502, Documents on Australian Foreign Policy, Australian Government Department of Foreign Affairs and Trade. http://www.info.dfat.gov.au/info/historical/HistDocs.nsf/(LookupVolNoNumber)/5~502.

72. Churchill to Curtin, 23 May 1942; PREM 3/150/7.
73. Evatt to Churchill, 25 June 1942; also Evatt to Brendan Bracken, Minister of Information, 28 June 1942; ibid.
74. Evatt to Churchill, 30 June 1942; ibid.
75. Air Vice Marshall Evill, RAFDEL, to CAS, 5 September 1942; AIR 19/349. Original date for concern given as '1942', but text indicates future production after April 1943 is more relevant.
76. Freeman to Tedder, 29 September 1941; AIR 20/2791. RAFDEL to Air Ministry, Caesar 610 WX.3964, 4 January 1942; AIR 8/413.
77. Arnold, p. 296.
78. Eisenhower, No. 1715, 1 September 1942; Arnold's Logs.
79. Alexander Seversky, *Victory Through Air Power* (New York: Simon & Schuster, 1942), pp. 235, 242. Seversky's belief that the high-altitude power-output problem of the Allison could be solved by the adoption of the notoriously unreliable Napier Sabre was somewhat misplaced but he confirmed the relative quality of the Spitfire: '. . . as all airmen knew, General Spaatz borrowed Spitfires because American fighter planes were unable to stay in the air with the Germans'; Alexander Seversky, *Air Power: Key to Survival* (London: Herbert Jenkins, 1952), p. 185. Arnold, pp. 296–8.
80. 'Design and Operation of United States Combat Aircraft', Office of War Information Advance Release for Monday Afternoon Papers, October 19, 1942, pp. 7–8; Lovett papers.
81. R. Keith Kane, Chief of the Bureau of Intelligence at the Office of War Information to Lieutenant Colonel George Brownell, Office of the Assistant Secretary for Air, 28 November 1942. 'Just How Good Are Our War Planes?', *The Daily Mirror*, 16 September 1942; Lovett papers.
82. Jeffrey Quill, *Spitfire: A Test Pilot's Story* (Manchester: Crécy, 1996), pp. 214–19. Comparative testing of a captured FW 190

against a Spitfire V indicated that it was 20–30 mph faster than the Spitfire V and more manoeuvrable in almost every respect. Appendix D, Chapter 10, Alfred Price, *The Spitfire Story* (London: Arms & Armour, 1999), pp. 143–4; Peter Caygill, *Flying to the Limit* (Barnsley: Pen & Sword, 2005), pp. 106–15.

83. Douglas and Wright, pp. 160–1.
84. Freeman to CAS, 6 June 1942. AIR 8/650.
85. Senior Air Staff Officer (SASO) Fighter Command, 17 May 1942. Memorandum 77; AIR 16/587.
86. Portal to Air Marshal Sir Douglas Evill, RAF Delegation in Washington, Webber W.394 and Webber W.465 12 April and 17 April 1942; AIR 9/165.
87. Chaney's correspondence with Arnold given below is anticipated in his correspondence with Portal, 2–20 May 1942; AIR 20/2836.
88. Chaney, No. 1284, 25 April 1942; Arnold's Logs.
89. 'P-38s have been in use long enough to demonstrate serviceability . . . buffeting and poor handling qualities corrected and speed increased.', WD 476 (PC 892) annotation to No. 1284, 26 April 1942; Arnold's Logs.
90. Chaney, No. 1373, 4 May 1942; attached note to No. 1373, 6 May 1942, Chaney No. 1473, 8 May 1942; Arnold's Logs. Chaney to Portal, 2 May 1942, and Slessor to Evill, Webber W.799, 9 May 1941; AIR 20/2836.
91. Arnold diary entry, 26 May 1942. 'Long discussion with Chaney and Winant re efficiency of US pursuit, P-39 especially. Chaney doubts the efficiency of both P-38 and P-39, thinks we are doing wrong by using either.', Huston, p. 296.
92. Leland Atwood, vice president of North American Aviation at the time, rejects the attribution of the Mustang's aerodynamic efficiency to the use of a laminar-flow wing. J. Leland Atwood, 'We Can Build You a Better Airplane than the P-40', *Aeroplane Magazine*, Vol. 27, No. 5 (May 1999), pp. 34–5.
93. Fifty-eight Mustangs out of 150 from a single Lend-Lease order were diverted to the USAAF immediately after Pearl Harbor; Meekcoms, p. 113. War Production Board plans included a total of 620 British-contract Mustangs and a further 150 on Lend-Lease procurement before the termination of production at the end of August 1942. Table A, War Production Board Aircraft Branch Report 8.1, 31 January 1942; Hopkins papers.
94. Arnold, p. 376; Wesley F. Craven and James L. Cate (eds), *The*

Army Air Forces in World War Two, Vol. VI, *Men and Planes* (Chicago: Chicago University Press, 1955), p. 217.

95. Undersecretary of State for Air to C.-in-C. of Army Co-operation Command, S.69372/DGO, 21 July 1941; AIR 39/25.
96. Item 8(c), 'Memorandum to Commanding General US Army Air Force' from CAS, 31 May 1942; ibid. Ironically, in view of Portal's comments, the RAF's Allison-engined fighter-reconnaissance Mustangs would eventually be replaced with Spitfires at the end of 1944. Christopher Shores and Chris Thomas, *2nd Tactical Air Force*, Vol. II (Hersham: Classic, 2005), pp. 310–11.
97. CAS to Slessor, Webber W.501, 17 June 1942; AIR 19/349.
98. Slessor to CAS, Marcus 129, 6 June 1942; ibid.
99. Slessor to CAS, Marcus 136, 8 June 1942; ibid.
100. Slessor to CAS, Marcus 332, 11 June 1942; ibid.
101. Section 2(b) and 2(c), Annex A: 'Allocations of Aircraft Other Than Fleet Air Arm Types to Great Britain', Craven and Cate, VI, p. 568.
102. Draft agreement, 'Allocations of American Aircraft', RAF Delegation to Air Ministry, Marcus 410, 13 June 1942; AIR 19/349.
103. Cairncross, p. 82.
104. Initial trials reports for Mustang I quoted by Ken Delve, *The Mustang Story* (London: Arms & Armour, 1999), p. 13 and David Birch, *Rolls-Royce and the Mustang* (Derby: Rolls-Royce Heritage Trust, 1987), pp. 9–30. The Merlin 60-series engines were based on the Merlin 20-series with the addition of a second, enlarged supercharger working in series with the first. The Rolls-Royce designer involved attributed to the installation of this engine in the Spitfire a 10,000 feet (3,050 m) increase in fighting altitude and a 70 mph increase in speed; Hooker, p. 56.
105. Slessor from CAS, Webber 283, 5 June 1942; AIR 19/349.
106. Rolls-Royce correspondence dated 3 June 1942 indicates that Winant 'instructed' Arnold to proceed with a Packard Merlin installation in the United States two weeks after Rolls-Royce first raised the idea with the MAP; Birch, pp. 11, 12–15.
107. Winant to Hopkins for General Arnold, Number 84, 5 June 1942; Hopkins papers.
108. Birch, p. 21; Furse, pp. 227–9.
109. Winant to Hopkins, ibid. Freeman to Ernest Hives, Director of Rolls-Royce, 30 June 1942, quoted in Birch, p. 21.
110. Birch, p. 16.

111. Paul Ludwig, *Development of the P-51 Mustang Long-Range Escort Fighter* (Hersham: Classic, 2003), p. 84; Whitney, p. 157.
112. Slessor to CAS, Marcus 136, 8 June 1942. AIR 19/349.
113. Delve, p. 32.
114. Churchill to Hopkins, 16 October 1942. Hopkins Papers.
115. With an additional two XP-51B development aircraft. 'Army Air Forces Aircraft Procurement Programs (Fiscal Year Funds 1941–1943). Number of Aircraft on Program, on Contract, Accepted and Delivered as of September 30, 1942', p. 10; Lovett papers.
116. Schedule 'B', 126-1 (J.C.S. 178), 'Joint Chiefs of Staff agreement on Air Supplies to the British in 1943', 25 December 1942; Lovett papers.
117. Item 8, 'Review of Fighter Resources', 20 October 1941; AIR 19/302.
118. Whitney minimises the extent of the problem by referring to the comparison of single-stage Allisons against two-stage Merlins; Whitney, p. 326. This ignores the adoption of the single-stage Packard Merlin 20 series in the Kittyhawk, and the Merlin 45 in the Spitfire V, as well as the later reliability issues of the turbo-charged V-1710-F.
119. British testing indicated that the P-40F was almost 4 minutes faster to climb to 20,000 feet (6,096 m) than the P-40D, and approximately 20 mph faster at that height, with the Spitfire V a further 20 mph faster than the P-40F and another 4 minutes faster to climb to the same altitude; Caygill, pp. 151–3; Price, p. 143. At that altitude the Packard Merlin V-1650-1 in the P-40F produced the same power as the Merlin 46 engine used in the Spitfire V.
120. Kelsey, p. 117; Bodie, p. 208; Eaker, No. 29, 19 November 1942; Doolittle, No. K-3763, 17 February 1944; Spaatz, No. K-3225, 22 January 1944; and Spaatz, No. E-3044, 30 May 1944; Arnold's Logs.
121. General Harmon, then in London as part of the USAAF observer mission, to Military Intelligence Division, Number 1133, 1 May 1941; Arnold to General Brett, 3 May 1941, Entry 22, Record Group 18; NACP.
122. Craven and Cate, Vol. VI, pp. 212–14. Matthews contradicts the assertion by Craven and Cate that the P-39 and P-40 were designed for coastal defence and ground attack; these roles sprang up after their shortcomings as interceptors had become apparent; Matthews, p. 104.
123. Wesley F. Craven and James L. Cate (eds), *The Army Air Forces in*

World War II, Vol. IV (Washington, DC: War Department, 1950), p. 41.

124. The Allison V-1710-E4; Table 5.8, Whitney, p. 149. The first operational tests in the south-west Pacific Area of a P-39D with the supercharger gearing changed to increase the FTH of the engine were not completed until February 1943, resulting in a request to replace the supercharger gearing in all existing P-39, P-400 and P-40 aircraft in the south-west Pacific area, an unnecessary step if the undesirable supercharger gearing was restricted to British-contracted P-400s in isolation; HQ, SWPA to Air Service Command, Brisbane No. XA 1085, 2 February 1943; Arnold's Logs.
125. The performance differential between the P-39 and the Spitfire is not discussed in the official history's account of the 31st Fighter Group's deployment to Britain. Craven & Cate, *I*, p. 642. The episode avoids treatment by Slessor's biographer. Orange, *Slessor*, pp. 91–2.
126. Neither Arnold nor Huston explain why Soviet allocations were considered inviolable, in contrast to British allocations. The fact that Arnold's position in April–May 1942 involved reneging on the existing first ATP agreement is not discussed, nor is the change in USAAF position towards the British requests between April and June. Huston, pp. 272–7.
127. Craven and Cate, I, p. 566.
128. Ibid., pp. 476–7, 642.
129. AMSO to Sinclair, 12 April 1942; AIR 19/286.
130. Memorandum, 9 September 1942; AIR 2/7762.
131. By April 1942, the RAF's targets for Spitfire reserves had been set at 320 to be achieved by 1 June 1942; Memorandum 29A, Douglas to Portal, 3 August 1942; AIR 2/3133.
132. About a third of average monthly Spitfire production at that time. Some 1074 Spitfires were produced between July and September 1942, or about 358 per month; AIR 20/2039.
133. By September 1942 Fighter Command's wastage allocation had been reduced from three hundred Spitfires per month to 225 and then down to 160 in the coming winter months; memorandum, 12 August 1942; AIR 20/2393.
134. RAFDEL to Air Ministry, Marcus 74, 9 May 1942; AIR 9/165.
135. Craven and Cate, VI, p. xv.
136. Winston S. Churchill, *The Second World War*, Vol. IV, *The Hinge of Fate* (London: Cassell, 1951), pp. 517–18. Spitfire Vs were

shipped via the Persian Gulf in November 1942; CAB 111/101. They were used by the Soviets in the Kuban bridgehead campaign in 1943; Price, pp. 140–2.

137. Air Marshal Roderic Hill to C. R. Fairey, BAC, 29 November 1941; AVIA 38/861.
138. Huston, p. 312.
139. Furse, p. 228.
140. For Chaney's relationship with Arnold, Craven and Cate, I, pp. 578–85 and Coffey, p. 273.

8 Collaboration and Interdependency

> We propose to consider first the single elements of our subject, then each branch or part, and, last of all, the whole, in all its relations – therefore to advance from the simple to the complex.
>
> *Carl von Clausewitz*[1]

The seminal military theorist Clausewitz wrote before the evolution of air power and did not pay much attention to the dynamics of the kinds of economic and maritime war traditionally waged by the British state in the eighteenth and early nineteenth centuries that were echoed in the maritime blockade and peripheral campaigns of World War II. Nonetheless, some of his ideas can be successfully applied to the British experience in that conflict. This narrative has used a series of case studies to provide a more general reappraisal of the Anglo-American aircraft supply relationship in the first half of World War II. All these case studies have identified factors operating to constrain the value of American aircraft supply. These constraints operated in the classical sense of Clausewitzian 'friction', or the accumulation of difficulties and circumstances that cause disappointment in any endeavour.[2]

The result of this friction was that American aircraft supply in 1940–2 fell short of the assertions associated with it at the time. Furthermore, subsequent historical accounts failed to recognise fully this friction and have perpetuated misperceptions concerning the importance of American aircraft supply to Britain. The key causes of that friction have been identified in political, quantitative and qualitative factors that have not been sufficiently explained in previous historiography. These can be recapitulated and summarised before giving a new explanation to provide a more accurate understanding of aircraft supply diplomacy and how this can inform our understanding of the wartime Anglo-American relationship.

The political influences bearing on aircraft supply fall under two broad headings. These are the diplomacy conducted to secure access to American supplies and exploit the full potential of American production, and the political and factional resistance to that diplomacy. The diplomacy involved and the resistance to it adapted and changed over time. At the beginning of this period, the French and British and then the British alone fought to establish and maintain a claim on large-scale American aircraft production but much of the rest of the period was spent defending that claim against USAAF resistance before the full extent of that production was realised.

The ultimate objective of this supply diplomacy was the full mobilisation of the United States economy on the Allied side, a mobilisation that was eventually achieved in 1943–5 and ensured that American production delivered an overwhelming quantity of high-quality aircraft which played a decisive role in winning air supremacy over Germany and Japan in 1944–5. But this does not account for the situation in 1939–42 and the full spectrum of diplomacy required to secure British objectives in that period. During this time, the British operated a qualitative deployment policy which often marginalised American aircraft at the same time as they struggled to increase the numbers and quality of aircraft supplied. This involved a complex and dynamic process in which the goals of British strategic diplomacy could be, and were, sometimes frustrated, and the British had to adapt their policy as a consequence.

British aircraft supply policy can be divided into several phases: 'marginal' supply in 1938–40, when the British followed the French lead; a period in 1940 and early 1941 when the 'critical dependency' thesis advanced by Lord Lothian became dominant; and a subsequent and lesser-known tertiary phase in 1941–2, where the British struggled to deal with the reality of American aircraft supply while conducting their own war effort. Incorporated within the second two stages of this process were two key issues:

the portrayal of British resistance as crucial to American interests, and the assertion of immediate American aid measures as critical to that resistance. This provided the framework for the 'mobilisation procurement' strategy of Monnet and Purvis to operate, which sought to use Allied purchase orders as the catalyst to mobilise American economic potential behind the Allies.

This process demanded that political resistance to aiding the Allies be overcome. That resistance ranged from the financial restrictions imposed by isolationist legislation, which were removed by Lend-Lease, to the resistance of the United States services to aircraft allocation to the British which dilated on the outbreak of war and remained a problem subsequently. The direction of this diplomacy would often proceed in a more complex manner than previous accounts of events in 1940 might suggest, being initially framed to provide the political gestures required to keep the French in the war, and then being informed by the dictates of American politics as understood by Lothian, Purvis and Morgenthau. Their initial objectives included the immediate supply of small numbers of aircraft, which were known to be of marginal operational value, in order to facilitate the political conditions necessary for the United States to become entangled in the British war effort. Their ultimate objective was to stimulate a massive expansion of American aircraft production which was believed to be essential for ultimate victory. A key element in this was the British commitment to an aircraft production programme that ultimately could be financed only by the United States and which was, therefore, instrumental in precipitating Lend-Lease. This was clearly indicated by Purvis, one of the main architects of the '3,000 per month' plan and the associated 'balance sheet', when he admitted later in 1941 that, 'This statement had been very useful in overcoming what was the main difficulty at the time – finance'.[3]

The critical dependency diplomacy of 1940 had shaped the subsequent perception of American aircraft supply to Britain but how valid is that perception? Were supplies of American aircraft critical for British survival? Did they make the difference between survival and defeat? What did the British believe at the time? Did American aircraft supply meet the diplomatic and military objectives set for it? These questions have been addressed by a detailed exploration of the context involved which reveals a far more complex and wide-ranging British supply strategy than the conventional wisdom assumes.

Aircraft supply diplomacy did not end with the evolution of Lend-Lease nor with the entry of the United States into the war. In the third phase of British aircraft supply diplomacy, the British attempted to reconcile an aircraft deployment policy that marginalised American types for secondary theatres and roles at the same time as they continued to assert the critical importance of American supply. The conflicts which resulted, and the manner in which they arose and were resolved, have illustrated the continuing operation of political constraints on American aircraft supply. These proceeded from the breakdown of the Slessor agreement, the failure to secure more heavy bombers at the Atlantic conference, and the situation in 1942 where the British had to supply their own aircraft to the USAAF to secure continuing supplies of American aircraft.

Continuing political constraints were also joined by enduring quantitative and qualitative constraints. Quantitative constraints, in the form of delayed deliveries due to the small scale of American industry and the problems of expanding production, were noted in the pre-war period and remained a constant problem from 1940 onwards. Qualitative constraints, in the form of equipment or performance shortcomings, limited the perceived value of American aircraft even before 1939. All these acted to restrict the utility of American aircraft in various ways and thereby determine their operational value. This is revealed by the manner in which the RAF adopted a qualitative deployment policy, most obviously in the case of American fighters in 1942. But this was, in fact, evident throughout the previous two years where even a versatile and useful aircraft such as the Hudson was not seen as an adequate replacement for available but obsolescent British types such as the Blenheim.

These qualitative and quantitative deficiencies, and the qualitative deployment policy that resulted from them, created an 'expectational gap' where the use of American aircraft contradicted the routinely extravagant assertions of the diplomacy employed to secure them. This gap required considerable attention in British supply diplomacy as it provided ammunition that could easily be employed to further USAAF resistance to supplying the British in the longer term.

The concept of the expectational gap turns us towards RAF deployment policy, the real indicator of the military value of American aircraft. The account here has attempted to illustrate how the RAF perceived American aircraft and how they fitted into British air strategy. The result can clearly be seen to diverge from the exhortatory targets of diplomacy in 1940 and even from RAF strategic requirements. Firstly, it must be observed that the RAF was more sceptical of exhortatory procurement targets than many assume, and this was obvious from the Slessor mission onwards. The prospect of huge levels of aircraft supply from the United States was obviously welcome but, while the RAF became an active participant in exhortatory United States plans in the heavy bomber diplomacy of 1941, the Air Staff generally did not allow the fevered imaginations of the politicians or procurement executives to dictate their deployment plans.

Where specific objectives can be identified for American aircraft supply, it failed to meet expectations. Examples detailed include providing 'insurance' against the loss of domestic production, relieving the need to supply overseas theatres, meeting the Soviet quota, and providing the enormous expansion in heavy bomber production demanded by British strategy in 1941. All these objectives required British aircraft supply to be substituted for American when the latter fell short of expectations. This is not to assert that American aircraft were unimportant, merely to observe that their military value diverged from their political and diplomatic importance. The diplomacy of American aircraft supply was infused with expectations of decisive levels of output, sufficient to play a war-winning role. Until much later in the war, the reality was somewhat different and the history of Anglo-American aircraft supply given here is one of how the British accommodated themselves to this reality.

It can be said from the outset that the political importance of American aircraft was perceived to be the inverse of their actual operational value. This could be seen in the tentative steps taken by the British towards developing American aircraft production in 1938–39. From the time of the Weir mission and the first French purchase mission, they were considered by the British, French and Americans to have a diplomatic significance beyond their marginal military value. British pre-war plans saw the United States as 'a contingent reserve'.[4] Though this would change in 1940, pre-war opinion that American industry was small, and their products expensive and of limited quality, would take a lot longer to change.[5]

The diplomatic value of American aircraft was particularly significant in the case of the French who experienced a military and political need for American aid which far outstripped that of the British in the same period. The French position can be contrasted with that of the British which was informed by a greater feeling of security in their own domestic air rearmament programme. A sense of the diplomatic importance of aircraft supply affected British procurement policy more subtly, never developing into the sense of immediate criticality demonstrated by the statements and personal diplomacy of Bonnet, Daladier and Monnet. It is, indeed, difficult to see Chamberlain matching Daladier's claim to be willing to 'sell Versailles' to get the American aircraft required for victory.[6]

While Roosevelt saw aircraft supply as a way of bolstering Allied resistance to Hitler's aggression, this was almost entirely concentrated on the French. British needs from American supply at this time were concentrated on particular niches (such as the machine tools required to expand British aircraft production, or the supply of training aircraft) which allowed British air rearmament to concentrate more heavily on operational combat aircraft. This pattern would persist after the British followed the French precedent of 'critical dependency' diplomacy.

The key obstacles to any substantial American supply programme were the constraints isolationist legislation placed upon Allied access to the American economy. The removal of the Neutrality Act embargo gave scope for Jean Monnet's arguments to prevail, which culminated in the joint Allied purchase programme of spring 1940. The importance of this programme to subsequent American aircraft supply cannot be overstated; it essentially defined the reality of American aircraft production which lay behind the diplomatic interactions for the next two years. It remains a remarkable fact, however, that the Air Ministry dedicated practically no thought to the employment of the aircraft from this programme until July 1940. The adoption of the plan had everything to do with politics: securing a visible gesture of American support for the Allies; bolstering French resolve; reinforcing the French air force which was perceived to be in dire need of modern military aircraft; and being seen to respond in a meaningful way to the administration's efforts to overcome isolationist legislation.

The crisis of 1940 saw the British adopt the thesis of criticality which had previously been used by the French. American aid was deliberately and repetitively characterised as being critical to continuing British resistance. While this had reflected the relatively urgent military and political needs in France, in the British case it was falsified by the reality of June–August 1940. Where France had been forced out of the war by German military success, regardless of American moral encouragement or material assistance, British resistance continued. It continued despite the understandable inability or unwillingness of Roosevelt to move forward on 'immediate aid' supply initiatives, such as releasing USAAC aircraft. This leaves a problem for historians seeking to emphasise the importance of American aid to Britain in 1940.

At the most basic level, using the correspondence between Churchill and Roosevelt as an accurate measure of British strategic supply requirements at face value can distort the contemporary reality. Referring to the British requests for arms and aircraft in this period as demonstrating British dependence upon the United States, Martin Gilbert observes that: 'The United States was already serving, however, as the essential arsenal for British war supplies'.[7] This is premature. The strategic need for American aid had been identified but there was, as yet, no evidence of it actually appearing. And yet the British did not draw the apparently obvious conclusion from this and sue for peace.

A key factor in the background context enabling this decision to be reached was British confidence in the capacity of Britain's sea and air power to defeat any invasion attempt. Even when the administration resumed more active support, after Britain's capacity to survive had been demonstrated, the British had no illusions about the number or quality of American aircraft immediately available, and even turned down the offer, made in August, of the P-40s that had been a central feature of supply diplomacy in May and June. The concept of a critical British military dependency on immediate American supply measures is therefore contradicted by the contemporary reality. The concept of a critical political dependency, however, is closer to the truth but still contradicted by the continuation of resistance into the winter of 1940 when disappointment and complaints about American supplies mounted and American policy lagged far behind the more optimistic hopes.

This marginality was reflected in the minimal contribution of American aircraft to the RAF's order of battle at the end of 1940 and which continued over the next two years. Instead, the diplomacy involved in the initial assertions of critical dependency can be related to the political and diplomatic efforts made to keep the French in the war and to entangle the United States in the future British war effort. During the Lend-Lease period, undoubtedly the apotheosis of critical dependency diplomacy, British concerns were primarily engaged on an aircraft production programme that would mature a year or more later, and were therefore irrelevant to the needs of immediate survival. This remains the fundamental example of exhortatory production planning with high-level political and diplomatic objectives.

The mobilisation procurement of Monnet and Purvis was clearly in long-term British interest. Those ambitions outstripped contemporary RAF plans, however, and were driven, in part, by the wishes of the administration. As Richard Overy has observed in relation to Roosevelt's use of unrealistic rhetorical targets for aircraft production: 'The figures bore no relation to what the industry was capable of producing, nor any relation to what the air forces were demanding.'[8] These targets would eventually be achieved, but not in the timescale initially set out for them, while the ability of the British to access even agreed levels of this production would prove to be problematic. It is worth repeating the words of Sir Arthur Salter's report to the War Cabinet at the end of July 1940, as they clearly reveal the British objectives behind the mobilisation procurement strategy.

> In general it is of urgent importance to 'talk big and at once'. It matters little if we over-estimate . . . The greater our estimate the greater will be the extension of America's productive capacity for our armaments. If sufficient productive capacity is created now, it matters little how it is allotted. Its products will be available for our war effort, if by us – good; if by the Americans themselves – better still.[9]

This approach was evident in 1940 and continued long afterwards in aircraft supply diplomacy. In January 1942, the BAC explained their use of inflated statistics in the negotiations leading up to the first ATP agreement. 'The reason for this was partly the desirability of over-estimating our needs from America at a time when it was known that a large new production programme was in prospect . . .'[10]

In the event, as the British official historians would note, the aircraft produced as a result of this diplomacy would largely be employed by the US services when they finally materialised.[11] Although American production would eventually rise to the extent that it would meet the ambitious hopes of 1940–2 and prove sufficient to meet most of the enormous global demands placed upon it, this took time to achieve. The limited and marginal value of American supplies in 1940–2 was certainly not a matter of surprise to the British government, even if the political obstacles encountered in the process of securing it and its slow delivery still attracted disappointed comment. In the meantime, we must account for British strategy and operations in the absence of the critical dependency asserted by diplomatic rhetoric. The fundamental reality was that an overarching diplomatic strategy of asserting critical dependency consistently overstated the value and significance of immediately available American aid.

There are several explanations for this. The most obvious is that the British wanted all the aid that they could get. This by no means detracts from the fundamental reality that the aid available was known to be of marginal significance. There were certain significant niches, such as the supply of flying boats where the

American Catalina was clearly superior to the defective British Saro Lerwick at a time when production of the only British alternative, the Short Sunderland, was insufficient for demand. In that area, at least, the British genuinely depended upon supplies of American aircraft to meet a significant strategic need.

Such examples are rare, however, and are not sufficient to explain fully the reality where many of the aircraft involved in appeals for immediate aid were known to be of minimal operational value to the RAF. Much of the rationale for this lies in the significance of such measures as stepping stones towards the greater collaboration that the British ultimately desired. This was openly acknowledged by the British in the form of the destroyers bases deal, and it is now suggested that a similar dynamic was present in the supply of other potentially useful but non-critical aircraft, such as the Curtiss P-36 and P-40. These aircraft might have had value in an extremis never reached by the British during the Battle of Britain but, more importantly, their supply involved the Americans accepting the political importance of delivering them to Britain, and set the precedent for future supply aid. By pressing for the supply of marginally important aircraft in immediate aid measures, the British forced the American administration to prioritise supplying the Allies above rearmament for American or hemispheric defence. Openly rejecting such aircraft would completely contradict the critical dependency thesis, undermine support within the administration, and restrict the future potential of American supply to Britain.

The advantageous position the British had apparently achieved in aircraft supply by early 1941 was not simply a question of the Roosevelt administration sharing a British perception of overall strategic needs rather than the USAAF's. In a very real sense, the British had paid for their position with hard cash. The administration, and Morgenthau in particular, set enormous store in evidence of Allied co-operation with American financial policy. This was evident from 1939 in Morgenthau's interest in French gold expenditure and British defence of the sterling–dollar exchange rate, all the way through to Lend-Lease in 1941 and beyond.[12] Aircraft supply became the principal vehicle for this policy to be pursued in 1940–1. That was evident in the huge sums involved in capital investment required for the '3,000 per month' scheme in August–September 1940, the ultimate output from which was known to be beyond the British ability to pay for and led directly to Lend-Lease. Financial investment was taken by the administration, and ultimately by the American public, as demonstrable evidence of the primacy of co-operation instead of selfish national self-interest on the British part. Alongside the demonstration of continuing British resistance in 1940, which was in American interest, British industrial investment was instrumental in allowing the influence of traditional antagonisms to be eroded to the point where isolationist legislation could be defeated.

On the British side, at a time when the cabinet was considering the likely hiatus in developments before the American election in November 1940 and the possibility of a new Republican administration taking up the reins in Washington in January 1941, this capital investment in American aircraft production was seen as a way of forcing the American administration to continue to finance that capacity. This would stimulate American aircraft production on a massive scale at the same time as resolving the crippling constraints of the Johnson Act and committing that production to the British war effort. This programme was the fundamental determinant in securing British access to American war production and the full economic collaboration identified as a prerequisite for eventual victory.

Committing to this programme would exhaust British financial resources within months at a point where Roosevelt had given no clear and unambiguous undertaking that the United States would assume the resulting financial commitment. This was, as Beaverbrook admitted, risk taking but it is clear that the risks involved were calculated ones to achieve a major objective of British statecraft.[13] Nonetheless, the specific outcome of such schemes was an issue of future importance with no relevance to meeting the needs of the current situation. As Beaverbrook stated, and as Slessor and the Air Ministry were to repeat on many occasions subsequently, the output from such plans would only fully materialise in 1942.[14]

Despite the fact that the administration's response was too late to avoid the interim finance crisis of spring 1941, British policy was successful. The remarkable thing about this is that the British went ahead with this programme on the basis of the most indefinite statements of approval from the administration. The capital investment involved in the joint Allied purchase programme of spring 1940 had been encouraged by an implicit understanding that the output of that capacity would be made available to the Allies for the remainder of the war.[15] 'This expansion will be at the expense of the Allied governments but its output would be available on option for the Allies for the duration of the war.'[16] When the British had to defend their expectations of continued supply from this capacity under Lend-Lease in 1941–2, there was apparently no formal agreement or undertaking available to support them beyond the statements of Roosevelt and Morgenthau to the press in 1940–1. This financial investment ultimately secured a bedrock minimum of American aircraft supply but it required continuous high-level political support to defend it.

That was usually invoked by the British to fend off encroachment by the USAAF on their claimed allocations. One example took place in July 1941 when Lend-Lease appropriations were being discussed to pay for the continuing production from British-funded capacity, and the BAC recorded the following story:

> We claimed the right of appeal to the President to establish whether the US departments were interpreting the President's public statements correctly. The US representatives then withdrew their objection and General Burns informed us that they accepted the principle and the programme went forward on this basis.[17]

This ability to escalate disagreements to Roosevelt via civilian officials, such as Morgenthau or Hopkins, provoked resentment from the USAAF at the time and criticism from historians of the USAAF subsequently.[18] What tends to be left unsaid is that these threats of escalation arose when the British were attempting to counter the unilateral abrogation of existing supply agreements at the behest of the USAAF. The necessity for this kind of escalation, born out of the difficulties of maintaining aircraft supply agreements in the face of USAAF competition, was reiterated by the head of the RAF Delegation as late as October 1942. 'There does not appear to be any really effective organisation below the President capable of reviewing and adjusting the conflicting interests of the services . . .'[19]

Such capacity did not always operate to British benefit and was determined by the political context of the moment. Indeed, Arnold himself was able to invoke the same process to increase USAAF allocations at British expense in the spring of 1942. As Hopkins and Harris observed in relation to heavy bomber supply, the British could not always rely on the capacity and willingness of civil officials in the administration to overrule the USAAF. This all sprang from the political difficulties created when dealing with chronic production shortfalls.

There were only two ways of resolving such quantitative shortcomings: implementing a higher priority for British allocations against USAAF resistance, or urging higher production with USAAF support. While the British employed both tactics, it should not be surprising that the need constantly to resort to them caused disenchantment. By November 1941, more than a year down the road of increasingly ambitious production targets, the Air Ministry had reached stark conclusions that emphasised that American production must be increased still further.

> At the root of the matter lies the hard fact that American production has not yet faced up to American policy. America has promised to be the arsenal of democracy and to send a vast flow of armaments to Great Britain, China and the other countries resisting aggression . . . These commitments cannot be faced with the capacity yet created in America, and no system of allocations will resolve a dilemma which springs from inadequate supply.[20]

In the same month, the MAP warned the BAC of the bitter disappointment of the Air Staff with the prospects of American supply. 'You know this but you may perhaps not realise the full depth of feeling on the subject on this side.'[21] This sense of disappointment was enduring. As the public rhetoric continued to outstrip the available resources, sharp conflicts arose and demanded constant attempts to resolve them. These would finally peak in mid-1942 and effectively settle American aircraft allocation for the rest of the war. The conflicts generally arose over two issues: quantity and quality. Quantity was the most obvious and easily calculated of these problems.

The negotiation of the Slessor Agreement had established British expectations at the time of Lend-Lease. In the event, neither the production nor allocation targets could be maintained, and this was the determining feature of all the aircraft allocation agreements that followed. Between the end of 1940 and the middle of 1942, the British received 6,974 operational aircraft against the promised number of 26,000; by the end of 1942 they received a total of 9,687 aircraft. In total, they eventually received less than 20 per cent of the background expectation of 50,000 aircraft involved in the supply diplomacy of 1940–1.[22]

The extent to which American aircraft supply continued to fail to meet British expectations in 1942 can be seen in Table 8.1. What makes these figures particularly significant is that they reveal the failure to meet the schedule agreed by Arnold in the first ATP Agreement which, in theory, accounted for the new commitments that arose by the end of 1941 in the form of the Soviet supply protocol and the entry of the United States into the war. By this time, January 1942, American production had a year in which to grow to meet the targets of 1941, and the commitments on that supply had now reached their fullest extent.

It should be noted that Bermudas and Lightnings were delivered to the BAC in the United States but only deliveries accepted by the RAF were recorded as 'deliveries' in Table 8.1. In fact, the situation was worse than it appeared because the Airacobras accepted by the RAF – including the fourteen aircraft used to maintain one flight of 601 Squadron on Airacobras between October 1941 and March 1942 – were all transferred to the USAAF or shipped to the Soviet Union, reducing the total number available for use by the RAF by 375 to 3,792 aircraft or 38.2 per cent of the number promised in the first ATP agreement.[23] The types in which the British were able to claim a high proportion of their original allocation, such as the Hudson, Baltimore and the Mustang, were the ones that were generally not subject to strong competition from the USAAF in 1942.

In total the British received 22.2 per cent of the total American

Table 8.1 First ATP agreement allocations of US aircraft supply and deliveries, 1942

Type	First ATP allocations for 1942 (Jan 1942)[24]	Deliveries to RAF in UK, 1942[25]	Deliveries to overseas commands and dominion governments, 1942	British receipts (percentage of first ATP allocation)	Total US production, 1942[26] (percentage British receipts of total)
B-17 Fortress	275	43	0	43 (15.6)	1,412 (3.0)
B-24 Liberator	314	124	5	129 (41.1)	1,164 (11.1)
B-25 Mitchell	390	76	0	76 (19.5)	1,554 (4.9)
B-26 Marauder	479	0	45	45 (9.4)	803 (5.6)
Ventura	875	144	163	307 (35.1)	913 (33.6)
A-20 Boston	199	180	5	185 (93)	1,785 (10.4)
Hudson (inc. transport version)	617	310	471	781 (126.6)	836 (93.4)
Baltimore	774	0	367	367 (47.4)	505 (72.7)
Vengeance	807	4	204	208 (25.8)	786 (26.5)
Bermuda	748	0	0	0 (0)	Not recorded
P-38 Lightning	647	3	0	3 (0)	1,479 (0)
P-51 Mustang	701	605	0	605 (86.3)	634 (95.4)
P-39 Airacobra	659	375	0	375 (56.9)	1,973 (19)
P-40 Kittyhawk	1903	10	1033	1,043 (54.8)	4,454 (23.4)
P-47 Thunderbolt	95	0	0	0 (0)	532 (0)
Total	9,935	1,874	2,293	4,167 (41.9)	18,830 (22.2)

Table 8.2 British aircraft production and total shipments overseas, 1942[27]

Type	Production in 1942	Shipped to overseas destinations (inc. Russia)
Halifax	802	41
Lancaster	693	0
Manchester	11	0
Stirling	461	0
Hampden	56	0
Wellington	2,702	708
Whitley	540	0
Blenheim	678	566
Mosquito (bomber variant)	131	3
Beaufort	317	218
Beaufighter	1,579	562
Hurricane	3,067	3,421
Mosquito (fighter variant)	297	0
Spitfire	4,144	1,911
Typhoon	686	0
Albemarle	165	0
Total	16,329 (inc. Albemarle)	7,430 (or 45.5 per cent)

production of the various types involved and 42 per cent of their expectations which had already been reduced from the Slessor agreement level. The total of just under 4,200 American aircraft the British received in 1942 can be contrasted with the figures for British production of comparable operational types and their shipment overseas in 1942 given in Table 8.2.

This indicates that the British were continuing to ship more operational aircraft overseas than they were receiving from the United States fully two years after American supply had originally been directed at relieving the British from meeting overseas supply needs.

All this leaves the inflated targets associated with the '3,000 per month' scheme and succeeding procurement plans irrelevant to the reality of American aircraft supply to Britain. Subsequent British allocations, from 1942 onwards, were then largely governed by the 'maintenance clause' in the ATP agreements, restricting supply to the level needed to replace losses of the units established by mid-1942. As the RAF delegation observed at the end of 1942, 'General effect of agreement is to give us bare minimum required to maintain squadrons at present equipped with USA types.'[28] What this meant is that the contribution made by American aircraft to RAF strength was determined by the level that contribution had reached by the summer of 1942. This level, in turn, was determined by the level that deliveries of American aircraft had achieved in 1940–1.

The primary explanation for this situation was the industrial difficulties involved in increasing production and incorporating equipment and armament modifications required in the field against a background of intensive military demand. There was nothing exceptional in the American experience with this; indeed, as British observers pointed out, they had undergone similar difficulties expanding their production in 1937–40 and were struggling to achieve a satisfactory production of heavy bombers well into 1942. Yet their relatively delayed start to rearmament left American production lagging behind the British for some time, despite the massive targets used in the rhetoric of procurement diplomacy. As a result, contemporary appreciations of American supply were marked by a sense of quantitative deficiency that could amount to failure.

The problem of insufficient output leading to allocation disputes was not immediately resolved in 1942. That December, John Jewkes, a senior MAP official responsible for planning, reported that the United States authorities were resorting to 'raising the tail of the graph', or increasing long-term output expectations to compensate for shortcomings in the short term in order to meet ambitious targets. As Jewkes put it, this illustrated how '. . . the Americans are proposing to put off the evil day when they must admit that they cannot achieve their programme'.[29]

While the Air Ministry could be forgiven for detecting a substantial degree of hypocrisy in this, given their previous experience of the MAP's exhortatory domestic production targets, it was true that the British had confronted the most egregious errors in production planning with the self-proclaimed 'realistic' programme by the end of 1942. Meanwhile, the failure to meet production targets had a direct consequence in the revision of

British allocations throughout this period. As Jewkes observed, American production falling below the planned programme had a predictable outcome:

> The allocations of aircraft from the United States to Great Britain are always likely to be shortlived if they are based on too optimistic a view of production. For when the inevitable happens there is no power in the world which will prevent the American Air Staff from revising, quite legitimately, their plans for the transfer of planes to us.[30]

It is clearly evident that this had happened previously and an obvious example was the question of allocations to the Soviet Union in 1942. While the USAAF had accepted the British concept of a 'common pool' of aircraft supply aid to the Allies by December 1941, this did not operate to British benefit in isolation, with the Soviets receiving roughly half of that allocation.[31] In fact, this overstates their position, as the diversion of Boston supplies to the Soviets from British purchase contracts indicates. The Air Staff summarised the Soviet supply situation on 1 May 1942. This listed a total of 1,852 aircraft shipped from their own production or from cash purchase deliveries from the United States to the Soviet Union. Over the same period, the United States had shipped 787, with most of the 355 bombers included in that total being diverted from British cash purchase contracts. In other words, of the 2,639 aircraft the Allies sent to the Soviet Union, 70 per cent were supplied from Britain, and 57 per cent were produced in Britain.[32] Clearly, most of the initial burden involved in supplying the Soviet Union fell on British aircraft production and British supply expectations. This had been anticipated by the Air Staff in November 1941: 'Over the whole field of aircraft supply acute difficulties are bound to arise owing to the failure of the American supply at a time when we have been forced to assume added responsibilities on account of Russia.'[33]

The problem continued in the negotiations involved in the second ATP Agreement in June 1942. The British had previously notified the Americans in October 1941 that the British contribution to the Soviet protocol would consist of deliveries of Lend-Lease Airacobras and Mustangs after an initial supply of

Hurricanes.[34] In the event, the RAF preferred to direct their cash purchase Airacobras rather than their cash purchase Mustangs to the Soviet Union, and they wanted to continue this arrangement with Lend-Lease-supplied Airacobras. In June 1942, however, Slessor discovered that the expected British allocation of Lend-Lease Airacobras had been omitted from the draft allocations, and were now scheduled to meet the American supply quota instead.

> I am sure there has been no question of bad faith but you will see how difficult this sort of thing makes it to arrive at reasonable agreements. In effect what is now happening is a repetition of past history in that they are now trying to meet their Russian commitments partly at our expense.[35]

This problem continued throughout 1942 and it added to the palpable sense of disillusionment in Whitehall with American aircraft supply policy. In September 1942, Oliver Lyttleton, then Minister of Production, reviewed a visit to the United States with a pessimistic evaluation of the history of American aircraft supply policy to date which noted the breach of successive allocation agreements. The continuing priority given to the Soviet Union did not escape comment. 'It should be noted that, whereas deliveries under the Soviet protocol are not affected by any failure in production, we have not been accorded such favourable treatment.'[36] The successful evolution of increasingly structured collaborative planning machinery in the combined boards in Washington did not completely eliminate this problem. When American production did rise, the British ability to secure larger allocations had already been compromised.

The outcome of all this was that American aircraft supply was regarded as unreliable. This had direct consequences on British aircraft deployment policy, such as the need to continue supplies of British aircraft to the Middle East and Far East to supplement American supply. There was a feeling abroad in the Air Ministry that letting C.-in-C.s in overseas theatres get their hands on the unreliable delivery schedules for American aircraft simply gave them a stick to beat the Air Ministry with when those deliveries fell short, much as Tedder did over Kittyhawk supply in 1942.[37]

This indicates that the RAF's belief in American aircraft production programmes must be qualified and this qualification extended from the general to the particular. This was apparent in the heavy bomber diplomacy surrounding the Atlantic conference which represented the RAF's first major attempt to change the orientation of American production towards the types of aircraft considered most effective and relevant to British plans. The outcome of the heavy bomber supply diplomacy in 1941 was the limited reorientation of USAAF production plans which were to prove of no direct benefit to the British attempts to reach their ambitious targets. Aside from political resistance to increased British allocations, the explanation for this was the time factor involved. The establishment of a Ford plant at Willow Run in Michigan in 1940 provides a salient example. While the Willow Run plant eventually turned out enormous numbers of Liberators, the excessive period of time involved in constructing, tooling and establishing the production line left the plant a 'pyrrhic triumph' because of the delay involved before mass production could begin.[38] Willow Run produced a total of twenty-four Liberators in 1943 rising to 1,291 in 1944, at a point where the vast majority of the bombers involved were being used to equip the USAAF and not the RAF.[39]

The Willow Run example is significant in a broader sense because, in the pre-war period, the grounds for belief in the eventual potential for aircraft production were largely based on the existing peacetime capacity for car production. Car production involved the use of semi-skilled labour to produce relatively complex machines on highly organised assembly lines. British production expansion during the rearmament period had created shadow factories at government expense, many run by motor companies, as well as allocating motor industry plants to aircraft production in wartime.[40] This was paralleled by the greater potential for aircraft production associated with the American motor industry which, in the 1930s, was the largest in the world.

Yet these expectations were not entirely borne out in practice; the appointment of the British car magnate, Lord Nuffield, to manage the shadow Spitfire factory at Castle Bromwich was a failure and, even under the direction of the armaments firm Vickers, the plant took considerable time to reach volume production. These experiences were encountered elsewhere in the British aircraft industry, and the Willow Run example demonstrates that the same problems existed in the United States. Indeed, given the widespread belief in the potential of the American automotive industry for aircraft production, the problems involved in converting that potential to actual production were particularly relevant to Allied hopes for it. The difficulties experienced in converting American mass car production to mass aircraft production struck at the very heart of the expectations underlying the American aircraft procurement programmes of 1938–42.

The heavy bomber diplomacy of 1941 also returns us to the issue of quality. This, like almost everything else, was determined by the RAF's relative position with regard to American aircraft supply and the operational deployment policy that resulted from it. Though the British subsequently wanted to maximise American supply to supplement British production and to provide insurance against the loss of their own production, it is clear that their distinctive position of relative strength continued into 1940–2 and informed British supply diplomacy. The key issue was that production was sufficient to meet essential RAF needs and begin the process of expansion even if American supply was expected increasingly to assist that expansion. Indeed, British production proved sufficient to meet essential needs and provide the backbone of overseas requirements for the RAF and diplomatic commitments to Allies in this period. But this was not just a factor of quantity, it involved the issue of quality.

The issue of quality revealed perhaps the clearest expression of the British perception of their distinctive position in aircraft supply in relation to the United States. As Portal stated in 1941, 'We are still, in the main, ahead of the Germans in the quality of our aircraft and equipment. It is quality which tells in air warfare.'[41]

Quality had been a major determinant of RAF deployment policy and this was evident in the employment of American aircraft in Britain and in their relegation to overseas theatres. It must be admitted that it was not the only consideration. Transporting American aircraft directly to overseas theatres economised on British shipping by using American or neutral-flagged ships on routes across the Pacific or across the south Atlantic to Africa which were not forbidden by the provisions of the Neutrality Act. The logistical advantage was not the only determinant, however. It is apparent from the general reluctance of the RAF to use American aircraft supplied overseas as direct substitutes for their own aircraft in Britain that aircraft deployment policy was also determined by aircraft performance, or quality. Richard Overy has observed that the effectiveness of an air force depends upon which enemy it is fighting. Likewise, aircraft effectiveness was also a relative matter, as the comparative success of clearly obsolete British aircraft against the Italians or Vichy French in the Middle East during 1940–1 indicated.

The clearest example of this process is in fighter supply and in the shortcomings of American fighters as perceived by the RAF in 1940–2. The first demonstration of this process was with the Tomahawk which was never considered a fully adequate substitute for the Spitfire or Hurricane and, as a consequence, was directed to overseas theatres. This is not to suggest that the Tomahawk was useless, merely that RAF deployment policy took account of its relative quality when compared with available British types. While the RAF in Britain could be expected to face the Luftwaffe in high-intensity combat, in 1940–1, the main opponents overseas were the Italians and Japanese. While Japanese air power was seriously underestimated before 1942, Italian air power was justifiably expected to be inferior to that of the Luftwaffe.

This perception of relative British strength and American weakness in the quality sphere informed aircraft deployment policy and, as a result, supply diplomacy. As Freeman stated to Sinclair in the spring of 1942, '. . . American production, although it may exceed current forecasts, will surely be in unwanted types'.[42] It might seem paradoxical that the British wanted to defend their allocation of 'unwanted types' in their fighter supply diplomacy of 1942 but this was to the benefit of the RAF's qualitative deployment policy. American fighters had clear value in the Middle East and Russia but their value as interceptor fighters in high-altitude combat was limited. Though the Spitfire and the American single-engined fighters lacked the range needed to be fully effective strategic escorts for the American strategic bombing force based in Britain, the Spitfire had sufficient high-altitude performance for that role while the American single-engined fighters did not. This was a subtle and complex deployment policy which required that aircraft quality be perceived on a relative spectrum defined by aircraft performance, operational need and the quality of enemy opposition.

The Spitfires involved in the 1942 and 1943 supply agreements were not isolated instances. In early 1943 the British were able to secure yet more Bostons to re-equip Blenheim squadrons in North Africa. This time, the aircraft offered in exchange were Beaufighter nightfighters to meet the USAAF's need to defend North African ports used in the Tunisian campaign against Luftwaffe night raids. As Arnold stated to the War Department,

> Conversations with Portal, Spaatz, and Doolittle have convinced me that the only satisfactory solution to the night fighter problem is to have the British train our night fighter combat crews and furnish Beaufighters until such time as they can provide us with Mosquitoes or until we can produce a satisfactory plane for the purpose. The above will release the A.20s [Bostons] to the British.[43]

Just as the offer of Spitfires in 1942 had been because of their superior performance at altitude, the offer of Beaufighters was also inspired by a similar weakness in the USAAF capacity to provide effective nightfighters in early 1943. Once again, this was thrown into sharp relief by discomfiting operational demands being made on Arnold from the Pacific theatre, this time by the United States Navy.

> You should know that Admiral McCain has just returned from tour of the Pacific theatre including Guadalcanal where he experienced some night bombing and as a result has persuaded Admiral King to re-open question of provision of RAF night fighter squadron for South Pacific.[44]

This is important, not just because it illustrates the continuing nature of the British capacity to meet US operational deficiencies, but because it confirms that the qualitative issue operated in both directions to meet mutual needs. The RAF wanted Bostons in 1943 to meet their continuing light bomber needs at a time when their Blenheims used in north-west Africa were painfully outclassed by Luftwaffe opposition, and their light bomber units in Libya had already been re-equipped (after lengthy delays) with more effective American Bostons or Baltimores.

In the case of the Beaufighters, as with the Spitfires in 1942 or the Mosquitoes which were additionally supplied to the USAAF later in 1944, the British were supplying aircraft to meet the requirements of specific qualitative niches in USAAF deployment policy. In no sense was American air power critically dependent upon British aircraft supply. It must be observed, however, that the same is true of the supply of American aircraft to the RAF in 1940–2 and, by contrast, the qualitative niches the British aircraft filled were at the apex of operational performance requirements.

Filling niches in the short term was not the only aspect of British fighter supply in 1942, however. It was also concerned with the need to raise the overall quality of American fighter production. Jewkes confirmed the role of the Merlin-engined Mustang in this process in October 1942 when he referred to one of the objectives of his visit to the United States as being: '. . . to have inserted in the American aircraft programme a larger number of Mustangs, preferably with the Merlin engine, so that the supply of first class fighters in the two countries might be increased'.[45] The subordination of quality to quantity was, in fact, a major consideration behind the mission, involving a series of visits to the United States by British technical experts in the latter part of 1942 under Oliver Lyttleton, then Minister of Supply.[46]

This gives rise to a fundamental question with regard to British supply policy. If the quantitative and qualitative shortcomings of American supply were so pronounced in 1940–2, why did the British compete so vigorously for an extensive share of American production? The problem was that, since losing 'the battle of the types' to get theirs introduced to American production planning in the autumn of 1940, the British had no choice but to accept USAAF-approved aircraft or none at all. Relinquishing their claim on continuing production of obsolete or relatively ineffective aircraft meant that they would lose that claim, never to regain it if and when more advanced types were brought into production. The case was made explicitly by the BAC in response to Air Ministry criticism in November 1941:

> . . . our appropriation is limited to capacity now engaged in on British orders, of which Curtiss and Bell are the outstanding firms. If we do not make a bid to hold our share of their output with continuation orders for latest types available the capacity will fall into other hands.
>
> We submit it is of prime importance to maintain our lien on output which gives us scope (as demonstrated in recent months) for determining distribution to fit in with British war plan even though types immediately available can only be usefully employed in remoter theatres of war. If the capacity is surrendered to other applicants corresponding engine and equipment capacity is likewise lost and there is no assurance that we can re-establish our claim for the new types when they come into production.[47]

A similar logic was evident in the apparent inconsistency whereby British supply diplomacy sought to continue the delivery under Lend-Lease of Airacobras which they had no use for and which would be redirected to supplying the Soviets. 'We must safeguard our inter-Governmental position to preserve these supplies as part of [the] British quota to Russia by virtue of our surrender of delivery expectations in their favour . . .'[48] This was a political argument designed to maximise the diplomatic leverage the British might receive from their Soviet supply quota while simultaneously retaining their claim over aircraft produced from the capital investment they had made in 1940.

This still left the British with the problem of dealing with the quality of American output. In the case of heavy bombers, the British made, with limited success, a renewed effort before, during and after the Atlantic conference in 1941 to improve the quality of American bombers, and to introduce British bombers into American production, an attempt that failed. In 1942, the

British tried to influence American production plans in favour of a Merlin-engined Mustang. This was successful, largely because the USAAF was now a combatant and no longer in a position to chose to ignore or discount British criticisms which had powerful diplomatic support. It is difficult to escape the conclusion that the early combat experience of the USAAF represented a rude awakening to some of the deficiencies in the American aircraft procurement programme which British experience, and British supply diplomacy, had already indicated. Another factor in British success was the fact that they had been prepared to supply Spitfires to the USAAF. In both these cases, this represented a success for the RAF's qualitative deployment policy.

This is not to suggest that the British point of view was unchallengeable. In terms of fighter quality, problems of production development and expansion were not limited to the United States. Early British mass production of the Spitfire in 1937–40 was dogged by similar issues.[49] British development of the Hawker Typhoon fighter, originally planned to replace the Hurricane, was plagued with problems of engine and structural reliability as well as poor high-altitude performance.[50] In terms of deployment policy, not only were American light and medium bombers clearly superior to the British alternatives, but defending the use of Bostons on Turbinlite operations during a period of intense shortage in supply in 1942 is challenging by any objective standard. Nonetheless, the British position remained informed by the overall positive impact of contemporary British production. The development of the Spitfire made the Mk V of 1941 and the Mk IX of 1942 competitive with the best enemy designs and gave the British a relatively advantageous position in fighter deployment policy and fighter supply diplomacy. The comparative British neglect of light bomber production was a consequence of their concentration on producing heavy bombers and their strenuous attempts to prevent them being diverted away from their strategic bombing campaign.

British officers and officials were not blameless when it came to the question of personal, factional or chauvinistic prejudices. But their influence on supply diplomacy can be contrasted with that of the USAAF, and Arnold in particular. Arnold's attitude has perhaps been best summarised by Huston:

> . . . Arnold's beliefs mirrored those of the American military officer corps . . . His Anglophobic sentiments were intensified in the three years before Pearl Harbor, when he struggled to prevent the bulk of increased US aircraft production from being sent to Great Britain at the expense of what he considered the necessary [US]AAF buildup.[51]

Arnold's opposition had a ready outlet in Congress and the press, both of which could be used to prejudice administration objectives of supplying the Allies before the USAAF. This resistance was institutional, however, and not just personal. Subordinate officers were also known to brief the press and hostile isolationist legislators against administration aircraft supply policy.[52] Despite the general success of the British strategy of developing individual contacts with American officers through the dispatch of observer missions, individual officers, such as Harmon, Brett and Strong, clearly had little difficulty in selectively representing their findings to undermine British claims to USAAF benefit. While increasing contact and collaboration reduced some of these tensions, particularly with the personal efforts of senior officers, such as Marshall, Dill or Eisenhower, their presence within the Anglo-American supply relationship and their impact on that relationship must be appreciated.

Arnold was striving to ensure that the USAAF met legislative establishments of aircraft and personnel set out by Congress during budgetary hearings, and also to meet USAAF expansion plans agreed in inter-Allied diplomacy. He therefore saw himself, not without good reason, as obliged to evaluate the British use of American aircraft as a consequence. 'I wanted to give the British all the equipment they could use, but not enough for a surplus.'[53] The relevant evaluation of how much the British could use and what could be considered surplus, however, remained within Arnold's subjective judgement which proved chronically hostile to the British position agreed in formal bilateral allocation agreements. The British wanted large reserves to meet operational wastage and compensate for potential losses of domestic production by German bombing or for losses of American supply by U-boat sinkings of their shipping. This was an issue to which Arnold was never fully reconciled and which was a source of friction between himself and his subordinate commanders in operational theatres when the USAAF began to participate in combat operations. The fundamental reality remained that Arnold and the USAAF remained in conflict with administration policy of aiding the Allies to the fullest extent of available aircraft supply.

Arnold's personal resistance was curtailed by direct threats of reassignment by Roosevelt in 1939–40 but it remained a covertly active force in aircraft supply diplomacy. This accounted for the technological exchanges demanded – supply of Spitfires, Merlin engines, and future combat reports – before Arnold would release the most modern types of combat aircraft ordered by the USAAF for export to the Allies in the spring of 1940. It also accounted for the British need to enter a series of 'horse-trading' arrangements to secure continuing supply of American aircraft; these began with the diversion of British-contracted Tomahawks to the Chinese in 1941, and continued with numerous examples all the way through to the Beaufighter–Boston deal of 1943.

The British were aware of this attitude and had little sympathy for it. General Brett's criticisms made in the Middle East led to Tedder privately wondering how '. . . he and all the American visitors could lay down the law about things of which they knew next to nothing'.[54] More seriously, criticisms of American officers coming to the Middle East '. . . with their minds made up as to the conclusions they would reach' were repeated by an irate minister to cabinet.[55]

These attitudes were repeated time and again throughout the evolution of American aircraft supply to Britain and were conclusively summarised by Arnold's rationale for the revision of the first ATP agreement in the spring of 1942 on the basis of the exceptionalism of American aircrew. Though Slessor felt able to reassure Portal that there was no question of bad faith involved in Arnold's negotiating tactics during the second ATP agreement, it is indicative that the question even arose. One contemporary British army witness was less sympathetic: 'I am afraid he is a complete twister'.[56]

The British were fully alive to the dangers these attitudes represented to their claims on American production. In the case of Brett's reports from Egypt, Churchill had observed that '. . . these criticisms, even if ill-founded, represented a dangerous factor'.[57] This was repeatedly echoed throughout British official correspondence during the period.

The strategy adopted to deal with this prejudice included increased personal contact and the provision of information to counter it, such as the supply of information on British pilot strengths and losses by Slessor to counter the assertions of General Strong in 1940. Another aspect of this policy was a constant emphasis on the criticality of American supplies which penetrated (at least to a limited extent) Arnold's scepticism of British needs during his first visit to Britain. It is instructive to note that this featured in his assumptions regarding British national character: 'The British were desperate – so desperate that for once their cloak of conservatism was cast aside; their inbred policy of understatement thrown into the discard. They needed help badly, and were frank to admit it.'[58]

Arnold and the British alike were largely at the mercy of a procurement policy in which the political ambitions of the administration outstripped the capacity of American industry. The diplomatic consequences of this were observed by the British embassy in December 1940 when presidential promises to assist Greece with the delivery of Grumman Wildcat naval fighters had to be integrated into procurement plans. This had caused 'some embarrassment' as '. . . the President seems to have committed himself to assist in the way of aircraft without having completely thought out how this could be implemented'.[59]

This can also be taken as representative of the approach to aircraft supply to Britain, with the consequence that allocation negotiations were required at regular intervals to bridge the increasing gap between supply expectations and the reality. For the British, this process meant that their expectations of American supply, drawn from the rhetoric of the economic mobilisation diplomacy of 1940–1, were consistently written down in the period that followed.

American aircraft had been intended to replace shipments of British-produced aircraft to overseas theatres but, in the end, they could not meet that requirement and British production provided the backbone of British air strength in overseas theatres. American aircraft had been identified as the means of meeting the Soviet supply quota but, initially, they were also unable to meet this demand. American heavy bomber production had been identified as a principal means of meeting the British requirement for strategic bombers in 1941–2 only for this expectation also to be deflated. By mid-1942, the British had faced three successive stages in aircraft supply diplomacy which revised and reduced the level of aircraft supply they had been promised in the Slessor agreement.

As a result, the British had to rely on their own domestic production to meet requirements that American supply could not fully satisfy for them. In the case of fighter supply to the Soviet Union and overseas theatres, the British had to continue Hurricane production at the end of 1941 when they had expected to end it. In the case of bomber supply, the British embarked on a further expansion of domestic heavy bomber production as a direct consequence of the American failure to increase their allocations of heavy bombers. By mid-1942 the British were even supplying their principal fighter to the USAAF at the point of maximal strategic overstretch when British fighter production was supporting the domestic needs of Fighter Command, the Soviet quota, most of the requirements of the Middle East and all the RAF's requirements for the new theatre in the Far East.

Central to this divergence between diplomacy and reality was the relative strength, quantitatively and qualitatively, of British aircraft production. This has largely escaped attention in a historiography dominated by the teleology of British decline and the diplomatic rhetoric of critical dependency. The existence of this divergence was, however, understood at the time. In 1942, a memorandum by a British official in Washington outlined the problem.

> On the production side the American has been taught that the United States is the arsenal of democracy. He does not know that until now Britain has, in fact, been the main arsenal. Still less does he know what an effort in planning, building, adaption of plant and man-power is represented by the fact that our total war output is equal to that of the United States or that for the years 1940 and 1941 we produced 50 per cent more military aircraft than the United States.[60]

It must be stated that this does not warrant an absolute dismissal of the various political, diplomatic, economic and military values of American supply aid to Britain. If binary, zero-sum characterisations of British 'dependency' are insufficient to explain the historical reality, this necessarily also applies to any attempt to deny that such dependency existed. What is required is a recalibration of a more complex process and not a chauvinistic contest to exaggerate or diminish the historical reality.

The intent behind British diplomacy in 1940–1 was to secure the level of material support required to defeat Germany at a point in time where German domination of western and central Europe had been achieved. As a result of that domination, the British were isolated and faced with the combined economic effort of not just the German economy but the German economy augmented by most of industrialised Europe. While German economic potential had therefore been increased by her conquests up to mid-1941, the British had to consider the potential impact of German bombing and the impact of the German submarine campaign on their own expanding war production. It should be noted that this strategic situation was significantly worse for Britain than it had been in World War I. With a hostile Italy in the Mediterranean, the Soviet Union supplying Germany until June 1941, and a tangible Japanese threat in the Far East, the British faced a level of global strategic overstretch never experienced before.

Before the industrial and military capacity of the Soviet Union to resist and occupy the bulk of the German armed forces had become apparent, there was no credible alternative for British strategy other than securing the full economic support of the United States. Without that support, there could be no realistic prospect of achieving a decisive victory, and it is not the purpose of this study to challenge that self-evident reality. This, however, was a strategy designed not to secure British survival but to secure German defeat in those circumstances. British survival was won by the military means available to resist Germany between the fall of France and the attack on the Soviet Union a year later which was determined by Hitler's inability to force a conclusion on the British. That inability was tied directly to two factors: British naval and air strength, neither of which was contingent upon

American aid. Most importantly of all, the situation evident in 1940 – the clear constraints on American supply and the relative importance of British production – continued into the period afterwards.

Warren Kimball has observed that the war can be divided into three separate struggles; as well as a Japanese–American conflict in the Pacific, the other two are identified as a preliminary British defensive struggle to survive until the spring of 1941 and then the eventual victory won by the Soviet Union against German forces on the Eastern Front.[61] While this reflects the crucial importance of the Soviet contribution to defeating Germany, it underestimates the British role. The British could never confront the same mass of German forces as the Soviets, by force of geography and circumstance, had to but they were able to do more than win the Battle of Britain.

Though a land invasion of the Continent to defeat the greater part of the *Wehrmacht* was a task beyond British capacity (and beyond American capacity) in 1940–2, British strategic ambitions did not end with that realisation. Instead, the RAF deployed an increasingly large bomber force in a strategic bombing campaign directly against the industrial cities of Germany. With hindsight, it is obvious that this strategy was based on unrealistic economic intelligence and wildly optimistic assumptions about the effectiveness of strategic bombing by night. Nonetheless, the campaign steadily grew in size and effectiveness and demanded an increasing investment in defensive resources for the Germans to contain it. The direct contribution of American aircraft supply to this campaign was minimal.

Furthermore, the British were also able successfully to project force in the Mediterranean. Though marked by periodic reverses, such as the loss of Greece and the fall of Crete in April–May 1941, and a three-year see-saw struggle in Libya, the British were able to defend their positions and build up their forces in the Mediterranean. These forces defeated the Italians from Ethiopia to Libya, overcame Vichy French forces in Syria, and attracted increasingly large diversions of German land and air strength throughout 1941–2. It is worth noting that, by December 1941 and the conclusion of the 'Crusader' offensive which relieved

Tobruk, the RAF had evolved effective tactical air power in the western desert. Whatever shortcomings of command and control bedevilled the British army's experiences of tank warfare against Rommel in this period were not repeated in the air. Though the Axis troop commitment to North Africa was always marginal, compared to their equivalent commitment to the Russian campaign, the quality of the forces involved (including several armoured divisions and a major Luftwaffe involvement) decreased this disparity.

In addition to this, the British were faced with the need to react to the Japanese offensive in the Far East and the political requirement to supply the Soviet Union. British strategy had, largely at Churchill's behest, been prepared to run risks in the Far East by delaying the completion of the air expansion and re-equipment programme known to be necessary there to the benefit of supplying the Soviets. These risks were exposed by the scale and speed of the British defeats in Malaya, Singapore and Burma. Lack of available aircraft played a direct part in British strategic misfortunes in that theatre but this defeat was less a product of aircraft deficiency than it was of strategic choice.

The decision to leave the Far East underequipped reflected an underestimation of the Japanese threat but also it reflected the decision to opt for supplying the Soviet Union ahead of the Far East, an option clearly chosen for political reasons against the preferences of the chiefs of staff. Opinions were expressed at the time that a fraction of the level of aircraft supply dedicated to the Soviet Union – at that time more heavily dependent upon British than American aircraft supply – could have saved Malaya and Singapore from the Japanese.[62] The end result of the Japanese offensives was the need to increase aircraft supplies to Burma and India at the same time as American supplies were cut back further, throwing the British back on the same reliance on Hurricane fighters and Blenheim bombers seen in the Middle East in 1940–1. An initial attempt to economise by underinvesting in the air defences in the Far East (in part by deploying American fighters which were known to be completely outclassed everywhere else) contributed to a catastrophe that then demanded much greater investment of British aircraft to counter.

Overall, American aircraft supply did have an impact on the course of the fighting in the Middle and Far East but it was never able to move beyond a position of supplementing British supply to relieve the British of their obligations as it had originally been intended to. In the meantime, quantitative and qualitative problems persisted with American aircraft supply and demanded that the question of allocation and development be revisited time and again, usually to the disappointment of British hopes. In the event, American aircraft were generally limited to secondary roles in subsidiary theatres while attempts to utilise American supply to meet specific needs in this period essentially failed. Equally, in their early stages of deployment, American forces found themselves dependent upon British aircraft supply for fighters, nightfighters and reconnaissance aircraft as the initial qualitative failings of the USAAF procurement programme became evident.

Richard Overy has identified four key roles for air power: air defence, strategic bombing, air–naval co-operation, and air support for ground troops; and two forms of air strategy, 'limited' and 'general'. A 'limited' air strategy undertakes one major role in support of other forces, while a 'general' air strategy pursues all four roles simultaneously.[63] What is striking about the British position in 1940–2 is that they pursued a 'general' air strategy on a global scale, with the massive investment of economic resources that that required, long before the United States economic mobilisation sought by British procurement diplomacy was achieved. Sir Arthur Salter's memorandum of July 1940, advocating the overestimation of British requirements to stimulate capital investment, identified a period of 'roughly a year' during which resistance from British resources, with limited aid from North America, would have to be sustained.[64] This study indicates that the existence of that period must be accepted and even extended through 1942 and into 1943 as the British adopted a general air strategy before they had secured the resources of American production to implement it.

The extent to which American aircraft supply contributed to RAF strength in this period is detailed in the tables in Appendix A. Taken into consideration with the facts provided in previous chapters, this reveals the actual impact of American aircraft supply on RAF operational strength. Qualitively, these indicate that American aircraft played a useful role replacing obsolete pre-war British types but were unable to supplant British aircraft at the apex of operational performance. On performance grounds, the British were unwilling to use American fighters and heavy bombers to supplant their own types. In quantitative terms, when compared to British production, American aircraft played a useful but minor role in expanding RAF strength. The qualitative and quantitative constraints on American aircraft production identified in the pre-war period continued to exert a determining influence on aircraft supply well into the early and mid-war period. The distinctive position of the British aircraft industry and the resulting British air strength, which had been evident in the pre-war and phoney war period, were maintained throughout the early and mid-war periods that followed.

In place of Warren Kimball's 'two-stage' view of the war in western Europe, this suggests a more complex, multistage framework. While the British role in the eventual concentration of overwhelming force to defeat Germany in the period 1944–5 can be seen only as a minor one compared to the US–Soviet one, and the Anglo-American role in 1941–3 can also be accepted as only a relatively minor one in comparison to the Soviet effort, the British role in 1940–2 amounted to more than a purely defensive stand. As such, an interim stage must be inserted between the 'defensive' battles of 1940–1 and the eventually decisive deployment of American forces in 1943–5. During this period, the outcome of the 'critical dependency' thesis and 'mobilisation' diplomacy was an American aircraft supply policy that was divergent from the operational reality of the value of the aircraft concerned. The aircraft resulting from this diplomacy did eventually materialise in the quality and quantity required, but not before 1943–4, and then generally in American hands. Crucially, *this was understood at the time.*

The last word in this study should perhaps be addressed to the relocation of aircraft supply diplomacy into the arena of diplomacy, given the dominance of political factors in aircraft supply. No account of aircraft diplomacy can account for the quantitative and qualitative constraints on aircraft supply without engaging with the political resistance to British and administration objectives. Subjective, and even prejudiced, political perceptions were relevant and live issues between the wartime Allies and the supply diplomacy conducted between them. These issues transcended strategic or military concerns, and this was so regardless of the relative strengths and powers of the particular nations concerned. This political dimension was particularly evident in the views of USAAF officers as well as among isolationist legislators who, against many of their ingrained political and historical instincts, were confronted with the movement of the United States into a close alliance with Britain.

To secure the level of industrial production needed to defeat the Axis powers, the British needed not only to initiate an enormous expansion of American industry on their behalf but also to overcome the instincts referred to above. To do so, they adopted a thesis of criticality and mobilisation procurement, exemplified by the '3,000 per month' aircraft production programme which lay at the heart of Lend-Lease. This programme was the context behind Morgenthau's claims to Congress in January 1941 that, without immediate financial aid, the British would have to stop fighting – financial aid centring upon an aircraft supply programme that he himself had advocated to Purvis the previous July as 'a bluff' to overcome American service resistance to British aircraft orders.[65]

The ultimate outcome of this programme was problematic and defined by political, quantitative and qualitative constraints that have not been sufficiently explored by the existing historiography. This historiography, from the declinist extreme to the responsible mainstream of diplomatic history, remains in the grip of the diplomatic rhetoric of the time. Reappraising the value of the American supply of combat aircraft to the RAF indicates that a new understanding of British air power, British production and the British economic contribution to the Allied war effort is required. As part of that process, the specific aims of British and American diplomacy designed to entangle the United States with the Allies must be disentangled from the various other diplomatic, political and military objectives to be attained. Between 1938 and 1942, aircraft supply was indivisible from the Anglo-French diplomacy conducted to secure fully mobilised American economic involvement with the Allies.

Ultimately, the British approach to American aircraft supply would play a significant part both in the process of mobilising the US economy for war and to supplement British air strength, albeit at a lower level than asserted by the supply diplomacy of the time. But it did not change the fundamental reality that British air power was contingent upon the enormous level of investment evident in pre-war rearmament policy. The resulting output from the British aircraft industry was, in a factual and economic sense, exceptional. Exceptionalism is also true of a selective focus on the combat aircraft it produced at the expense of the relative neglect of naval carrier aircraft, transport aircraft or even tank design and production, all of which involved much more positive contributions from American supply.

Nonetheless, behind the rhetoric of critical dependency diplomacy and the mobilisation procurement policies of 1940, the historical reality of Anglo-American aircraft supply was one of a complex collaborative relationship of asymmetrical interdependency which does not easily fit within the framework of a competitive and zero-sum British dependency upon rising American power. Understanding the strategic purpose and ultimate impact of British financial investment in the American aircraft industry, alongside a qualitative evaluation of the aircraft involved in Anglo-American aircraft supply, reveal that the creation and deployment of the Arsenal of Democracy was more of a transatlantic collaboration than history has admitted to date.

Notes

1. Carl von Clausewitz, *On War*, trans. J. J. Graham and F. N. Maude (Ware: Wordsworth, 1997), p. 5.
2. Clausewitz, pp. 66–9.
3. Note of informal meeting held in Mr Purvis's Office in War Cabinet offices on Monday, 11 August 1941; AVIA 38/576.
4. Cabinet 21 (38), 27 April 1938; CAB 23/93.
5. Confidential annexe, WM (40) 74, 7 November 1939; CAB 65/4/6.

6. Bullitt to Secretary of State, 23 November 1939, *FRUS 1939* II, p. 520.
7. Gilbert, p. 376.
8. Overy, *Air War*, p. 153.
9. 'Armaments Programme', note by Sir Arthur Salter, 31 July 1940; CAB 115/78.
10. 'Visit of Prime Minister and Chiefs of Staff to Washington, 22nd December 1941–14th January 1942'; AIR 20/4092.
11. Hall, Wrigley and Scott, p. 112.
12. R. A. C. Parker, 'The Pound Sterling, the American Treasury and British Preparations for War, 1938–1939' in *The English Historical Review*, Vol. 98, No. 387 (1983), pp. 261, 274–8.
13. Cabinet discussion on 'The Exchange Position', WM (40) 232, 22 August 1940; CAB 65/14/23.
14. 'Creation of New Aircraft Capacity in USA', WP (40) 354, 3 September 1940; CAB 66/11/34.
15. 'Report by Anglo-French Mission on Aircraft Production in US', 25 March 1940; AVIA 10/127. Colonel Greenly to Sir Arthur Street, Cable No.1, 21 March 1940; AVIA 38/4.
16. Colonel Greenly to Sir Arthur Street, Cable No.1, 21 March 1940; ibid.
17. 'Memorandum by Sir Henry Self Regarding Moral Right to Output Created on Anglo-French Account', AT/42/22, 18 May 1942; AIR 19/348.
18. Huston, p. 215.
19. Evill to CAS, 5 September 1942; AIR 19/349.
20. 'Allocation of US production', Sinclair to Churchill, 8 November 1941; AIR 19/275.
21. Craven to Self, 14 November 1941; AVIA 38/1245.
22. Figures of operational aircraft supplied to the United Kingdom, dominions and overseas commands are from AIR 20/2039.
23. Fourteen aircraft allocated to 601 Squadron. MAP to BAC, MAP 1040, 1 February 1942. AIR 9/436.
24. Figures for ATP expectations from 'Allocations of American Aircraft during 1942'; AIR 8/413.
25. Deliveries to UK and overseas from AIR 20/2039.
26. US production figures from Table 76, USAAF *Statistical Digest*, p. 118. The figures for P-38 Lightning production include 214 F-4 and F-5 photographic reconnaissance variants of the Lightning to reflect the inclusion of similar variants in the comparable totals of British Spitfire and Mosquito production.

27. Production and delivery figures from AIR 20/2039. Shipments include end users other than the RAF (e.g. Indian Air Force, Soviet naval and air forces), and include stocks accumulated from previous production.
28. RAFDEL to AOC-in-C. Middle East, 29 December 1942; AIR 23/1315.
29. John Jewkes, Deputy Director General of Statistics and Programmes, 8 December 1942; AVIA 9/40.
30. 'The Consequences of an Inflated Programme', Jewkes, 8 December 1942; ibid.
31. Craven and Cate, I, p. 134.
32. Figures from 'Aircraft for Russia. Summary of Allocations to 1st May 1942.', AT/42/17. AIR 19/348.
33. 'American Supply and the Royal Air Force Expansion Programme', anonymous Air Ministry memorandum, 27 November 1941; AIR 19/275.
34. Air Marshal Harris and Harold Balfour, Undersecretary of State for Air, to Sinclair and Beaverbrook, Caesar 666 WX.2155, 17 October 1941; AIR 9/436.
35. Slessor to CAS, Marcus 332, 11 June 1942; AIR 19/349.
36. 'The Working of the Combined Boards', Annex 1, 'Non-fulfilment of the Arnold–Towers–Portal Air Agreement, initialled by the President and the Prime Minister in Washington on June 22, 1942', memorandum by the Minister of Production WP (42) 434, 29 September 1942; AIR 19/284.
37. Ivelaw-Chapman to Director of Plans, 6 November 1941; AIR 9/436.
38. Zeitlin, p. 57.
39. Figures from USAAF *Statistical Digest*. The RAF did eventually receive over four hundred Ford-built Liberators in 1944–45; Meekcoms, pp. 85–6.
40. Sebastian Ritchie, *Industry and Air Power: The Expansion of British Aircraft Production, 1935–1941* (London: Routledge, 1997), pp. 57–61.
41. Portal to Craven, 15 September 1941; AIR 20/2689.
42. VCAS to Sinclair, 14 April 1942; AIR 19/286.
43. Quoted by Air Marshal Foster, RAFDEL, to ACAS (P), Troon 93, MS.7376, 5 February 1943; AIR 20/864.
44. Air Marshal Foster, RAFDEL, to ACAS (P), Troon 93, MS.7376, 5 February 1943; AIR 20/864.
45. 'Note on Visit to the United States', Summary I 'Achievements

of the Lyttleton Mission', Jewkes, 8 December 1942; AVIA 9/40.

46. 'Report by ACAS (TR) upon visit to USA', R. Sorley, 11 December 1942; AIR 19/282.
47. BAC to MAP, Briny 10885, 15 November 1941; CAB 115/78.
48. Self to Scott, Briny (Mossy) 11004, 19 November 1941; AVIA 38/576.
49. McKinstry, pp. 70–97, 128–35, 150–7.
50. Postan, p. 329. Though an effective low-level interceptor, and later a successful ground-attack fighter, judged by the same standards applied to US fighter procurement in 1942, it was a failure for similar reasons.
51. Huston, pp. 61–2.
52. Cole, *Roosevelt and the Isolationists*, p. 338.
53. Arnold, p. 233.
54. Tedder, p. 160.
55. Report by the minister of state, WM (41) 96, Confidential Annexe, 24 September 1941; CAB 65/23/20.
56. Alex Danchev, *Establishing the Anglo-American Alliance: The Second World War Diaries of Brigadier Vivian Dykes* (London: Brassey's, 1990), p. 161.
57. WM (41) 96, Confidential Annexe, 24 September 1941; CAB 65/23/20.
58. Arnold, p. 235.
59. Neville Butler to FO, 19 December 1940; AIR 19/487.
60. 'British Publicity in the United States', memorandum by H. B. Butler, WP (42) 208, 15 May 1942; CAB 66/24/38.
61. Kimball, *Forged In War*, pp. 32–3
62. Henry Probert, *The Forgotten Air Force: The Royal Air Force in the War Against Japan 1941–1945* (London: Brassey's 1995), p. 35.
63. Overy, *Air War*, p. 204-205.
64. 'Armaments Programme', Sir Arthur Salter, Chairman of the North American Supply Committee, 31 July 1940; CAB 115/78.
65. 'No Dollars Left' by Harold B. Hinton, *New York Times*, 29 January 1941; Morgenthau's remarks to Purvis on 23 July 1940 from Blum, p. 175.

Appendix

RAF Strength by aircraft type on 3 September 1939, 1940, 1941 and 1942[1]

The tables below include all aircraft except those listed as trainers and communications aircraft which have been excluded entirely. Aircraft known to have been operationally used at the time in question have been listed; those not in operational use but not listed as trainers or communication aircraft have been listed in Table A.5.

There are minor discrepancies between these figures and cumulative delivery totals and serviceable aircraft strength given elsewhere in the text, notably for the figures of Fortress Is in RAF hands on 3 September 1941. These are the most comprehensive contemporary figures on overall aircraft strength available, however. Strength includes all aircraft of given type on RAF charge on the dates in question, including damaged aircraft under repair and unserviceable aircraft within units. Aircraft in MAP hands have been excluded. Changes have been made to the classification of types from the original source as noted in the footnotes.

Table A.1 reveals the growth in the numbers of American fighters between 1940 and 1940; 0 per cent in 1940, to 12 per cent in 1941 and 17 per cent in 1942. The percentage of American fighters split between the UK and overseas changed from 7.6 per cent and 36.2 per cent in 1941 to 11.8 per cent and 32.5 per cent in 1942.

Significant changes in the figures include the Defiant which was still being used as an operational nightfighter in September 1941

Table A.1 RAF fighter and PR strength by type in UK – overseas and dominions[2]

Type	3 Sep 1939	3 Sep 1940	3 Sep 1941	3 Sep 1942
Airacobra	Nil	Nil	Nil	2 – 0
Buffalo	Nil	Nil	0 – 167	Nil
Havoc I and II	Nil	Nil	168 – 0	159 – 0
Kittyhawk (all marks)	Nil	Nil	Nil	11 – 511
Mohawk	Nil	Nil	68 – 16	10 – 108
Tomahawk	Nil	Nil	215 – 199	183 – 241
Mustang	Nil	Nil	Nil	559 – 0
Total American fighters (UK + overseas)	Nil	Nil	451 – 382 (833)	924 – 860 (1,784)
Beaufighter (all marks)	Nil	14 – 0	406 – 30	1,029 – 254
Defiant	Nil	169 – 0	589 – 0	Nil
Gladiator	208 – 151	83 – 154	Nil	Nil
Hurricane (all marks)	377 – 2	1,718 – 20	2,996 – 643	2,128 – 1,317
Mosquito II	Nil	Nil	4 –0	7 – 0
Spitfire (all marks)	247 – 0	628 – 0	1,414 – 0	3,389 – 266
Typhoon	Nil	Nil	1 – 0	311 – 0
Whirlwind	Nil	5 – 0	68 – 0	73 – 0
Total British fighters (UK + overseas)	832 – 2 (834)	2,617 – 174 (2,791)	5,478 – 673 (6,151)	6,937 – 1,837 (8,774)
Combined British and American total (UK + overseas)	832 – 2 (834)	2,617 – 174 (2,791)	5,929 – 1,055 (6,984)	7,861 – 2,642 (10,558)

but was regarded as obsolete in 1942; and the Gladiator which was obsolete by September 1941.

Table A.2 details RAF bomber strength by type but there was some overlap in roles; all the Fortresses and some of the Liberators listed in 1942 (and all the Liberators listed in 1941) were, in fact, used by Coastal Command as GR types but have been included here and in the original source as bomber designs.

Table A.2 RAF bomber strength by type in UK – overseas and dominions[3]

Type	3 Sep 1939	3 Sep 1940	3 Sep 1941	3 Sep 1942
Baltimore (all marks)	Nil	Nil	Nil	0 – 292
Boston III	Nil	Nil	294 – 0	219 – 116
Fortress I and II	Nil	Nil	12 – 0	46 – 0
Liberator (all marks)	Nil	Nil	18 – 0	79 – 26
Maryland I and II	Nil	0 – 2	39 – 127	8 – 83
Mitchell	Nil	Nil	Nil	99 – 0
Ventura	Nil	Nil	Nil	141 – 0
Vengeance	Nil	Nil	Nil	0 – 9
Total American bombers (UK + overseas)	Nil	0 – 2 (2)	363 – 127 (490)	592 – 596 (1,188)
Battle	986 – 0	Nil	Nil	Nil
Blenheim (all marks)	794 – 226	1,147 – 269	897 – 467	1,380 – 604
Halifax (all marks)	Nil	Nil	586 – 0	291 – 19
Hampden	195 – 0	437 – 0	550 – 0	405 – 0
Lancaster	Nil	Nil	Nil	243 – 0
Manchester	Nil	Nil	44 – 0	99 – 0
Stirling	Nil	7 – 0	47 – 0	198 – 0
Wellington (all marks except VIII)	147 – 0	725 – 4	1,398 – 149	1,986 – 264
Whitley (all marks)	172 – 0	419 – 0	474 – 0	787 – 0
Mosquito B.IV	Nil	Nil	Nil	34 – 0
Total British bombers (UK + overseas)	2,294 – 226 (2,520)	2,735 – 273 (3,008)	3,996 – 616 (4,612)	5,423 – 887 (6,310)
Combined British and American total (UK + overseas)	2,294 – 226 (2,520)	2,735 – 275 (3,010)	4,359 – 743 (5,102)	6,015 – 1,483 (7,498)

Table A.3 RAF maritime reconnaissance (GR) and flying boat strength by type in UK – overseas and dominions[4]

Type	3 Sep 1939	3 Sep 1940	3 Sep 1941	3 Sep 1942
Catalina	Nil	Nil	58 – 31	83 – 26
Hudson (all marks)	65 – 27	248 – 39	363 – 38	621 – 157
Total American GR aircraft (UK + overseas)	65 – 27 (92)	248 – 39 (287)	421 – 69 (490)	704 – 183 (887)
Anson	622 – 10	Nil	Nil	Nil
Beaufort	Nil	274 – 0	304 – 9	277 – 76
Sunderland	22 – 17	37 – 15	39 – 7	94 – 5
Vildebeest	41 – 58	10 – 52	0 – 48	6 – 0
Wellington VIII	Nil	Nil	14 – 0	116 – 30
Total British GR aircraft (UK + overseas)	685 – 85 (770)	321 – 67 (388)	357 – 64 (421)	493 – 111 (604)
Combined British and American total (UK + overseas)	750 – 112 (862)	569 – 106 (675)	778 – 133 (863)	1,197 – 294 (1,491)

Table A.2 reveals the growth in the numbers of American bombers between 1940 and 1940; 0 per cent in 1940 to 9.6 per cent in 1941 and 15.8 per cent in 1942. The percentage of American bombers split between the UK and overseas changed from 8.3 per cent and 17.1 per cent in 1941 to 9.8 per cent and 40.2 per cent in 1942.

The tables do not reflect operational service as the figures for the Mitchell, Ventura and Vengeance in 1942 indicate; none of these aircraft was used on operations at that point. The removal of the Battle from the totals reflects the same process of recognised obsolescence noted with the Defiant figures in Table A.1; the aircraft was available as a trainer and target tug after 1940.

Table A.3 reveals the growth in the numbers of American

Table A.4 RAF strength in miscellaneous types in UK – overseas and dominions[5]

Type	3 Sep 1939	3 Sep 1940	3 Sep 1941	3 Sep 1942
Douglas DC2 and DC3	Nil	Nil	0 – 13	0 – 24
Lockheed Lodestar (all variants)	Nil	Nil	0 – 9	6 – 35
Albemarle	Nil	Nil	Nil	76 – 0
Audax	0 – 105	0 – 43	0 – 85	Nil
Bombay		27 – 11	10 – 22	0 – 22
Gauntlet	93 – 44	0 – 21	Nil	Nil
Hardy	0 – 31	Nil	Nil	Nil
Hart	0 – 47	Nil	Nil	Nil
Hind	0 – 25	Nil	Nil	Nil
Lerwick	2 – 0	12 – 0	11 – 0	8 – 0
London	22 – 6	11 – 8	7 – 0	4 – 0
Lysander	195 – 37	490 – 47	559 – 85	Nil
Mosquito PR.I and PR.IV	Nil	Nil	Nil	17 – 0
Singapore	10 – 7	7 – 8	3 – 5	3 – 2
Stranraer	14 – 0	15 – 0	7 – 0	3 – 0
Spitfire PR.III and PR IV	Nil	Nil	Nil	196 – 0
Valentia	4 – 67	3 – 42	2 – 28	0 – 19
Vincent	21 – 113	0 – 60	Nil	Nil
Wapiti	Nil	0 – 55	Nil	Nil
Wellesley	0 – 95	2 – 55	Nil	Nil
Wirraway	Nil	0 – 18	0 – 16	Nil

GR aircraft between 1939 and 1940; 10.7 per cent in 1939 to 42.5 in 1940 to 57 per cent in 1941 and 59.5 per cent in 1942. The percentage of American aircraft split between the UK and overseas changed from 8.7 per cent and 24 per cent in 1939 to 44 per cent and 37 per cent in 1940 to 54 per cent and 52 per cent in 1941 and finally 59 per cent and 62 per cent in 1942.

These figures indicate that American aircraft were able to supplant the Anson (which became obsolete and counted under 'Communication and Training' types as early as September 1940)

Table A.5 Overall RAF strength in British and American operational types

	3 Sep 1939	3 Sep 1940	3 Sep 1941	3 Sep 1942
Overall strength	4,216	6,476	12,949	19,547
American aircraft	92	289	1,813	3,859
American aircraft as percentage of overall strength	0.2 per cent	4.5 per cent	14.0 per cent	19.7 per cent
Increase in overall strength (percentage of previous year's overall strength)	N/A	2,260 (53.6 per cent)	6,473 (100 per cent)	6,598 (51 per cent)
Increase in American strength (percentage of American aircraft in increase of overall strength)	N/A	197 (8.7 per cent)	1,524 (23.5 per cent)	2,046 (31 per cent)

and provided a far more significant percentage of RAF strength in this area than in fighters and bombers covered in Tables A.1 and A.2.

Table A.4 includes miscellaneous types present in small numbers in the relevant strength returns. This table is included for completeness though the aircraft have been excluded from the totals in Table A.5.

Many of the types involved (e.g. the Wapiti, Vincent, Wellesley) were obsolete but were used in operations in the Middle East until 1941.

The Harrow has been excluded, despite the fact that it was listed under flying boats and transports in 1941, as it was included in the totals for communications types in the other years and its use did not change in 1941. Lockheed 18s, purchased in 1940, and

Lodestars, supplied in 1941, have been grouped together as the same aircraft design.

No figures for PR types are given before 1942, as conversions from Spitfires delivered as fighters, the aircraft may be included in the fighter figures in Table A.1.

The Hertfordshire, which contributed precisely one aircraft to RAF strength in September 1940, has been excluded.

Table A.5 presents a summary of the figures from Tables A.1 to A.3, inclusive. Table 10-4 has been excluded owing to the minimal operational use many of the types involved saw after 1940 and to eliminate potential errors stemming from the status of the PR aircraft in 1940–1. This reduces the proportionate totals of British aircraft in 1939–41 but ensures that the available data are used conservatively to support the conclusions advanced in the text.

From these figures it can be seen that RAF strength increased from 4,216 aircraft in September 1939 to 19,547 in September 1942, an increase of 463 per cent. The contribution of American aircraft to the total grew from less than 1 per cent to nearly 20 per cent in the same period.

The removal of obsolete types, such as the Gladiator, Audax and Wellesley, indicates how the value of aircraft supply cannot be measured in simply numerical terms. If the figures for the types listed for September 1941 in Table A.4 are included in the totals given in Table A.5, overall aircraft strength would rise by 862 aircraft, only twenty-two of which would have been American. This would have decreased the percentage of American aircraft from 14 per cent to 13.3 per cent.

From the above tables, it can be seen that American aircraft played a useful role in replacing obsolete types, such as the replacement of the Battle by the Boston, the Gladiator by the Tomahawk, the Anson by the Hudson, the British flying boats (the Lerwick, London and Stranraer) with the Catalina, and the Lysander by the Tomahawk and Mustang. This was generally not because the British did not have aircraft available, however; even disregarding the obsolete types the American aircraft replaced, the British usually had aircraft available with sufficient performance to fulfil the roles involved (except in certain cases, such as the Catalina). The RAF's qualitative deployment policy reserved Spitfires for use in Britain against the Luftwaffe and British heavy bombers for their strategic bombing offensives.

While American aircraft did have value, this was primarily in the replacement of obsolete types in secondary roles, relieving the British of the necessity to divert better-performing aircraft to such roles. This, alongside the limited extent to which American aircraft supply played in RAF expansion indicated in Table A.5, reveals the role of American aircraft supply to have been supplemental to British strategy.

Notes

1. Data from AIR 20/2022.
2. The Mosquito B.IV was the bomber variant in service with 105 and 139 Squadrons in 2 Group; the type has been moved from the 'fighter' figures in Table A.1 to the 'bomber' figures in Table A.2. The Mosquito T.III trainer has been removed from the 'fighter' figures. PR variants of the Mosquito, totalling seventeen aircraft, have been excluded. PR variants of the Spitfire, totalling 196 aircraft, have also been excluded.
3. Mosquito B.IV added from Table A.1. Wellington VIII (GR variant) moved to Table A.3. Fortress I strength is not given for 3 September 1941 in AIR 20/2022 but operations were conducted by ninety squadron in September and Bomber Command reported four serviceable Fortress Is on 30 September 1941. Five RAF Fortress Is had been lost by 3 September 1941, out of seventeen delivered by the end of September, and so the figure of twelve Fortress Is has been added to the data. This is speculative though based on contemporary evidence. It would not be reasonable to ignore aircraft actually being used on operations.
4. Wellington VIII (GR) moved from Table A.2. Table A.2 does not include bomber types used in the GR role, such as the Fortress I and Liberator III, which have been included in Table A.2.
5. Excludes all communications aircraft and trainers.

Unpublished Sources Cited in Text

Churchill College Archives, Cambridge
Prime Minister's Records, The Chartwell Papers
CHAR 20/13
CHAR 20/15

FDR Library, Hyde Park, New York
Map Room Files
Harry L. Hopkins Papers
James H. Rowe Papers

The United Kingdom National Archives, Kew

Admiralty files (ADM)
ADM 116/4409

Air Ministry files (AIR)
AIR 2 – Registered Files
AIR 2/1686
AIR 2/3133
AIR 2/7244
AIR 2/7272
AIR 2/7498
AIR 2/7762
AIR 2/7789

AIR 8 – Department of the Chief of the Air Staff: Registered Files
AIR 8/293
AIR 8/404
AIR 8/411
AIR 8/413

AIR 8/414
AIR 8/446
AIR 8/563
AIR 8/591
AIR 8/637
AIR 8/650
AIR 8/865

AIR 9 – Directorate of Operations and Intelligence and Directorate of Plans: Registered Files
AIR 9/165
AIR 9/436

AIR 14 – Bomber Command: Registered Files
AIR 14/340
AIR 14/629
AIR 16 – Fighter Command: Registered Files
AIR 16/587

AIR 19 – Private Office Papers
AIR 19/173
AIR 19/204
AIR 19/274
AIR 19/275
AIR 19/282
AIR 19/284
AIR 19/286
AIR 19/287
AIR 19/302
AIR 19/348
AIR 19/349
AIR 19/473
AIR 19/487

AIR 20 – Papers accumulated by the Air Historical Branch
AIR 20/864
AIR 20/880
AIR 20/1774
AIR 20/1834
AIR 20/1892
AIR 20/1980

AIR 20/1904
AIR 20/2016
AIR 20/2039
AIR 20/2068
AIR 20/2113
AIR 20/2393
AIR 20/2689
AIR 20/2779
AIR 20/2791
AIR 20/2836
AIR 20/2868
AIR 20/2915
AIR 20/2999
AIR 20/3461
AIR 20/4092
AIR 20/5519
AIR 20/5777

AIR 22 – Periodical Returns, Intelligence Summaries and Bulletins
AIR 22/34
AIR 22/38
AIR 22/280

AIR 23 – Royal Air Force Overseas Commands: Reports and Correspondence
AIR 23/1315
AIR 23/1722

AIR 27 – Operations Record Books, Squadrons
AIR 27/2069

AIR 39 – Army Co-operation Command: Registered Files
AIR 39/25

Ministry of Aircraft Production Files (AVIA)
AVIA 9 – Ministry of Aircraft Production: Private Office Papers
AVIA 9/40

AVIA 10 – Air Ministry and Ministry of Aircraft Production: Miscellaneous Unregistered Papers
AVIA 10/39

AVIA 10/119
AVIA 10/120
AVIA 10/122
AVIA 10/124
AVIA 10/125
AVIA 10/126
AVIA 10/127

AVIA 15 – Ministry of Aircraft Production: Registered Files
AVIA 15/652
AVIA 15/921
AVIA 15/1025

AVIA 38 – Ministry of Supply and Ministry of Aircraft Production: North American Supply Missions, Second World War, Files
AVIA 38/4
AVIA 38/14
AVIA 38/39
AVIA 38/452
AVIA 38/476
AVIA 38/483
AVIA 38/576
AVIA 38/732
AVIA 38/735
AVIA 38/794
AVIA 38/797
AVIA 38/861
AVIA 38/1245

Cabinet Office papers (CAB)
CAB 21 – Registered Files (1916 to 1965)
CAB 21/766
CAB 21/1406
CAB 21/1413
CAB 23 – War Cabinet and Cabinet: Minutes
CAB 23/93

CAB 65 – War Cabinet and Cabinet: Minutes (WM and CM Series)
CAB 65/4/6
CAB 65/6/49
CAB 65/7/13

CAB 65/7/36
CAB 65/7/40
CAB 65/7/46
CAB 65/8/22
CAB 65/8/41
CAB 65/9/2
CAB 65/9/6
CAB 65/9/40
CAB 65/13/42
CAB 65/14/23
CAB 65/18/8
CAB 65/19/20
CAB 65/19/26
CAB 65/23/20
CAB 65/24/4

CAB 66 – War Cabinet and Cabinet: Memoranda (WP and CP Series)
CAB 66/5/20
CAB 66/7/48
CAB 66/9/18
CAB 66/10/7
CAB 66/10/36
CAB 66/11/34
CAB 66/11/35
CAB 66/12/17
CAB 66/13/7
CAB 66/13/27
CAB 66/14/19
CAB 66/14/35
CAB 66/17/6
CAB 66/18/5
CAB 66/18/25
CAB 66/24/38

CAB 68 – War Cabinet: Memoranda (WP(R) Series)
CAB 68/1/16
CAB 68/6/1
CAB 68/6/30

CAB 85 – War Cabinet: Anglo-French Committees: Minutes and Papers
CAB 85/14
CAB 111 – War Cabinet and Cabinet Office: Allied Supplies Executive: Correspondence and Papers
CAB 111/101

CAB 115 – War Cabinet: Central Office for North American Supplies: Minutes and Papers
CAB 115/78
CAB 115/83
CAB 115/317

CAB 120 – Cabinet Office: Minister of Defence Secretariat: Records
CAB 120/352

Foreign Office files (FO)
FO 371 – Foreign Office: Political Departments: General Correspondence from 1906–1966
FO 371/24192
FO 371/24239
FO 371/24246
FO 371/24249
FO 371/24256
FO 371/24250

Prime Minister's files (PREM)
PREM 3 – Prime Minister's Office: Operational Correspondence and Papers
PREM 3/150/7
PREM 3/422/1
PREM 3/476/10

The Scottish National Archives, Edinburgh
Papers of the Eleventh Marquess of Lothian
GD 40/17/372
GD 40/17/398
GD 40/17/402
GD 40/17/444

United States National Archives and Records Administration, College Park, Maryland

Papers of Robert Lovett, Assistant Secretary of War, Records Group 107, Entry 210

General Arnold's Message Logs, Record Group 18, Entry 6 and additional material from General Arnold to General Head Quarters USAAC in 1941 from Record Group 18, Entry 22

Bibliography

Addison, Paul and Crang, Jeremy (eds), *The Burning Blue* (London: Pimlico, 2000).

Air Ministry, *The Decline and Fall of the German Air Force, 1933 to 1945* (London: His Majesty's Stationery Office, 1948).

Allan, Michael, *Pursuit Through Darkened Skies* (Shrewsbury: Airlife, 1999).

Allen, R. D. G., 'Mutual Aid Between the U.S. and the British Empire, 1941–45' in *Journal of the Royal Statistical Society*, Vol. 109, No. 3 (1946).

Atwood, J. Leland, 'We Can Build You a Better Airplane than the P-40', *Aeroplane Magazine*, Vol. 27, No. 5 (May 1999).

Bailey, Gavin, 'The Narrow Margin of Criticality: The Question of the Supply of 100-Octane Fuel in the Battle of Britain', in *The English Historical Review*, Vol. 123, No. 501 (2008).

Bailey, Gavin, '"An Opium Smoker's Dream": Anglo-American Heavy Bomber Diplomacy at the Atlantic Conference 1941', in the *Journal of Transatlantic Studies*, Vol. 11, No. 4 (2013).

Barnett, Corelli, *The Audit of War: The Illusion and Reality of Britain as a Great Nation* (London: Macmillan, 1987).

Bercuson, David J. and Herwig, Holger H., *One Christmas in Washington: Churchill and Roosevelt Forge the Grand Alliance* (London: Weidenfeld & Nicolson, 2005).

Birch, David, *Rolls-Royce and the Mustang* (Derby: Rolls-Royce Heritage Trust, 1987).

Bodie, Warren M., *The Lockheed P-38 Lightning* (Hayesville: Widewing, 1991).

Blum, John, *From the Morgenthau Diaries: Years of Urgency 1938–1941* (Boston: Houghton Mifflin, 1965).

Bond, Brian (ed.), *Chief of Staff: The Diaries of Lieutenant-General Sir Henry Pownall*, Vol. 1 (London: Leo Cooper, 1971).

Bowers, Peter M., *Curtiss Aircraft, 1907–1947* (Annapolis: Naval Institute Press, 1979).
Bowyer, Michael J. F., *2 Group RAF* (Somerton: Crécy, 1992).
Bowyer, Michael J. F., *Aircraft for the Few* (Yeovil: Patrick Stephens, 1991).
British Library, *The American War of Independence 1775–1783* (London: British Museum Publications, 1975).
Brown, Robin, *Shark Squadron: The History of 112 Squadron 1917–1975* (Cornwall: Crécy, 1994).
Bullitt, Orville H. (ed.), *For the President Personal And Secret: Correspondence Between Franklin Roosevelt and William C. Bullitt* (London: André Deutsch, 1973).
Burns, James MacGregor, *Roosevelt 1940–1945: The Soldier of Freedom* (San Diego: Harcourt, 1970).
Butler, J. R. M., *Grand Strategy*, Vol. II, *September 1939–June 1941* (London: Her Majesty's Stationery Office, 1957).
Butler, J. R. M., *Grand Strategy*, Vol. III, Part 2, *June 1941–August 1942* (London: Her Majesty's Stationery Office, 1964).
Butler, J. R. M., *Lord Lothian (Philip Kerr) 1882–1940* (London: Macmillan, 1960).
Butterfield, Herbert, *The Whig Interpretation of History* (New York: W. W. Norton, [1931] 1965).
Cairncross, Sir Alec, *Planning in Wartime: Aircraft Production in Britain, Germany and the USA* (London: Macmillan, 1991).
Caygill, Peter, *Flying to the Limit* (Barnsley: Pen & Sword, 2005).
Charmley, John, *Churchill: The End of Glory, A Political Biography* (London: Sceptre, 1993).
Charmley, John, *Churchill's Grand Alliance: The Anglo-American Special Relationship 1940–1957* (London: Hodder & Stoughton, 1995).
Christie, Carl A., *Ocean Bridge* (Toronto: University of Toronto Press, 1995).
Churchill, Winston S., *The Second World War*, Vol. II, *Their Finest Hour* (London: Cassell, 1949).
Churchill, Winston S., *The Second World War*, Vol. III, *The Grand Alliance* (London: Cassell, 1950).
Churchill, Winston S., *The Second World War*, Vol. IV, *The Hinge of Fate* (London: Cassell, 1951).
Clausewitz, Carl von, *On War*, trans. J. J. Graham and F. N. Maude (Ware: Wordsworth, 1997).
Coffey, Thomas, *Hap* (New York: Viking Press, 1982).

Cole, Wayne S., *Senator Gerald P. Nye and American Foreign Relations* (Minneapolis: University of Minnesota Press, 1962).

Cole, Wayne S., *Roosevelt and the Isolationists 1932–45* (Lincoln: University of Nebraska Press, 1983).

Colville, John, *The Fringes of Power: Downing Street Diaries, 1939–1955*, Vol. I, *September 1939–September 1941* (Sevenoaks: Sceptre, 1986).

Copp, DeWitt S., *Forged in Fire: Strategy and Decisions in the Air War over Europe 1940–1945* (New York: Doubleday, 1982).

Connell, John, *Auchinleck: A Biography of Field-Marshal Sir Claude Auchinleck* (London: Cassell, 1959).

Craven, Wesley F. and Cate, James L. (eds), *The Army Air Forces in World War II*, Vol. IV (Washington, DC: War Department, 1950).

Craven, Wesley F. and Cate, James L. (eds), *The Army Air Forces in World War Two*, Vol. VI, *Men and Planes* (Chicago: Chicago University Press, 1955).

Craven, Wesley F. and Cate, James L. (eds), *The Army Air Forces in World War Two*, Vol. I, *Plans and Early Operations January 1939 to August 1942* (Washington, DC: Office of Air Force History, 1983).

Cross, Sir Kenneth, *Straight and Level* (London: Grub Street, 1993).

Dallek, Robert, *Franklin D. Roosevelt and American Foreign Policy, 1932–1945* (New York: Oxford University Press, 1995).

Danchev, Alex, *Establishing the Anglo-American Alliance: The Second World War Diaries of Brigadier Vivian Dykes* (London: Brassey's, 1990).

Danchev, Alex and Todman, Daniel (eds), *War Diaries 1939–1945: Field Marshal Lord Alanbrooke* (London: Phoenix, 2002).

Dasso, Dik Alan, *Hap Arnold and the Evolution of American Airpower* (Washington, DC: Smithsonian, 2000).

Dean, Sir Maurice, *The Royal Air Force and Two World Wars* (London: Cassell, 1979).

Delve, Ken, *The Mustang Story* (London: Arms & Armour, 1999).

Dilks, David (ed.), *The Diaries of Sir Alexander Cadogan 1938–1945* (London: Cassell, 1971).

Dobson, Alan P., *US Wartime Aid to Britain 1940–1946* (Beckenham: Croom Helm, 1986).

Dobson, Alan P., *Anglo-American Relations in the Twentieth Century* (London: Routledge, 1995).

Dobson, Alan P., *FDR and Civil Aviation: Flying Strong Flying Free* (New York: Palgrave, 2011).

Douglas of Kirtleside and Wright, Robert, *Years of Command* (London: Collins, 1966).
Draper, Theodore, *A Struggle for Power: The American Revolution* (London: Abacus, 1997).
Dutton, David, *Simon: A Political Biography of Sir John Simon* (London: Aurum, 1992).
Dutton, David, *Neville Chamberlain* (London: Arnold, 2001).
Edgerton, David, *The Warfare State: Britain, 1920–1970* (Cambridge: Cambridge University Press, 2006).
Ellis, John, *Brute Force: Allied Strategy and Tactics in the Second World War* (London: André Deutsch, 1990).
English, Richard and Kenny, Michael (eds), *Rethinking British Decline* (London: Macmillan, 2000).
Evans, Richard J., *The Third Reich at War* (London: Penguin, 2009).
Feiling, Keith, *The Life of Neville Chamberlain* (London: Macmillan, 1947).
Ford, Daniel, *Flying Tigers: Claire Chennault and the American Volunteer Group* (Washington, DC: Smithsonian, 1991).
Freeman, Roger, *B-17 Fortress at War* (London: Ian Allen, 1977).
Fukuyama, Francis, *The End of History and the Last Man* (London: Penguin, 1992).
Furse, Anthony, *Wilfred Freeman* (Staplehurst: Spellmount, 2000).
Gilbert, Martin, *Finest Hour: Winston S. Churchill 1939–1941* (London: Mercury, 1989).
Gillison, Douglas, *Australia in the War of 1939–1945*, Series 3, *Air*,Vol. I (Canberra: Australian War Memorial, 1962).
Guinsburg, Thomas N., *The Pursuit of Isolationism in the United States from Versailles to Pearl Harbor* (New York: Garland Publishing, 1982).
Gwyer, J. M. A., *Grand Strategy*, Vol. III, Part 1, *June 1941–August 1942* (London: Her Majesty's Stationery Office, 1964).
Haight, John MacVickar, 'France, the United States and the Munich Crisis', in *The Journal of Modern History,* Vol. 32, No. 4 (1960).
Haight, John MacVickar, *American Aid to France, 1938–1940* (New York: Athanaeum, 1970).
Hall, H. Duncan, *North American Supply* (London: Her Majesty's Stationery Office, 1955).
Hall, H. Duncan, Wrigley, C. C. and Scott, J. D., *Studies of Overseas Supply* (London: Her Majesty's Stationery Office, 1956).
Harriman, W. Averell and Abel, Elie, *Special Envoy to Churchill and Stalin 1941–1946* (New York: Random House, 1976).

Harris, Sir Arthur, *Bomber Offensive* (London: Greenhill Books, 1998).

Harrison, Mark (ed.), *The Economics of World War II* (Cambridge: Cambridge University Press, 1998).

Harvey-Bailey, Alex, *The Merlin in Perspective – The Combat Years* (Derby: Rolls-Royce Heritage Trust, 1995).

Herodotus, *The Histories*, trans. A. de Selincourt, revised A. R. Burn (Harmondsworth: Penguin, 1983).

Hooker, Sir Stanley, *Not Much of an Engineer* (Marlborough: Airlife, 2002).

Hudson, H. U. (ed.), *Lord Lothian Speaks to America* (London: Oxford University Press, 1941).

Hughes, Thomas Alexander, *Over Lord: General Pete Quesada and the Triumph of Tactical Air Power in World War II* (New York: The Free Press, 1995).

Huston, John W. (ed.), *American Airpower Comes of Age: General Henry H. 'Hap' Arnold's World War II Diaries*, Vol. I (Maxwell Air Force Base: Air University Press, 2002).

Lord Ismay, *The Memoirs of General the Lord Ismay* (London: Cassell, 1960).

James, Lawrence, *The Rise and Fall of the British Empire* (London: Abacus, 1997).

Jordan, Elizabeth (ed.), *The Collected Writings of John Maynard Keynes*, Vol. XVI (London: Macmillan, 1971)

Keegan, John, *The Second World War* (London: Pimlico, 1997).

Kelsey, Benjamin S., *The Dragon's Teeth?* (Washington, DC: Smithsonian Books, 1982).

Kennedy, Paul, *The Rise and Fall of the Great Powers: Economic Change and Military Conflict from 1500 to 2000* (London: Fontana, 1989).

Kershaw, Ian, *Hitler, 1889–1936, Hubris* (London: Penguin, 1999).

Kimball, Warren F., *The Most Unsordid Act: Lend-Lease, 1939–1941* (Baltimore: Johns Hopkins University Press, 1969).

Kimball, Warren F., '"Beggar My Neighbour": America and the British Interim Finance Crisis, 1940–41', in *Journal of Economic History*, 29: 4 (December 1969), p. 770.

Kimball, Warren F., '"1776". Lend Lease Gets a Number', in *The New England Quarterly*, Vol. 42, No. 2 (1969).

Kimball, Warren F. (ed.), *Churchill and Roosevelt: The Complete Correspondence*, Vol. I. *Alliance Emerging October 1933–November 1942* (Princeton: Princeton University Press, 1984).

Kimball, Warren F., *Forged in War: Churchill, Roosevelt and the Second World War* (London: HarperCollins, 1998).
Lane, Ann and Temperley, Howard (eds), *The Rise and Fall of the Grand Alliance 1941–45* (London: Macmillan, 1995).
Lash, Joseph P., *Roosevelt and Churchill 1939–1941* (New York: W. W. Norton, 1976).
Leighton, Richard M. and Coakley, Robert W., *Global Logistics and Strategy 1940–43* (Washington, DC: War Department, 1955).
Lloyd, Ian, *Rolls-Royce: The Merlin at War* (London: Macmillan, 1978).
Luce, Henry R., 'The American Century', reprinted in *Diplomatic History*, Vol. 21, No. 2 (1999).
Ludwig, Paul, *Development of the P-51 Mustang Long-Range Escort Fighter* (Hersham: Classic, 2003).
Lund, Erik, 'The History of Industrial Strategy: Reevaluating the Wartime Record of the British Aviation Industry in Comparative Perspective, 1919–1945', in *The Journal of Military History*, Vol. 62, No. 1 (1998).
MacDonald, C. A., *The United States, Britain and Appeasement, 1936–1939* (London: Macmillan, 1981).
McKinstry, Leo, *Spitfire: Portrait of a Legend* (London: John Murray, 2008).
Matthews, Birch, *Cobra! Bell Aircraft Corporation 1934–1946* (Atglen: Schiffer, 1996).
Meekcoms, K. J., *The British Air Commission and Lend-Lease* (Tunbridge Wells: Air Britain, 2000).
Middlebrook, Martin and Everitt, Chris, *The Bomber Command War Diaries: An Operational Reference Book 1939–1945* (Leicester: Midland, 1996).
Milward, Alan S., *War, Economy and Society* (Harmondsworth: Penguin, 1987).
Murray, Williamson, *The Luftwaffe 1933–45: Strategy for Defeat* (London: Brassey's, 1996).
National Maritime Museum, *1776: The British Story of the American Revolution* (London: Times Books, 1976).
Nicolson, Nigel (ed.), *Harold Nicolson: Diaries and Letters 1939–1945*, (London: Collins, 1967).
Orange, Vincent et al., *Winged Promises: A History of No. 14 Squadron RAF 1915–1945* (Fairford: RAF Benevolent Fund, 1996).
Orange, Vincent, *Slessor: Bomber Champion* (London: Grub Street, 2006).

Overy, Richard, 'German Air Strength 1933 to 1939: A Note', in *The Historical Journal*, Vol. 27, No. 2 (1984).

Overy, Richard, *Why the Allies Won* (London: Pimlico, 1996).

Overy, Richard, *The Battle* (London: Penguin, 2000).

Overy, Richard, *The Air War 1939–1945* (Dulles: Potomac Books, 2005).

Parker, R. A. C., 'The Pound Sterling, the American Treasury and British Preparations for War, 1938–1939', in *The English Historical Review*, Vol. 98, No. 387 (1983), pp. 261, 274–8.

Peden, G. C., *British Rearmament and the Treasury: 1932–1939* (Edinburgh: Scottish Academic Press, 1979).

Pope, Stephen W., 'Combined Ops', in *Flypast* magazine, June 2002.

Postan, M. M., *British War Production* (London: Her Majesty's Stationery Office, 1952).

Price, Alfred, *The Hardest Day* (London: Cassell, 1988).

Price, Alfred, *The Spitfire Story* (London: Arms & Armour, 1999).

Probert, Henry, *The Forgotten Air Force: The Royal Air Force in the War Against Japan 1941–1945* (London: Brassey's, 1995).

Probert, Henry, *Bomber Harris* (London: Greenhill Books, 2003).

Quill, Jeffrey, *Spitfire: A Test Pilot's Story* (Manchester: Crécy, 1996).

Rae, John B., 'Financial Problems of the American Aircraft Industry, 1906–1940', in *The Business History Review*, Vol. 39, No. 1. (1965).

Renwick, Robin, *Fighting With Allies* (Basingstoke: Macmillan, 1996),

Reynolds, David, *The Creation of the Anglo-American Alliance, 1937–1941: A Study in Competitive Co-operation* (Chapel Hill: University of North Carolina Press, 1982).

Reynolds, David, *Britannia Overruled* (Harlow: Pearson, 2000).

Reynolds, David, *In Command of History: Churchill Fighting and Writing the Second World War* (London: Penguin, 2005).

Richards, Denis, *Royal Air Force 1939–1945*, Vol. I, *The Fight at Odds* (London: Her Majesty's Stationery Office, 1974).

Richards, Denis, *Portal of Hungerford* (London: Heinemann, 1977).

Ritchie, Sebastian, 'The Price of Air Power: Technological Change, Industrial Policy, and Military Aircraft Contracts in the Era of British Rearmament, 1935–39', in *The Business History Review*, Vol. 71, No. 1 (1997).

Ritchie, Sebastian, *Industry and Air Power: The Expansion of British Aircraft Production, 1935–1941* (London: Routledge, 1997).

Roberts, Andrew, *The 'Holy Fox': The Life of Lord Halifax* (London: Phoenix, 1991).

Roberts, Priscilla (ed.), *Lord Lothian and Anglo-American Relations, 1900–1940* (Dordrecht: Republic of Letters, 2010).

Roskill, Stephen, *Hankey: Man of Secrets*, Vol. III, *1931–1963* (London: Collins, 1974).
Rowland Peter, *Lloyd George* (London: Barrie & Jenkins, 1975).
Scott, Stuart R., *Mosquito Thunder: No. 105 Squadron RAF at War 1942–5* (Stroud: Sutton Publishing, 2001).
Sellar, W. C. and Yeatman, R. J., *1066 And All That* (London: Methuen, 1930).
Seversky, Alexander, *Victory Through Air Power* (New York: Simon & Schuster, 1942).
Seversky, Alexander, *Air Power: Key to Survival* (London: Herbert Jenkins, 1952).
Sharp, Alan J., 'The FO in Eclipse 1919–22', *History*, 61, No. 202 (June 1976).
Sherwood, Robert E., *Roosevelt and Hopkins* (New York: Harper, 1948).
Sherwood, Robert E., *The White House Papers of Harry L. Hopkins*, Vol. I, *September 1939–January 1942* (London: Eyre & Spottiswoode, 1949).
Shores, Christopher, *Dust Clouds in the Middle East: The Air War for East Africa, Iraq, Syria, Iran and Madagascar, 1940–42* (London: Grub Street, 1996).
Shores, Christopher, *Air War for Burma: The Allied Air Forces Fight Back in South-East Asia* (London: Grub Street, 2005)
Shores, Christopher, Cull, Brian and Izawa, Yasuho, *Bloody Shambles*, Vol. 1, (London: Grub Street, 1998).
Shores, Christopher, Cull, Brian and Izawa, Yasuho, *Bloody Shambles*, Vol. 2, (London: Grub Street, 2000)
Shores, Christopher, Cull, Brian and Malizia, Nicola, *Malta: The Hurricane Years 1940–1941* (London: Grub Street, 1987).
Shores, Christopher, Cull, Brian and Malizia, Nicola, *Air War for Yugoslavia, Greece and Crete 1940–41* (London: Grub Street, 1999).
Shores, Christopher and Thomas, Chris, *2nd Tactical Air Force*, Vol. II (Hersham: Classic, 2005).
Skidelsky, Robert, *John Maynard Keynes*, Vol. 3, *Fighting for Britain 1937–1946* (London: Macmillan, 2000)
Slessor, Sir John, *The Central Blue* (London: Cassell, 1956).
Smith, Malcolm, 'The Royal Air Force, Air Power and British Foreign Policy', in *The Journal of Contemporary History*, Vol. 12, No. 1 (1977).
Taylor, A. J. P., *Beaverbrook* (London: Hamish Hamilton, 1972).
Taylor, A. J. P., *English History 1914–1945* (Oxford: Oxford University Press, 1992).

Lord Tedder, *With Prejudice* (London: Cassell, 1966).

Terraine, John, *The Right of the Line* (Ware: Wordsworth, 1997).

Thorne, Christopher, *Allies of a Kind: The United States, Britain and the War Against Japan 1941–1945* (Oxford: Oxford University Press, 1979).

Tooze, Adam, *The Wages of Destruction* (London: Penguin, 2007).

Turner, John (ed.) *The Larger Idea: Lord Lothian and the Problem of National Sovereignty* (London: Historians' Press, 1988).

USAAF, *Army Air Forces Statistical Digest World War Two* (Washington, DC: War Department, 1945).

US Government, *Foreign Relations of the United States, Diplomatic Papers 1939*, Vol. II (Washington, DC: US Government Printing Office, 1956).

US Government, *Foreign Relations of the United States 1939*, Vol. III, *General, the British Commonwealth and Empire* (Washington, DC: US Government Printing Office, 1956)

USSR Ministry of Foreign Affairs, *Stalin's Correspondence with Roosevelt and Truman, 1941–1945* (New York: Capricorn, 1965).

Walpole, Horace, *Letters of Horace Walpole, Earl of Orford, to Sir Horace Mann, his Britannic Majesty's resident at the court of Florence, from 1760 to 1785*, Concluding series, Vol. 2 (London: R. Bentley, 1843).

Wark, Wesley K., 'British Intelligence on the German Air Force and Aircraft Industry, 1933–1939', in *The Historical Journal*, Vol. 25, No.3 (1982).

Wheeler-Bennett, John W., *King George VI: His Life and Reign* (London: Macmillan, 1958).

Whitney, Daniel, *Vees for Victory!* (Atglen: Schiffer, 1998).

Wilson, Theodore, *The First Summit: Churchill and Roosevelt at Placentia Bay 1941* (London: Macdonald, 1969).

Wood, Derek and Dempster, Derek, *The Narrow Margin: The Battle of Britain and the Rise of Air Power 1930–1940* (Tiptree: Arrow, 1967).

Young, Robert J., 'The Strategic Dream: French Air Doctrine in the Inter-War Period, 1919–39', in *The Journal of Contemporary History*, Vol. 9, No. 4 (1974).

Young, Robert J., *In Command of France: French Foreign Policy and Military Planning, 1933–1940* (London, 1978).

Zeitlin, Jonathan, 'Flexibility and Mass Production at War: Aircraft Manufacture in Britain, the United States and Germany, 1939–1945', in *Technology and Culture*, Vol. 36, No. 1 (1995).

Index

EU Authorised Representative:
Easy Access System Europe Mustamäe tee 50, 10621 Tallinn, Estonia
gpsr.requests@easproject.com

Printed and bound by CPI Group (UK) Ltd, Croydon, CR0 4YY
06/07/2026
02160622-0003